Praise for *Oops! Why* 1

'*Oops! Why Things Go Wrong* is essential reading for every person who wants to improve their leadership and teamwork skills, be resilient and survive crises. Downey's unique knowledge from years of experience commanding commercial airline cockpits and surgeries puts you into the Captain's seat to maximise safety, quality and save lives.' – *Captain Richard de Crespigny, Retired Airbus A380 Captain at Qantas, author of* **QF32**

'Niall takes the reader on a fascinating journey through a condition we all suffer from – human error. From sport and surgery to aviation and agriculture, this book details both the unfortunate and the catastrophic, why error happens and, most importantly, what we can do about it.' – *Mark Gallagher, author of* **The Business of Winning: Strategic Success from the Formula One Track to the Boardroom**

'Human connections are essential to delivering person-centred care and sometimes the care environment, culture or the way we do things creates harm. In healthcare this can be catastrophic. This book provides safety critical insights and methods to help eliminate avoidable harm. A must read for healthcare teams.' – *Professor Charlotte McArdle, Deputy Chief Nursing Officer, NHS UK*

'In this book, Niall Downey takes a look at error through multiple lenses: from aviation to sport, justice to politics. As a surgeon-turned-pilot, Downey has skin in the game and he casts his net wide to find answers for why things go wrong.' – *Dr Steven Shorrock Chartered Human Factors Specialist, Editor in Chief of* **Hindsight** *magazine, Honorary Clinical Tutor at the University of Edinburgh*

'Niall's perspective in this new book is just what the doctor ordered! His insight on what we need to do to radically transform how we all react to human error is urgently needed in healthcare systems across the world.' – *Ariana Longley BS, MPH, Technical Consultant, World Health Organisation, Geneva*

'I've made mistakes, every doctor will make mistakes, but how can we limit them? Niall Downey's unique perspective as both pilot and doctor has enabled him to apply the lessons learned by the airline industry to modern medicine. This book should be mandatory reading for everyone with an interest in healthcare, i.e. everyone.'– *Dr Liam Farrell, author of* **Are You the F**king Doctor?**

'Trainee to Captain ... from inside the chest with hands on the heart, to inside the cockpit with hands on the side-stick, Niall Downey offers unique insights into mitigation of errors and human factors. We need this in healthcare now.' – *Professor David J. O'Regan, Retired Consultant Cardio-Thoracic Surgeon*

'Captain Niall Downey originally qualified in medicine, training in cardiothoracic surgery, before deciding to change career for commercial aviation. In this great new book, Niall shares his unique expertise and insight from both professions to help healthcare colleagues learn how to reduce their chance of medical error.' – *Professor Peter Brennan, Consultant Oral & Maxillo-Facial Surgeon*

'We so often sleepwalk through life, assuming the systems around us work for the best. Being attentive to human error not only wakes us from that stupor, but makes us realise the ways we can be attentive to our own mistakes. As relevant to big business, industry and elite sport as it is to the individual, error management and how to be alert to it is an important conversation to be had in all walks of life. Niall's vast experience makes him the perfect person to write this book.' – *Orla Chennaoui, journalist and Lead Presenter for Eurosport's cycling coverage*

'Niall has spent his entire career studying human error, initially as a surgeon in training and in the last number of years as an airline captain. It is critical that such knowledge and training is adopted in the health service to reduce the risk and impact of error and to ensure that a just culture exists to prevent problems in the future. This book is a vital part of the armoury required.' – *Professor Mark A. Taylor, Consultant General and Hepato-Biliary Surgeon*

'I have known Niall for many decades, as a medical student in Trinity ... a potential Olympic cyclist, a Surgical Registrar and a pilot. He has always ... been an excellent researcher with great integrity which is reflected in his book *Oops! Why Things Go Wrong*. I recommend that everyone should read this book.' – *Fellow Emeritus Professor Moira O'Brien, Retired Professor of Anatomy, Trinity College, Dublin, Founding Fellow of the RCPI/RCSI Faculty of Sport & Exercise Medicine*

'Infused with hard-won wisdom, Captain Downey has a flair for dazzling scene-setting and an arsenal of startling facts. If you care deeply about making your systems safe and seek to design long-term reliability, then put this book on your required reading list. I greatly appreciate this no-nonsense guide to mitigating against errors and speaking the truth to power about designing safer systems.' – *Professor Paul Barach MD, Former Editor* BMJ, *Critical Care Specialist*

About the Author

Capt. Niall Downey FRCSI attended St. Columb's College in Derry and qualified as a doctor from Trinity College, Dublin. After twelve years of medical training, Niall decided to change course and retrained as an airline pilot with Aer Lingus, initially combining aviation with medicine by working as an Accident & Emergency doctor before focusing full-time on aviation. He currently operates on Aer Lingus' Airbus A330 fleet flying on their transatlantic network. Niall provides courses and speaks at major conferences on the topic of error management, in particular how it relates to the healthcare industry. He lives with his family in Newry, Northern Ireland.

Oops! Why Things Go Wrong

Understanding and Controlling Error

Niall Downey

The Liffey Press

Published by
The Liffey Press Ltd
'Clareville'
307 Clontarf Road
Dublin D03 PO46, Ireland
www.theliffeypress.com

A catalogue record of this book is
available from the British Library.

ISBN 978-1-7397892-6-8

Printed in Northern Ireland by W&G Baird.

Contents

Acknowledgements

Many, many people have been instrumental in the production of this book, both knowingly and unknowingly. I'm going to attempt to single out some of them but will undoubtedly overlook some important contributors – isn't that the main message of the book?

Firstly, I'd like to thank my parents, Jackie and Anna, both no longer with us unfortunately, for encouraging me to pursue the education which has given me the opportunities I hope I have taken full advantage of. I would also like to thank the many teachers I have had the privilege of learning from over the last five decades. This includes not only schoolteachers and university lecturers, but the many colleagues from both my healthcare and aviation careers and beyond. Between healthcare staff of all disciplines, patients and their families as well as my airline colleagues including pilots, cabin crew, ground staff, engineers and behind the scenes staff who keep the system operating, I have been humbled both by their breadth of knowledge and their generosity in sharing it.

I must pay tribute to the pioneers of the Human Factors approach which has transformed aviation and will, I believe, eventually transform healthcare too. Many of the lessons were written in the blood of the victims of accidents – hopefully this book builds on the learning from the errors found and can help continue to reduce them.

I'd like to thank Jack Ramm for his initial editing of the early manuscript, restructuring it into a more coherent format, and to David Givens of The Liffey Press for the final polishing and for the vote of confidence in publishing it. The book which you have in your hand has benefitted greatly from their input. Any errors which have escaped editing and proof reading however are indisputably mine, thus proving the point of the book – error is inevitable so let's just deal with it!

Lastly, I would like to thank my wife, Judith, and my children Méabh, Aoife, Daire and Conor who have tolerated me spending too much time reading about error, listening and/or contributing to podcasts and seminars on the topic and more recently, writing this book then trying to convince someone to publish it, all at the expense of family time. Thank you for your patience.

Oh, and one final mention must go to Bailey, our Labrador, who followed me into my study every night as I was writing this and kept me company by sleeping under my desk.

Foreword

Brian Goldman, MD

The people who run hospitals and healthcare around the world know the system has a big problem with preventable harm caused by medical errors. In 1999, the U.S. Institute of Medicine (IOM) published a landmark report into medical errors entitled 'To Err is Human: Building a Safer Health System'. Citing data from two major studies, it estimated that between 44,000 and 98,000 patients die each year of preventable harm at American hospitals – at an estimated annual cost of between $17 billion and $29 billion.

The report listed factors that contribute to what it characterized as 'the nation's epidemic of medical errors', including fragmented health care, lack of timely access to the patient's full health record, lack of education on preventing errors, a medical insurance system with no financial incentive to reduce errors, and a legal system that acts as a serious impediment to uncovering and learning from mistakes. Concluding that the know-how to prevent many mistakes exists, it called for a 50 per cent reduction in errors over the next five years.

Adverse events are generally accepted as occurring in 10 per cent of admissions with 10 per cent of those suffering serious injury (impairment lasting 12 months or more) and 5-7 per cent leading to their death. In Ireland (population 5 million), that's 5,000 deaths per year.

I practice medicine in Canada, with a population of just over 38 million. If our error rate is similar to that of Ireland, it would mean 38,000 deaths per year. That's just under 230 Airbus A320s per year, 20 per month, crashing.

The comparison to deaths caused by the crashing of passenger planes is highly pertinent. As I described in my book *The Power of Teamwork: How We Can All Work Better Together*, the aviation industry went through a period (from the 1960s to the 1980s) in which a series of air disasters threatened to ground the entire industry. Those mishaps did not arise mainly from the burgeoning technology on board increasingly sophisticated aircraft. The main causes of those crashes had much more to do with the behaviour of the people who fly them.

The people who make commercial aviation a reality figured out that to make air transportation as safe as possible, they'd have to confront the errors committed on a disturbingly frequent basis by human beings.

Human factors engineering refers to the science that deals with the application of information on physical and psychological characteristics to the design of devices and systems that are used by people. Aviation got much safer the moment the people who run the system began adopting the principles of human factors engineering.

What's true of aviation has become true of other critical industries – from nuclear power plants to giant oil tankers. Error also occurs in many other industries but, like aviation, they have a strategy for managing it.

Sadly, we are still waiting for that moment in medicine.

There are several reasons for this. One is the widespread belief that physicians are somehow different from airline pilots and the people who run nuclear power plants. That mistaken belief in 'medical exceptionalism' has led some to opine that surgeons are somehow better equipped than other shift workers to handle sleep deprivation.

I believe there is a core psychological issue that makes it difficult to impossible for physicians to confront the human frailty at the heart of medical errors. That issue is toxic shame, which is different from the healthy kind. Humans are hard-wired to need to belong to a group, and to believe we will not survive physically or emotionally unless we're included in the group. In that context, shame is good. Do something wrong or bad, get criticized, rectify the problem, and get back into the good books.

Toxic shame is very different. Brené Brown, a research professor at the University of Houston Graduate College of Social Work, has written extensively on the maladaptive form of shame. She defines shame as the 'intensely painful feeling or experience of believing that we are flawed and therefore unworthy of love and belonging'. Brown argues that the most direct way of avoiding such an unpleasant experience is to keep the act that led to that judgement a secret.

I believe that medicine's general reluctance to confront medical errors arises from feelings of shame that are triggered by the acknowledgment of those errors. 'If you put shame in a petri dish, it needs three ingredients to grow exponentially: secrecy, silence, and judgment,' Brown writes. Moreover, shame blocks the very empathy we need to align ourselves with our patients, and to be the kind people we are hard-wired to be.

The first step to overcoming shame and its stifling impact on confronting medical errors is to talk plainly about errors with colleagues, patients and their loved ones.

In 2010, I gave a talk at TEDxToronto entitled 'Doctors make mistakes. Can we talk about that?' For 19 minutes, I talked publicly about errors I have committed over the years as an emergency physician. Since appearing on the TED.com web site, my talk has been viewed more than 1.7 million times. Talking about my own errors and apologizing to patients for those human errors has made me a better and kinder physician.

We need to fundamentally change our approach to how we manage adverse events. We need society to accept error as inevitable too and not to immediately seek retribution for it. No fault compensation and mediation are options which are being trialed and may improve outcomes for patients, staff and hospitals. Kindness can go a long way.

Dr. Niall Downey's new book reaffirms that errors are inevitable, and nothing of which to be ashamed. Rather, it is something that can and should be managed. This book provides a toolkit on how to do just that.

The book explains how our brains have developed while factoring in shortcuts which introduce errors. It outlines the science behind the classifications of error to help us understand and categorise them. With margins ever tighter in healthcare, these errors which were previously very efficient from an energy use point of view are now lethal. The goal posts have moved. We need to move too.

Finally, the book provides a toolbox which we can apply to many areas of our work life and personal life to help us manage error and make our lives and those of others a little safer and easier.

Foreword

Niall Downey is the best and perhaps the only person in the world who could write his important new book. As a cardio-thoracic surgeon and a commercial pilot, Downey gives us an inside look at two of the most critical industries in which error has serious consequences. He shows how errors are inevitable in every part of life. It's how you deal with them that makes all the difference. His book is an owner's manual on how to work, play and live safer by knowing how and why errors happen.

Dr. Brian Goldman is an emergency physician at Sinai Health System in Toronto, Canada. His latest book, The Power of Teamwork: How We Can All Work Better Together, *is published by HarperCollins Canada.*

Chapter 1

Come Fly With Me!

I am thirty miles south of London's Gatwick Airport, the world's busiest single-runway airport, when one of the seven flight control computers fails in my Airbus A320 aircraft. The plane politely 'bings' and flashes an unthreatening amber light to alert me to this fact. I co-ordinate with my co-pilot to ensure the safety of the flight is assured, and that the plane is performing as expected under the circumstances. We check if there are any relevant checklists to perform. There aren't. Reassured, I push a button to acknowledge via our computer interface on the ECAM control panel that I'm aware of the failure and then again to acknowledge that I am aware of the status of our aircraft systems.

And that's pretty much it! This could have been a big problem, but thankfully, the flight control computer's error, whatever it was, has minimal impact.

Our $100 million airplane is designed around the concept of redundancy. We expect that things will go wrong, so we have back-ups for more or less everything. If a computer or a system fails, its back-up takes over with little or no fuss. Our A320 is a Fly-By-Wire (FBW) aeroplane, which means that our controls (side-stick, rudder pedals, thrust levers and so on) are not physically connected to the

1

flight controls, but via multiple levels of computing power which allows some pretty nifty programming to smooth out my inputs making me look better than I actually am. It also provides protections to stop me exceeding the limits of the aeroplane, for instance banking or pitching beyond pre-determined limits, flying too fast or too slow and so on. It also saves weight by removing quite a few cables, pulleys and levers which were previously needed to link us to the control surfaces. This means we save on fuel, and thereby our plane is more economical.

There are seven flight control computers, namely, two Elevator and Aileron Computers (ELAC 1 & 2), three Spoiler and Elevator Computers (SEC 1, 2 & 3) and two Flight Augmentation Computers (FAC 1 & 2). In a reassuringly paranoid mindset, each computer in a set is supplied by a different vendor, uses software provided by a different vendor and each processor is even programmed in a different computer language, all to minimise the chance of everything failing at once.

These sophisticated bits of kit mean that the aeroplane operates in what Airbus calls Normal Law most of the time. This is designed to approximate what a conventional aeroplane feels like to fly, although fewer and fewer of us are getting the opportunity to fly one of those, as many pilots start their careers in a modern FBW aircraft and never revert to anything else. We take off in Ground Mode which gently transitions into Flight Mode a few seconds after getting airborne. On final approach to landing, it moves into Flare Mode as we approach touchdown, again to make it feel more like a conventional aeroplane, and so it behaves as our brains expect machinery to behave. As noted, it protects me from over-speeding, under-speeding, stalling, excessive g-loads, pitch and bank angles. It adjusts how it interprets my input according to our speed, altitude and so on. Overall, it's an incredible bit of kit, although it's not fool-proof.

The failure of our ELAC 1 has minimal impact on our day except that we have lost a layer of redundancy. This becomes of more interest to us when we hear a second bing shortly afterwards to let us know that our second computer, ELAC 2, has come out in sympathy with its friend. We go through the same procedure again and assess that we are still in good shape except that the plane has now degraded into what is called Alternate Law. This is similar to Normal Law but with fewer protections. We retain our g-load protection but lose our bank angle and pitch protections. Our low and high-speed protections are not as comprehensive but we have some support. This is a slightly bigger deal; it means we have to become more alert, but the aeroplane still flies normally.

Unfortunately, our day then gets progressively worse. The plane informs us with increasing levels of urgency (continuous high pitched chimes and red flashing lights) that further flight control computers have dropped out, leaving us in Direct Law, which essentially turns the plane into a normal, conventional aeroplane with all our protections lost and no autopilot to help me fly.

As a final insult, we lose all electrical power which drops us into the lowest available flight mode, Mechanical Back-up. This leaves us with only two, fairly crude connections to our flight controls, namely our trim wheel in the centre pedestal which moves the elevator on the tail-plane allowing us some control to point the plane up or down, and the rudder pedals, again connecting us to the tail of the aeroplane and the rudder giving us some left/right turn control. This is designed to enable us to fly roughly straight and level to buy enough time to get at least one computer re-booted and give us enough control to land the plane safely. Our engines are still working but without our Autothrust mode (our cruise control, if you like). These three inputs are all we have left.

It's a bad day at the office, but it could have been a lot worse. Aviation's attitude to error has provided us with many layers of protection to allow us to navigate our way safely back from multiple failures. In this book I will explore these and show how, with minimal modification, they can be used to achieve a similar goal in both our professional and personal lives, regardless of what field we work in or our circumstances.

*   *   *

I've always been fascinated by mistakes. In the late 1970s my brother gave me a book, *The Book of Heroic Failures* by Stephen Pile, the President of the Not Terribly Good Club of Great Britain. It opened my eyes to such glorious errors as the prisoners in Saltillo Prison in Mexico who spent five months digging a tunnel in an audacious escape plan only to find upon surfacing that it led into the nearby courtroom where many of them had been sentenced – all seventy-five were swiftly returned to prison. Or the equally impressive error Mrs Beatrice Park made by mistaking the accelerator for the clutch during her fifth attempt at her driving test in 1969, which resulted in her and her examiner sitting on the roof of the car in the middle of the River Wey in Guildford waiting to be rescued. The examiner had to be sent home and when Mrs Park enquired whether she had passed she was told, 'We cannot say until we have seen the examiner's report.'

It also exposed truly brilliant errors like Decca Records (as well as Pye, Columbia and HMV, in fairness to Decca) who turned down The Beatles with the now legendary quote, 'We don't like their sound, groups of guitars are on the way out'. This great tradition has been carried on by the twelve publishing houses who turned down J.K. Rowling's book about a young wizard named Harry Potter in the 1990s. Error is not simply a historical curiosity. It's alive and well.

My interest in error dwindled as I progressed through my education as the emphasis was on the need to avoid it. This reached its zenith as I trained as a cardio-thoracic surgeon in Belfast and Dublin, where the idea of error was simply anathema. The underlying message seemed to be: 'Don't make a mistake. If you do make a mistake, don't admit to it and don't make the same mistake again.' I think this attitude is fairly ubiquitous around the world.

But my view on error was challenged when I left health-care to retrain as an airline pilot in 1999. In aviation, there is the idea that error is inevitable, and therefore something integral to our whole Safety Management System. When I went through our Command Training and Check process in 2010, an arduous series of simulation training and real flights taking around two months, I gradually realised that the position of the captain, the person in command of the flight, was not all about technical aircraft knowledge (although obviously a certain level is essential) but more about the anticipation and management of error. My interest in error, and the broader Human Factors and ergonomics field encompassing it, was reborn. I realised belatedly that many of the ideas I'd suggested whilst a surgical trainee were in fact the same ones which aviation had embraced as the bedrock of their entire safety philosophy, and that healthcare could benefit hugely from the implementation of a similar approach.

During the following year, 2011, I established Frameworkhealth Ltd, which focused on the transfer of the aviation approach to error management into healthcare with the aim of reducing avoidable harm from adverse events. What follows is an exploration of what I have learnt over the last decade from experts on the subject of error, and how we can use this learning in many areas including healthcare, transport and maybe even how we engage with our social and political leaders.

This book will explore how we have become quite exposed by twenty-first century advances. We have pro-gressed much faster than evolution can cater for, resulting in a brain structure and function which increases the likelihood of error. In the past this was of little consequence, and may even have been a good trade-off in cost/benefit terms, but in our current environment the stakes are much higher. We will look at how error affects various industries and what defences have been erected to try to address the problem. We will start by studying aviation, since it is generally seen as the Gold Standard which other industries aspire to, and learn how aviation's Error Management System actually works. We will then move on to exploring error in other industries to see if some areas of overlap can be found.

Later, we will see how the same principles apply in soci-ety in general, not just industry. This is perhaps best seen in the concept of Fake News, where truth and lies are now all but indistinguishable, and how social media enables world-wide distribution of falsehoods almost instantaneously.

Finally, we'll explore what we can do about it. There are well-tested approaches we can use to counteract the huge problem of error, but first we need to acknowledge its existence. Too often, we refuse to talk about mistakes, refuse to admit that they might happen, which leaves us destined to repeat them. But it's not an insurmountable problem as several Safety Critical industries have demonstrated, and the potential upside is huge with green shoots already pushing through. Further success would deliver the rare win/win scenario of improved quality of life alongside reduced costs.

Before we get started, though, I think it's important we define what an error is. If we search through dictionaries (or more likely nowadays, Google) for a definition of error, we find a seemingly endless list of options depending on the specific context. For our purposes, we are going to take a fairly simple approach:

> *Error is a mistake, an inaccuracy, an incorrect*
> *belief or judgment.*

This covers most of the cases of error that I intend to focus on, namely human error, which by definition we can influence in order to either prevent it or at least mitigate its impact.

Any errors in the text are, I'm proud to say, mine alone thus carrying on the glorious tradition which this book explores and celebrates. So now that we have glimpsed the prize, let's get started!

LEARNING THE HARD WAY – LESSONS FROM AVIATION

Aviation has supplied us with a template which has been created and honed through bitter experience, starting from Alphonse Chapanis's pioneering work in the 1940s, accelerated after the Tenerife Disaster of 1977 and fine-tuned constantly by a twenty-first century industry which now boasts a phenomenally successful Error Management strategy. It consists of a deceptively simple three-stage framework starting with Just Culture, an acceptance of the inevitability of error and thus, logically, no reason to be ashamed of it or to conceal it. Indeed, in aviation, we celebrate error as it's how we learn and how we avoid potentially hazardous situations.

Secondly, we look for 'what went wrong', not 'who went wrong'. This involves assessing the system the staff member was working in to discover why they made an error despite having successfully navigated the same system many times before. We usually find a succession of small, seemingly minor mistakes which, when combined, leave serious gaps in our safety system (like the holes in Swiss cheese lining up – a memorable model pioneered by Professor James Reason of the University of Manchester). We then try to eliminate the flaws where possible and add in safety nets to create extra layers which will hopefully interrupt the error if the same circumstances arise again. Each event is seen as an opportunity for an incremental gain, a system popularised in recent years by the Sky Cycling team under Sir Dave Brailsford, but actually used in aviation for decades before that.

Finally, we teach our staff an operating philosophy known as Crew Resource Management which is a toolkit to help anticipate, spot and deal with error on an ongoing basis.

The most difficult part of this strategy is the first part – the acceptance of error as inevitable and therefore something to be managed, not hidden. Industries which haven't successfully implemented Error Management often fall at this first hurdle.

*   *   *

Back in our aeroplane, I'm cautiously using the trim wheel and rudder pedals to keep the plane straight, level and airborne. I need, though, to do something pretty drastic if we are going to get back down on the ground safely. We need to come up with a plan to dig ourselves out of this ever deepening hole. Perhaps a whistlestop tour through aviation history may unearth something of value that we can apply to our situation. And there is – it's the Safety Management System.

Expectation of error is the default position in aviation and the basis of the spectacular safety performance of the industry. On average, less than 1,000 people per year lose their lives in commercial jet aviation accidents despite over 4 billion passenger journeys. So what is aviation's secret? How did we achieve this level of safety? Let's go back in time and track aviation's relationship with error.

The Wright Brothers, Wilbur and Orville, launched modern aviation with the first powered flight of a heavier than air aircraft in December 1903. The original aeroplane, the *Wright Flyer*, is on display in Washington DC in the Smithsonian National Air and Space Museum. They improved their design and started a business selling planes. They achieved little success initially, so in 1908 Wilbur moved to France where he found a more receptive audience. Orville joined him in 1909, along with their younger sister Katherine, where the family became celebrities feted by royal families and heads of state. European sales increased before the Wrights moved back to the USA later in 1909 where they achieved some success before Wilbur's premature death from typhoid fever in 1912, aged only 45.

The original Wright Flyer on display in the National Air and Space Museum in Washington, DC.

Aviation was under way. It received a huge boost in funding during the First World War which increased the number of aeroplanes and engines available.

After the war ended in 1918, there was suddenly a glut of aeroplanes which could be picked up relatively cheaply. There was no regulation as such at that stage and no such thing as a pilot's licence. In the USA, operations such as barnstorming (flying short pleasure flights from a local farmer's field for $5.00 a trip before moving on to the next town), crop dusting and bootlegging alcohol during the Prohibition era of the 1920s were a pilot's staple diet. Some developed an air-taxi service because it was difficult to provide a regular scheduled service between two destinations that could compete with railways. Trains were faster, more comfortable and more efficient. Airmail provided some work in the 1920s too, but again, the railways did it better. It has been said that a pilot's biggest risk at this time was starving to death.

Things were a little better in Europe. The railways had suffered extensive damage during the war and links between Britain and continental Europe were complicated due to the UK being an island. Flying as a purely commercial venture still wasn't cost effective though, so the era of national airlines began. Governments provided subsidies to airlines, a commonplace practice until quite recently.

The first shoots of long-haul flying also appeared with the first trans-Atlantic crossing being achieved in 1919, six years after London's *Daily Mail* newspaper offered £10,000 to the first pilot to fly non-stop from North America to Ireland or the UK in less than 72 hours. Unfortunately, the First World War had gotten in the way, but shortly afterwards several teams vied for the honour. In June 1919, John Alcock and Arthur Whitten-Brown successfully flew from St. John's, Newfoundland to a field outside Clifden in the West of Ireland where they landed in a bog after just under sixteen hours of fairly eventful flying. On a reasonable night, I can cover the same ground in around four hours before landing in Shannon or Dublin.

The first solo flights for a man (Charles Lindbergh, 1927) and a woman (Amelia Earhart, 1932) followed and Earhart's flight provided my family with an early tantalising taste of error when, on the day after her landing just outside my home town of Derry in Northern Ireland, my father, then only one-year-old, was taken to visit the field where she had landed to see her red Lockheed Vega aeroplane. The occasion was immortalised with a photo of him in his pram, but unfortunately my Grandparents failed to include the plane in the photo! I partially righted this heinous omission when I visited Earhart's original plane in its current home in the Smithsonian Museum in Washington DC and became

The Amelia Earhart display and her Lockheed Vega aircraft

the first Downey to successfully take a picture of Amelia Earhart's aeroplane!

Development continued as Pan Am started flying passengers across the Pacific in 1936 and began the first transatlantic passenger service in 1939. Then another World War intervened, essentially stalling most commercial development as aviation focused on the war effort.

A notable event early in the 1940s, however, was the birth of the Human Factors or ergonomics movement with Alphonse Chapanis, the first psychologist employed by the US Air Force. Ergonomics started by being primarily focused on the design and improvement of products, but it has evolved into a specialty which now involves a much broader remit, including designing systems that minimise the risk of errors and reducing their impact if they do occur. Chapanis worked on projects including cockpit displays, visual disturbance due to hypoxia (the reduced availability of oxygen) at altitude and tolerance of g-forces.

But what he is most remembered for today was prompted by a series of accidents in the B-17 bomber, the Flying Fortress. The B-17 had an unfortunate history of accidents on approach and landing. Planes kept crashing and nobody was quite sure why. Chapanis spotted that the control which operated the landing gear (the plane's wheels) was positioned right beside an almost identical control for the flaps (extendable panels which increased the size of the wings to generate lift at slower speeds and make landing safer). The proximity and similar design of these two controls made it almost inevitable that even experienced pilots would eventually select the wrong one – usually at a critical moment when about to land.

Chapanis introduced the modification that the landing gear lever would have a wheel at the end of a handle and the flap lever would be shaped like a flap in order to minimise the risk of confusion. This simple change resolved the problem and accidents due to selecting the wrong control ceased. This convention is followed to this day, even in the biggest of commercial jets. Pictured here is the landing gear lever on an Airbus A330. Chapanis' way of thinking is now at the heart of modern aircraft design in general.

Landing gear lever on an Airbus A330 aircraft

After WWII, commercial aviation picked up again. By 1950, the transatlantic route was the world's busiest and

1952 saw the introduction of the first commercial passenger jet, the DeHaviland Comet. The Comet, unfortunately, was also a high-profile example of design error. Three of the planes crashed in the first year, including two which broke up in flight. The fleet was grounded while investigations progressed. The fault was metal fatigue, which was relatively unknown at the time and due partly to the design of the large square windows. The sharp corners led to stresses in the structure which rapidly progressed to cracks.

The window redesign involved smaller windows and rounded corners giving an oval shape, which is still the design standard on modern airplanes. The problem of metal fatigue was an early example of error due to what US Secretary for Defense Donald Rumsfeld famously called 'unknown unknowns', a phrase which has become synonymous with him but actually existed previously. It also frames our need to understand error in complex systems, as resolving one error can unknowingly create a completely new one, the Law of Unintended Consequences.

The steady growth of the industry through the 1950s, 1960s and 1970s was matched by new airports, navigation equipment and surveillance radar, all reducing the risk of mid-air collisions. Accidents, however, continued and the trend closely followed the upward trend in traffic as the graphs below show.

The graphs show a steady climb in the number of accidents and a corresponding increase in the number of deaths, albeit with spikes in both, coincident with WWII. However, something odd happens from the late 1970s onwards. Total traffic increases dramatically – total passengers carried in 1977 was around 0.5 billion whereas levels in 2020 (before the Covid-19 pandemic) were around 4.3 billion,

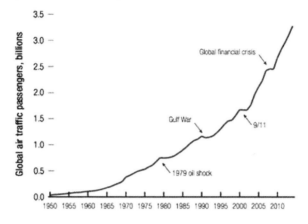

Figure 1: Global air passenger traffic trend, 1950-2014
(IATA Forecast for 2014)

Source: IATA.

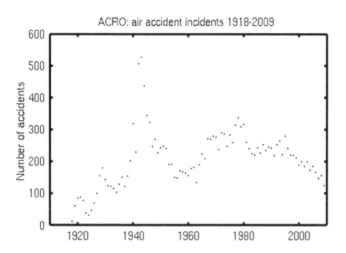

around 9 times higher. Total deaths in commercial jet aviation in 1977 numbered around 3,000 and was following a steady upward trajectory. Projecting forward should have shown a current mortality rate therefore of around 30,000 annually. But the actual figures are consistently below 1,000 deaths per year, a staggering 97 per cent lower than predicted. Indeed, in 2017, the global total number of deaths was zero! So, what happened in the late 1970s?

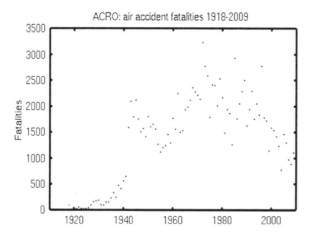

Source for figures: Aircraft Crashes Record Office (ACRO), Geneva.

Tenerife happened.

On 27 March 1977, aviation suffered its deadliest ever accident. Aircraft inbound to Gran Canaria were diverted to the small regional airport of Los Rodeos on the nearby island of Tenerife due to a terrorist attack at the airport. A small bomb had exploded in the terminal injuring eight people. A phone call had warned of a further device which led to the airport being temporarily closed. This resulted in several flights, including five large international ones, being diverted to Los Rodeos. There followed a series of errors which led to aviation's biggest disaster, but was also the turning point in its safety culture and the development of one of its greatest successes: Crew Resource Management.

The small Los Rodeos airport wasn't designed to handle this level of traffic and was forced to park some aircraft on taxi ways disrupting normal traffic flow. When Gran Canaria finally reopened, a Dutch KLM Boeing 747 had commenced refueling in order to speed up its turnaround before heading back to Amsterdam. Following traffic was unable to get past it and was forced to wait for 35 minutes. These crucial 35 minutes changed everything.

The KLM Jumbo was given clearance to taxi along the runway before performing a 180 degree turn at the end due to the partial blockage of taxi ways. A second 747, a Pan Am Clipper, was cleared to taxi down behind but to turn off at an intermediate taxiway to clear the runway for the KLM aircraft's departure. A series of errors ensued.

Firstly, the Pan Am aircraft missed its turn-off, although the turn-off was unsuitable for an aircraft of its size anyway, a mistake probably made by an air traffic controller inexperienced in working with this type of traffic. At the same time, the KLM was being instructed on what to do after take-off. These instructions were misinterpreted, and a query by the controller and the Pan Am was lost in garble due to the nature of the VHF radio signal when two stations broadcast simultaneously. Queries by the KLM co-pilot and flight engineer to their captain were dismissed. The KLM plane's captain continued the take-off roll. Neither plane could see the other as the Pan Am was in a fog bank. The airport wasn't equipped with ground radar so, back in the ATC tower, neither plane could be seen either visually or electronically by the controller.

The Pan Am crew raced for the next turn-off when they became aware of what was happening. By the time the KLM crew realised the error, they were going too fast to stop so tried to get airborne. They succeeded but didn't gain enough height to clear the other aircraft and their left engines and wheels tore through the mid-section of the Pan Am cabin whilst their right wheels hit its upper deck. It crashed to the ground just beyond and exploded in a fireball due to the large amount of fuel they had taken on. Fire crews were initially unaware that a second aircraft was involved. The accident cost the lives of all 248 passengers and crew on the KLM aircraft as well as 335 on the Pan Am, a horrific total of 583 people.

Study of the accident showed a litany of errors, including airport size and design, and the circumstances of the diversions. Procedures in low visibility weather conditions led to aircraft being in potential conflict. Poor radio discipline, including non-standard and potentially confusing or misleading wording, compounded things.

Crew interaction displayed a very steep authority gradient, where the input of more junior crew members was dismissed without any clear assessment. All in all, it was clear that the accident was down to layer upon layer of human error which came together catastrophically when the KLM plane tore into the Pan Am.

There had been accidents before the Tenerife disaster, but Tenerife galvanised the aviation industry to reassess its whole approach to safety, and to make sure accidents like this wouldn't happen again.

Some of the major players in aviation attended the Resource Management on the Flight-deck Conference in June 1979 in California which was convened by the National Aeronautics and Space Administration (NASA). It studied research into the causes of various commercial aviation accidents. Airlines went away determined to implement what they had found to reduce the impact of human error on their operations. The approach they came up with was christened Cockpit Resource Management (CRM). United Airlines was the first to launch a training programme in 1981 which included classroom-based and flight simulator training known as Line Orientated Flight Training (LOFT), which allowed pilots to deal with technical problems but focused on their personal interactions.

Many pilots hated this. It was quite corporate management-focused and involved role-play and games. Lots of pilots felt this was irrelevant. But United Airlines had experienced an accident in 1978 caused partly by the captain not listening to the co-pilot and so was keen to emphasise accepting input from juniors. Indeed, this first generation CRM could be described as convincing captains to relinquish their 'God-like' status and accept the possibility that they may actually be fallible! CRM was aimed at being more than a one-off course and United planned to incorporate it into their annual training programme. It met with some success but also quite a bit of resistance from pilots who branded it a 'charm offensive'. They felt that they were being manipulated.

Other airlines gradually introduced CRM and by the time NASA hosted a follow-up conference in 1986, the aim was that CRM would simply be absorbed into airline operations and wouldn't need to be trained specifically. At this stage, CRM was entering its second stage as the concept started to broaden beyond the cockpit into Crew Resource Management with the realisation that a lot of what happened beyond the cockpit had an impact on safety. Courses became a bit more aviation-orientated, but the focus was on team synergies so it still elicited criticism although, overall, CRM was gaining acceptance.

In the early 1990s, CRM entered its third iteration with cabin crew and pilots training together as the focus on broadening the concept gathered momentum. Non-technical skills (NTS) were given more prominence as it was realised that these 'soft skills', that is, personal and social skills not involving the technicalities of flying the aeroplane, were actually critically important. This had already been shown by NASA in a 1979 study when they put 18 crews into a Boeing 747 simulator and recorded that crews who interacted and communicated more effectively had better outcomes when problems were thrown at them. The way in which crews communicate in an aeroplane today has become much more formalized – clearly we can train people to communicate more effectively without having to rely on their innate personality. Human Factors were becoming more prominent by this point and now underscore everything we do in CRM. Human Factors specialists now work in aviation at the level of manufacturers, Air Traffic Control, as well as in airlines themselves.

Generation four came in the mid-1990s with airlines being given the freedom to develop their own programmes suited to their company's operation and culture, but within specific parameters. It encouraged Line Orientated Evaluations, which meant assessing people when they were flying their usual routes. The idea was to understand what was happening out in the real world on a normal day as opposed to the slightly artificial setting of the flight simulator where the focus is on big events, such as major system failures and extreme conditions.

The fifth generation at the turn of the twenty-first century gave the concept of Error Management more prominence, especially with the complexity of aeroplanes increasing and the pilot's job becoming more of a management role. The pilot needed the input of a second crew member to allow cross-checking and supervision of each other, and to challenge decisions to avoid tunnel vision and confirmation bias, especially in more stressful situations.

We are now in the sixth iteration of CRM, the main additional feature being the formalisation of Threat and Error Management (TEM) thinking. We are encouraged to constantly troubleshoot our operation to anticipate where issues may arise and to have a plan in place to deal with possible problems. Aviation is now well down the line to an Evidence Based Training (EBT) model, allowing us more flexibility in our use of valuable training time. We are gradually reducing the amount of time spent repeating standardised failures such as engine fire on take-off which, although serious, don't happen all that often with the current generation of planes. We can now use the time freed up to incorporate more of what is currently leading to accidents globally and to make training less predictable, more relevant and more beneficial to the crew. Many airlines are making progress to having this new approach approved by their national regulators. CRM is an integral part of this assessment and, as well as impacting on all aspects of the operation, it is also now assessed in a stand-alone way too. If a crew handles an incident successfully but the CRM is felt to be inadequate, the crew fails the check.

So, what does CRM look like in the modern aviation environment? In essence, it is a generic Human Factors, or Human Limitations-based method which focuses on a standardized approach to Error Management. Over the course of this book, we're going to fully unpack that, take away the jargon and see what it means in the real world. We're going to see how this same approach can be easily transferred to other industries, and indeed to our own lives. So often, despite having their very own 'Tenerife' moments, industries, businesses, governments and individuals have failed to learn the lessons and introduce a systematic way to reduce error.

It's my mission to change this. This book is a rallying cry to reduce error. The tools are there, we just need to persuade people to use them, both in their work environment but equally, in their personal lives.

*   *   *

But before we plunge in, let's nip back to London to see how I'm getting on with my rapidly deteriorating aeroplane.

We're still where we started, thirty miles south of Gatwick. To be more precise, we are in an industrial estate, thirty miles south of Gatwick in a CAA Approved Full Motion simulator costing around $20 million. I'm finishing Day 1 of my reconversion back onto an Airbus after spending two years flying a conventional aircraft, a Boeing 757, on our transatlantic service. In 2000, after spending a little over a year between classroom lessons and flying small training aircraft (a Piper Cherokee, a Piper Arrow and finally a Piper Seneca) based at Oxford Air Training School in Kidlington Airport, I was trained on our Airbus A320 fleet. Between flying over thirteen years on the A320 and three and a half years on our A330 fleet, I spent the next sixteen and a half years on Fly-by-Wire aircraft before getting the chance to fly a 'conventional aircraft' for two years.

This simulator session was my re-introduction to the luxuries I had forsaken. As well as re-learning the aircraft systems, this session was to emphasise just how many levels of redundancy we have and to convince me that, ultimately, it's still an aeroplane which can fly after all the toys are removed, albeit with a little more attention necessary than normal. In essence, we can summarise our aviation Safety Management System approach for slow learners like me as:

'Where Can This Go Wrong?' and 'What's Plan B?'

This underlying logic is one that underpins aviation and is the foundation of our Safety Management System, that of expecting error. We work on the assumption that things will go wrong and prepare a back-up plan to compensate to give us safe, viable options. This includes the design of aeroplanes and airports, but also our basic operating philosophy and decision-making processes.

Just to be clear, I'm not a Human Factors professional. I am, however, a professional whose very survival (and that of my 300+ passengers and crew) depends largely on my successful application of Human Factors. Human Factors/ergonomics (HF/E) is a specialty in itself whose principles are now deeply embedded in the aviation industry and has largely been responsible for the spectacular improvements in safety in our industry. In contrast, healthcare, another Safety Critical industry, has been much slower to adopt HF/E principles. The NHS in the UK, an employer with over 1.3 million staff, employs around only 10 HF/E professionals. In the absence of any imminent change, it is up to others to try to fill that void. I hope this book contributes to that aim.

In the next chapter we're going to explore this basic premise in a little more detail, before checking out its application to other industries and, indeed, society in general.

Chapter 2

It's Not Your Fault!

Let's nip back a hundred thousand years or so. Homo sapiens has been around for roughly twice that time so we are mid-way in our 'modern' evolution. We are in the plains of Africa hunting with our buddies. Out of the corner of our eye we see something moving quickly. We turn and see a lion running towards us. We analyse the animal and conclude that it is indeed a lion and check our memory database to assess where do lions fit into our risk assessment ladder. On concluding that they are pretty much at the top, we decide that running would probably be a good course of action and start doing just that!

Of course, this is not what we do at all – we would be eaten long before concluding that we are in a spot of danger. Instead, we operate initially on pattern recognition. The 'big animal running at me pattern' immediately triggers a freeze, fight or flight response which rapidly turns on a neurological and physical response which optimises our chances of survival. A successful outcome also gives us a chance at passing these very useful genes on to the next generation. Only if this initial approach doesn't give me an appropriate response do I move to the analytical option and start formulating ideas. In short, we don't think the way we think we think!

We use this pattern-finding technique in many aspects of our lives without even being aware of it and therein lies the problem. If we are unaware that we are doing it, it's very difficult to be alert for errors.

For instance, if you turn up at your local Emergency Department with severe chest pain, the doctor will ask questions such as where is the pain, what brought it on, does it radiate anywhere else, does anything help or worsen it? All these questions help her to match it to a pre-learned pattern allowing her to surmise whether it is most likely to be angina or a heart attack. She must also be alert to the possibility that it belongs to a similar pattern of symptoms which fit the indigestion algorithm. Only around 30 per cent of chest pain which presents to hospital is cardiac-related. Another 30 per cent is musculo-skeletal and most of the other 40 per cent is due to gastric reflux. Pattern recognition involving history, examination and investigations such as blood tests help narrow the available patterns down and tip the odds in the doctor's (and the patient's) favour. No pattern is fool-proof but you can give yourself a fighting chance.

The brain itself errs in the case of referred pain – severe discomfort in the jaw or down the left arm even though there is no injury to these areas. The cause still isn't fully understood but the thinking is that the autonomic (or unconscious) nervous system which supplies the heart (making it speed up and/or beat more forcefully when we get excited, for instance) gets stimulated, possibly through pain nerve fibres, or maybe by local release of chemical transmitters due to the underlying cell damage, and carries signals back to the spinal cord where they transfer to different pain fibres which lead to the brain. Since the brain isn't programmed to interpret pain from internal organs it assumes that the pain is coming from external parts of the body which have conscious sensation. It matches the incoming signal to the level it originated in the spinal cord. The level where the cardiac fibres enter (mid to lower cervical spine) is the level that sensation from the jaw and arm originates so the brain mistakenly assumes the pain to be originating from there. Patients who have been recipients of a heart transplant have disrupted nerve fibres so don't register the typical central chest pain that 'normal' patients feel, making it difficult to spot cardiac disease which is problematic because up to half develop coronary artery disease in their new heart within five years of transplant.

A critical investigation in central chest pain is the 12 lead ECG trace (which is actually produced using only 10 leads but looks at the heart from 12 directions, hence the name), giving various patterns of electrical disruption on the twelve pictures characteristic of the underlying cause. Junior staff can work through the various leads of the trace to reach a conclusion. Experienced staff can glance at it and almost instantly recognise a pattern through greater practice. Again, however, a healthy dose of scepticism is useful to prevent misdiagnosis. We'll look at this more closely when discussing error mitigation.

Pattern matching rather than painstaking assessment is common in our everyday lives too. We can generally assess a situation and extract the gist of what's happening in around a tenth of a second. This is very useful but comes at the cost of a woeful lack of detail. The problem is that we are often unaware that we have missed the detail and therefore rely more heavily on our assessment than we should. We overestimate our abilities. This is known in psychology as a cognitive bias, in this case Illusory Superiority, sometimes known as the Lake Wobegon effect after the fictional town on radio where 'all the women are strong, all the men are good looking and all the children are above average'. Above average, by definition, means in the top 50 per cent. An American study showed that 65 per cent of people consider themselves to be above average intelligence and 80 to 90 per cent consider themselves to be above average drivers!

The Dunning-Kruger effect is a manifestation of this, describing people who are so confident in their abilities that they are totally unaware of their limitations and can wreak havoc if promoted to an influential position. I'm sure we all have faces which spring to mind for this scenario! An extreme version of this is the mental illness which leads to one having 'grandiose delusions', that is, grossly over-estimating one's intelligence, wealth, authority and so on, although 10 per cent of the population verge on this but fall short of the clinical criteria.

We also display bias in our assessments, a tendency which predisposes us to error and one which is deftly manipulated by the advertising industry. If we see some-one we admire using a product, we are likely to rate that product more highly than an alternative, hence the value of celebrity endorsements. This bias can have more serious implications which we will see later as we have a look at our legal system. Memories also are less clear cut than we think and aren't a direct recalling of the events we experienced, but often a reproduction of what we think happened which can evolve and change over time. We take an overview of a situation and omit a lot of detail which allows us to be manipulated into incorrect decisions based on erroneous memories.

In summary, our brain design and function predisposes us to error. The greatest danger though is that we are often blissfully unaware of this so not only commit errors but are often oblivious to the fact and see no reason to question what we say or do. Even when we do question our actions, our brain tends to help us see what we expect or want to see, allowing the error to continue unabated, the 'confirmation bias' phenomenon.

The first step in dealing with this situation (which in Safety Critical industries can be a life or death scenario) is through awareness of its existence. Following from this, we have developed tools and techniques which we can apply to reduce the incidence of error. We can aim to reduce error as much as possible but need to accept that total victory is impossible – we are human beings so will always be prone to err. Even if we address all possibilities, new ones will appear, the phenomenon of 'unintended consequences'.

Human error involves misprocessing information gleaned from our surroundings and/or misuse of that information. Taking the first part, how do we manage to misinterpret what should be relatively straight-forward information absorbed through our senses? Surely we are pretty good at that? Let's have a brief look at how our brains have developed so we can understand why error is inevitable.

We can partly explain this by considering the timeline of evolution as outlined in Yuval Noah Harari's excellent book *Sapiens*. A quick overview of the history of time shows the beginning of the universe as being around 13.5 billion years ago. Fast forwarding to 4.5 billion years ago saw the formation of the Earth and then evidence of life 3.8 billion years ago. The earliest humans appeared only about 2.5

million years ago and our species, Homo sapiens, made its first appearance a comparatively recent 200,000 years ago.

To put that in perspective, let's think of the Earth's existence to date as a 24 hour day. We humans have so far been here for less than two hundredths of a second of that day! Fast forwarding rapidly shows domestication of animals and plants 12,000 years ago, the Scientific Revolution 500 years ago and the Industrial Revolution 200 years ago. Healthcare as we recognise it is younger again. Again, for perspective, consider human existence as a 24 hour day. The time since the Industrial Revolution is less than 90 seconds of that day. In short, our society's development has accelerated at warp speed over recent centuries and shows no signs of slowing down as we race through this one.

Evolution unfortunately travels at a rather more sedate pace and the neuroanatomy of our brains is now a long way behind what we need to successfully handle the challenges we currently find ourselves confronting every day. In short, we are trying to function in a highly complex, rapidly changing environment whilst still running on caveman software!

We sense our environment in five ways – sight, sound, smell, taste and touch. These inputs are processed via sense organs (eyes, ears etc.) into our brains to create a perception of what we experience. Our brain then presents this to us as 'reality'. It is, however, simply a suggestion to our consciousness of what is there. There are a multitude of ways this can go wrong. Also, the spectrum of what we experience is only a section of the continuum of what is actually there.

Let's briefly get a little technical so we can better understand how we can't but fail. Consider sight as representative of the other senses (as it's easier to reproduce visual examples in a book than it is, for instance, olfactory or auditory ones). We see the colour red but there is a range of frequencies below this such as infra-red and beyond. There is also ultra-violet and others in the higher frequency range which are beyond our visual capabilities – it doesn't mean they aren't there, just that we can't see them. Individual people also have differing capabilities – some have ranges a little beyond what others can see. Some are colour blind and can't perceive certain colours at all.

The retina is composed of two major light sensitive cell types called rods and cones. Rods outnumber cones by around twenty to one in the human eye with around 100 million rods and only 5 million cones. Cones are concentrated in one small area about 1 millimeter in diameter called the macula (also known as the fovea centralis) and provide photopic vision, that is, they work in bright light, perceive colour and are good at sensing detail. Rods, on the other hand, provide scotopic vision, work in dim light, cannot perceive colour and aren't good at differentiating detail. The small macular area is the only part of the retina capable of 'seeing' detail so we are actually focusing on an area roughly the size of our thumbnail in our field of vision, the rest is blurred.

Our eyes continually dart around taking snapshots for our brain to piece together whilst filling in the gaps producing what it 'thinks' we need to see so we are generally unaware of this blurring. This resultant creation of error has, as we shall see later, important implications in monitoring changing parameters which is essential in both aviation and healthcare. There is also a blind spot due to the area where the optic nerve plunges out of the retina en route to the brain which, again, our conscious brain edits out but can be found by tricks such as focusing on your thumbnail whilst moving it towards your face till it 'magically' disappears!

The visual signals are carried initially to the primary visual cortex near the back of the brain (which is why we 'see stars' if we get hit on the back of the head, stimulating this area). When anatomists sliced sections of this area in early studies of the brain, they noted the striped colouration so named the area the 'striate' or striped cortex. A handy feature of anatomy is that early anatomists generally decided what various features looked like or reminded them of, then simply changed the term into Latin which sounded much more impressive.

The Three Pound Universe by Judith Hooper and Dick Teresi explains the function of this area very neatly. They describe how American neuroscientists David Hubel and Torsten Wiesel, whose work led to their Nobel Prize for Physiology in 1981, studied the six layers of the visual cortex and discovered that rather than simply reconstructing the picture as a photograph would do, there are layers of cells working as 'feature detectors'. Some cells detected only horizontal lines, others only vertical, and many the various angles in between. It was like 'a neat ledger-book column of neurons that respond to lines or edges of a particular orientation'.

Francis Crick described the system as a 'pre-engineered machine' rather than 'a general purpose computer'. He said:

> The brain has been engineered to do a specific job. Mammals have been looking at the same sort of visual world for a long time, a world that consists of solids with surfaces. So, through natural selection we have evolved some special gadgetry for that.

We then process what we see into faces, words, land-scapes and so on. This gadgetry is very useful in finding short-cuts to speed up our processing capabilities but at the cost of occasional inaccuracies such as seen in optical illusions when we 'see' something but are conscious that what we are perceiving cannot be so. Examples abound such as those shown below (illusionindex.org) where our brains get tricked into misreading the lengths of comparable lines, misread colours depending on their surroundings and even fill in gaps to 'see' things which are clearly not actually there. It appears that seeing is not believing after all!

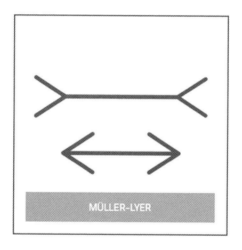

Which line is longer? On first inspection, the upper line appears longer. Measuring them however shows they are equal in length.

If we focus on the lines in the second image on the previous page, a 'solid' white triangle gradually becomes visible in the middle of the picture even though it is clearly not actually there.

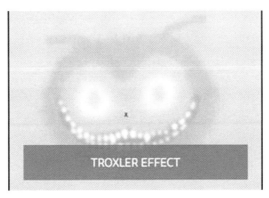

First glance shows a smiling Cheshire Cat but focussing intently on the x will see the cat slowly disappear until only its grin is left as in Lewis Carroll's *Alice in Wonderland*.

First inspection of the image below would suggest that Square A is much darker than Square B. Covering up the surrounding areas will show that they are in fact identical.

Adelson's Checker-Shadow Illusion

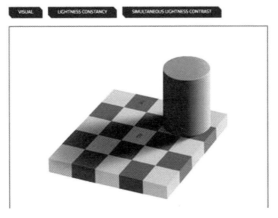

More examples and explanations can be found on the hugely entertaining illusionsindex.org website.

Artists have known about these tricks and illusions for many years and have used them in paintings such as Rembrandt's 'Philosopher in Meditation' where our eye is tricked into focusing on the main figure in the picture by the interplay of light and dark by his window. By covering the bright area we remove this bias and almost immediately see another figure in the foreground to the right of the painting which had been almost hidden until then.

We can already see at this early stage of our analysis how we can get duped into making errors simply due to the nature of our neuroanatomy and the shortcuts our brain takes in the interest of efficiency. In our ancestors' world, these distortions probably went unnoticed as they had little or no impact on their lives. The Safety Critical industries we have created in our modern world, however, have upped the stakes somewhat leaving less room for error before major consequences ensue. Having at least a passing awareness of their existence would probably be a good start for us twenty-first century dwellers.

The other four senses also feed signals into the brain and are just as capable of misinterpretation. For instance, to dupe your temperature sensors, try the experiment on heat sensation where we have one hand in hot water and the other in cold. When we transfer both into a container of lukewarm water, each hand registers a different sensation showing that we are programmed to register change, not absolutes.

The five senses also link up with other areas of the brain. Smell, for instance, can trigger long dormant memories which can bring us various associations and emotions, a trick which shops exploit by having particular scents blown through the air conditioning to encourage us to part with our money.

Think of the classic smell of freshly baked bread or brewed coffee when an estate agent shows us the house of our dreams! I haven't smelt freshly baked bread in the house since!

Our brains are also capable of doing the reverse of this and blocking us from registering a smell at all, a sensation christened by Proctor & Gamble as going 'nose-blind'. P&G, an industry leader in cleaning products with revenues which were already topping $35 billion per year in 1996 (which have since almost doubled), developed a revolutionary new product which they named 'Febreze', a combination of the words fabric and breeze which conjured up the image they wanted to portray for a product which, instead of masking a smell like other air fresheners, actually absorbed the molecules causing the smell and neutralised them (blew them away on the breeze). The active agent had been discovered three years previously by one of P&G's research chemists. The researcher was a smoker and at home that night his wife remarked that he no longer smelt of cigarettes. He pursued the idea and sprayed a solution on fabrics exuding a selection of common unsavoury scents such as sweaty shirts and wet dogs. The product absorbed the odours leaving the fabric much more pleasant-smelling. Febreze launched to great fanfare in 1996 but with no commercial success – sales were atrocious.

A group of scientists were drafted into the marketing team in an attempt to salvage the wonder product. They discovered that the customers they targeted, those with smelly dogs on their furniture for instance, generally couldn't smell what visitors to their house were almost gagging on. Their brains had created a useful (for them) error by removing awareness of a smell which was constantly there – they'd gone 'nose-blind'! P&G added a fresh scent to their previously neutral smelling product and re-shot the TV ads with Febreze shown as the 'reward' at the end of the housework leaving a happy home owner inhaling a noticeably improved scent. The manufacturer had side-stepped the 'error' of the brain attenuating the smell. Within a year, Febreze sales reached $230 million and in 2011 it passed the $1 billion annual turnover milestone. The brain responds better to changes in stimuli and tends to become almost unconscious to a constant stimulus (such as city-dwellers not noticing traffic noise). To our caveman ancestors, something which hadn't eaten you right away probably wasn't going to so it was safe to let your attention move on to more pressing matters.

Awareness of this tendency of the brain to err can prove very useful as our story shows. The various areas of the brain add together all these inputs and provide us with a consciousness it has determined to be of best use to us. Evolution has focused on self-preservation. Our twenty-first century dwellers have created something a little more sophisticated which our marketing industry use to manipulate what we buy, who we socialise with and who we vote for. A little knowledge of how the brain's shortcuts can lead to errors is useful both for us and the advertising industry who 'guide' our decisions. It may surprise you that the average person is now exposed to between 5,000 to 10,000 ads per day but that our brain doesn't register at least half of them – probably one of our more useful errors! We generally need exposure to a product or idea seven times before actually noticing it. The global spend on advertising is now around $560 billion annually so failing to understand our error-prone brain can be a costly matter!

A New Acceptance of Error

After years in the wilderness, error is beginning to emerge from the shadows and shake off the negative connotations generally associated with it. Several contemporary commentators have been instrumental in accelerating this sometimes grudging acceptance that error and failure are actually among the most useful traits we possess. Let's look at three of the most influential people contributing to this phenomenon.

How to Fail with Elizabeth Day

I spend quite a bit of time commuting to and from work and have a number of regular podcasts I listen to which make my time pass more productively. One of my favourites is called 'How to Fail with Elizabeth Day'. Day is a writer living in London who grew up near my home town in Northern Ireland. She is performing what I consider to be one of the most important public services in society at the moment, namely, to make error acceptable and, dare I say it, even somewhat cool!

Day describes in her book *How to Fail* the genesis of her podcast. She explains how she ended up in Los Angeles in late 2017 after the failure of a relationship which had come hot on the heels of her divorce two years previously. She had begun listening to podcasts whilst in California including one by renowned relationship therapist Esther Perel. Day was taken by how anonymous couples would reveal their most vulnerable sides to Perel. She began to consider the possibility of recording a series of interviews with people asking what they had learnt from things going wrong. She knew from her own experience that she learnt much more from things going wrong, her errors, than she did from her successes. What if she could persuade people to talk openly about their own failures?

We live, as Day says, in an era of 'curated perfection'. We post filtered images on Instagram, Facebook and Twitter of our fun, action-packed lives and proudly advertise our achievements. We tend to be less open about the failures along the way and when we do acknowledge them, it tends to be in a 'humble-bragging' way which is actually intended to show that we really are just like you, only a little more amazing.

Society tends not to be very tolerant of mistakes. Day describes the instant on-line condemnation if a mistake in one of her newspaper articles slipped through the fact-checking net, usually totally disproportionate to the error. The natural response to this of course is to play things safe and not to try anything outside our comfort zone. This makes for a reliable but rather dull existence unfortunately. Day describes a civil rights lawyer in the USA in the 1960s who became dispirited by newly qualified lawyers who were reluctant to take on cases unless there was a high probability of a victory.

Since failure often now leads to public shaming (and even to calls for resignation) it's no wonder that we are so reluctant to admit our mistakes. Unfortunately, this also means we are throwing away some of our best opportunities for self-improvement and growth, for developing 'resilience' to use one of our favourite management buzzwords of the moment! Some schools have started teaching the acronym FAIL – First Attempt In Learning.

This was the premise Day used in developing her podcast. She would ask outwardly successful people to describe three failures or errors from their lives. The guest had full control over what they discussed so the type of error they considered worth talking about was as revealing as the error itself. She found that most men struggled to come up with something they had failed at whereas women had no such problem. Day feels that this can be traced back to the neuro-anatomy we discussed earlier in this book. The amygdala, the primitive brain's fear centre, is activated more easily by negative emotional stimuli in women than men and their anterior cingulate cortex of the brain that processes errors is larger so women tend to own their failures more so than men. They are often plagued by self-doubt while less capable and less self-aware men can charge on, blissfully oblivious to their failings. A number of politicians spring to mind!

Day interviewed Canadian writer Malcolm Gladwell on the podcast and he shared a memorable story about the American political scientist Charles Murray, a controversial alternative thinker who co-authored a book in 1994 called *The Bell Curve* which, in one section, essentially argued that people of colour were less intelligent than white people. Gladwell wrote an article for *The New Yorker* about Murray and quoted comments which shared Murray's belief that just because he feels coloured people are of inferior intelligence, it does not mean they should be rounded up, segregated and barred from procreating. Gladwell failed to supply the magazine's fact-checker with the source material and the article went through the editorial process and into the magazine. Unfortunately, he omitted the word 'not' thereby accusing Murray of these egregious opinions in an internationally feted magazine.

Gladwell explains how his disdain for Murray bred some unconscious bias against his opinions which prevented him from seeing the error right in front of him. Apologies were issued but the event clearly demonstrates our mind's ability to 'see what it wants to see', especially if emotions are running high – Gladwell's mother is Jamaican so he was acutely offended by Murray's underlying premise. Awareness of this possibility would go a long way towards actually trapping the error before damage is done.

The political campaigner Gina Miller has a very healthy outlook on failure:

> Yes, I am very good at failing because I think I take risks and I push myself to try new things. And when you do that, you open yourself up to failure, but it's a way of really living life…. In life we're all going to fail, and my view is you've just got to get used to it. It's going to happen, so you might as well have a strategy for how you deal with failure, and then once you've got that in your back pocket, you can go out in life and really take risks.

This resonates with the famous quote attributed to inventor Thomas Edison:

> I have not failed 10,000 times – I've successfully found 10,000 ways that will not work.

Black Box Thinking by Matthew Syed

Journalist and former UK table tennis number one, Matthew Syed released his best-selling book, *Black Box Thinking,* in 2015 which has profoundly changed the way many people now view error. Drawing on his own experiences at the top level of his sport, and subsequently on interviewing many outwardly successful and confident individuals, Syed gradually realised that the common theme linking them was a healthy attitude to failure. He develops this into a description of a 'Growth Mindset' in contrast to a 'Fixed Mindset', an idea he has developed in subsequent books aimed at children and young people such as *You Are Awesome*. Changing the mindset towards error at this early stage could be a game changer in how society reacts to mistakes. It potentially could lead to a more open and tolerant community, an approach I have been advocating in healthcare for a decade now where it has the potential to be truly transformative.

Syed describes how Jason Moser, a psychologist at Michigan State University, studied the neural reactions of volunteers who made mistakes using electro-encephalogram readings. He and his team studied two particular neural responses. Error Related Negativity (ERN) is an involuntary signal discovered in 1990 originating from the anterior cingulate cortex which, as we saw earlier, is activated in the event of error. Error Positivity (Pe) is the response that occurs less than half a second after an error.

They had used a questionnaire to split the volunteers into two groups: one with a Fixed Mindset who believe that qualities such as intelligence or talent are fixed traits, and the other with a Growth Mindset who believe that these traits can be developed and continually improved upon.

The study simply involved the volunteers identifying the middle letter in a sequence of five letters such as BBBBB or BBGBB. Errors inevitably happened as the volunteers lost focus, got distracted and so on, and both groups showed a strong ERN signal when they did – the brain sits up and pays attention when we get things wrong. There was a striking difference however in the Pe response. The spike in the Growth Mindset was three times higher than in the Fixed Mindset group. The amplitude of the spike was also directly correlated to improvement in performance following the mistake. Building on what we discussed earlier, this shows that there is an actual neuro-physiological difference in people who learn from their mistakes compared to those who don't. This gives them an evolutionary advantage and is a common trait in high performing teams, an example of the 'marginal gains' approach so successfully applied by the Sky Cycling team under Sir Dave Brailsford.

Follow-up studies have confirmed Moser's findings, including work by psychologist Carol Dweck on 11- and 12-year-old school children. The children were presented with twelve tests, eight easy ones and four difficult ones. The dichotomy became very apparent when the two groups reached the hard tests.

Those in the Fixed Mindset category assumed they had reached the limits of their ability and simply gave up. Eighty per cent of those in the Growth Mindset rose to the challenge and tried more and more sophisticated strategies to solve the problems; 25 per cent improved their outcomes, some even solving the problems which were supposedly beyond their capabilities.

Mark Gallagher, a Belfast-man who has been working in Formula 1 motor racing for over 25 years, describes his time as Head of Marketing for Eddie Jordan, the Dubliner who headed up the Jordan F1 team. Jordan was an underdog competing against more established and better funded teams so he used his entrepreneurial spirit to position the team so that it punched well above its weight in race results, as well as offering great visibility for sponsors whether the team was winning or not. Gallagher gives a clear insight into the mindset of a successful entrepreneur like Jordan in his 2014 book, *The Business of Winning*, which describes how Jordan's team adopted the shallow authority gradient approach used in aviation, allowing all members of various sections to contribute information and opinions but have a leader with final authority to make the decision. All sections met together regularly to share information to avoid the 'silo thinking' which dogs many bigger businesses.

Gallagher attributes the team's success to this blend of communication, devolved leadership and sharing a common purpose and goal, a mindset that was missing in many of the better funded, yet less successful, squads. Eddie Jordan is a classic example of the 'Growth Mindset' Syed describes, starting as a bank official in Dublin and ending up owning one of the best loved F1 teams of recent decades. A small insight into his approach is the tattoo he apparently has on his wrist, hidden under his watch strap, reading 'FTB', an abbreviation of 'F**k The Begrudgers'.

The Checklist Manifesto by Atul Gawande

While Day normalized error and Syed championed the advantages of diverse teams in improving decision-making, an American surgeon introduced one of aviation's best known tools to healthcare – the checklist.

Atul Gawande will appear again in our healthcare chapter but his scope is broader than just health. He has written extensively in *The New Yorker* magazine on topics outside of medicine but which have something to contribute to the field such as what he learnt about standardisation and SOPs (Standard Operating Procedures) from spending a night in the kitchen of a Boston branch of The Cheesecake Factory. His classic 2009 book, cited in the heading above, explores how a concept as simple as a checklist is essential in industries dealing with complex systems such as construction, aviation and, somewhat grudgingly it would seem, healthcare.

He summarises the underlying problem much more eloquently than I can:

> Here, then, is our situation at the start of the 21st century. We have accumulated stupendous know-how. We have put it in the hands of some of the most highly trained, highly skilled and hard-working people in our society. And, with it, they have indeed accomplished extraordinary things. Nonetheless, that know-how is often unmanageable. Avoidable failures are common and persistent, not to mention demoralising and frustrating, across many fields – from medicine to finance, business to government. And the reason is increasingly evident: the volume and complexity of what we know has exceeded our individual ability to deliver its benefits correctly, safely or reliably. Knowledge has both saved us and burdened us.

That means we need a different strategy for over-coming failure, one that builds on experience and takes advantage of the knowledge people have but somehow also makes up for our inevitable human inadequacies. And there is such a strategy – though it will seem almost ridiculous in its simplicity, maybe even crazy to those of us who have spent years carefully developing ever more advanced skills and technologies.

It is a checklist.

Flying a plane involves quite a few steps which must be carried out in sequence. If a step is missed, consequences can be catastrophic so aviation developed 'Workload Management' as part of its CRM armoury. Perhaps the best known item in this subset is the checklist which takes on several formats depending on the specific area and circum-stance of use. In its basic format, the A4 sheet summarises the critical steps necessary for a safe flight, in a 'challenge and response' format. That means I carry out a series of tasks, for example preparing the aircraft for take-off, then ask my co-pilot to read out the challenges to which I respond by confirming each task has been accomplished (or if not, cor-rect it now while still in a safe environment).

The origins of the idea of a checklist seems to have been in the aftermath of a crash on 30 October 1935 of a Boeing Model 299 which was determined to be 'too much airplane for one man to fly' by one report at the time. It was much more complex than what had gone before and cockpit layout and ergonomics weren't on the agenda in the 1930s. Boeing had designed a new plane it hoped to sell to the US Army Air Corps and had laid on an elaborate show for them at Wright Field in Dayton, Ohio to convince them. The aircraft took off, banked and promptly nose-dived into the ground, bursting into flames. It subsequently transpired that no one had released the mechanical gust-locks from the flight controls which protect the plane while parked in strong winds, thus rendering it uncontrollable.

The solution which Boeing introduced was a simple list of things to check at various stages of the flight. The plane went on to be known as the B-17 Flying Fortress bomber which was used to great effect in World War II. Incidentally, the B-17 was also the star of another Human Factors development you may recall from our aviation chapter. This was the design feature of having the landing gear lever look like a wheel and the flap lever resemble a flap, an idea proposed by one of the fathers of ergonomics, Alphonse Chapanis, in response to a series of accidents due to two similar switches being regularly confused.

The Construction Industry. Gawande describes how checklists are used in the construction industry for building skyscrapers. Figures from Ohio State University in 2003 show that out of 70,000 new commercial building per year and around 1 million new homes, the rate of 'building failure' – a partial or full collapse of a functioning structure – is around 20 per year, that is about 0.00002 per cent. Building standards are continually increasing with energy efficiency, incorporation of new technologies and so on, and skyscraper construction is certainly a complex system, yet failures are remarkably rare. The reason stems from a Human Factors approach involving precisely organised communication, SOPs, shared decision making and checklists ensuring that no critical step has been missed.

Up until the middle of the twentieth century, construction was dominated by Master Builders – experts who designed, engineered and supervised construction from start to finish. Master Builders built cathedrals such as Notre Dame in Paris and St Peter's Basilica in Rome, but the sheer amount of advances in construction overwhelmed the abilities of any one individual to master. The era of specialists was born as teams developed incorporating architects, engineers and sub-specialist construction workers who later sub-divided even further in the same manner doctors have specialised and sub-specialised.

Gawande visited a construction site in Boston where the old Russia Wharf building on the waterfront was being renovated into a 32 story skyscraper with a footprint covering two acres. Lead structural engineer Joe Salvia took him on a tour and introduced him to Finn O'Sullivan, the 'project executive' for the building. O'Sullivan explained that he had up to 500 workers on site any day including up to 60 sub-contractors. He explained how he needed to co-ordinate these teams and make sure their work all meshed so that, despite the enormous complexity, the building would come together correctly. It was obvious that no one, including O'Sullivan, could possibly understand the details of all the individual jobs so a system needed to be developed that would overcome this hurdle.

The solution was a series of large checklists hung on the wall of the conference room outlining the sequence of steps to be carried out, colour-coded to highlight critical steps, without which the others couldn't be achieved. As each task was achieved, a tick was entered in the computer scheduling program and each week or so a new schedule/checklist would be produced. Each of the sixteen trades contributed to creating the checklist and then subcontractors double-check it to spot any errors or omissions. There was a second checklist, a 'submittal schedule', outlining communication schedules dealing with unanticipated events – nothing this complex can be expected to run smoothly! In the absence of a Master Builder who could make a decision on how to resolve problems, various teams would contribute their input and other teams could assess if this had an unintended impact on their work. This draws on the concepts discussed by James Surowiecki in his 2005 book, *The Wisdom of Crowds*, namely, that a group decision is often better than that of an individual, no matter how talented that individual may be. Although we all make mistakes, different people tend to make different mistakes so the group approach maximises the chance of spotting and managing errors before irreversible damage is caused.

Gawande was then introduced to another member of the team who loads each trade's information into a 3-D computer rendering of the building which allows him to 'walk' through the building to try to spot conflicts before they actually happen. Another program called Clash Detective double checked him, spotting conflicts between over-lapping teams' plans and building regulations. The clashes are highlighted in a different colour to draw attention to them. The program follows through on the issue by flagging it up on the next submittal schedule and e-mailed each of the affected teams to let them know their input was required to resolve a discrepancy. A different program called Project Centre allows any worker to flag a problem and trigger the system – an electronic Andon Cord to borrow from the Toyota Production System if you like.

Again, the underlying philosophy was that such a complex project was beyond the abilities of any one person to manage and therefore all available resources, including technology, were employed to aid dissemination of information and track outcomes making use of a Human Factors approach at each step of the way – an Error Management strategy in other words. O'Sullivan says, 'The biggest cause of serious error in this business is a failure of communication', an issue we have already seen to be at the heart of 70 per cent of errors in Safety Critical industries. The checklist system is exceptionally efficient but not foolproof (since they are created and used by humans), a reminder that we can never realistically hope to reach a zero-error state, hence the need to train in Error Management to minimise errors and, failing that, reduce their impact.

Checklists are useful in complex environments like the ones we have described but they also have uses in our everyday lives. Before I leave the house every day I run my standard checklist on the way to the door – 'keys, wallet, phone, glasses, ID'. I drum the same concept into my children when leaving for school in the morning (with varying results!) but the concept is equally valid. Have you a recurring error in your life that could be addressed by a simple checklist?

So, we can see that we are not the first to explore the rich seam of Human Error but, given its almost constant recurrence, we obviously haven't taken in the message fully yet. Let's study error in the world of sport now in order to get a flavour of its impact before we assess what we can do to manage it. Remember, we don't even consider eradicating error – it's too deeply ingrained in us for that – but we can restructure our systems, in industry, sport and elsewhere, to minimise its effects.

Chapter 3

A Good Sport

'You can't be serious man, you cannot be serious!
The ball was on the line, chalk flew up! It was clearly
in. How can you possibly call that out? How many
are you going to miss?'

John McEnroe's first round match in the 1981 Wimbledon tennis tournament brought human error in tennis (and sport generally) to the public's attention. During the match against Tom Gullikson, umpire Edward James ruled McEnroe's serve out. A native New Yorker, McEnroe was already renowned for his short temper and vociferous opinions on officiating mistakes, and had been christened 'Superbrat' by the media.

> Everyone knows it's in, this whole stadium and you call it out? Explain that to me, will you? You guys are the absolute pits of the world!

McEnroe was docked a point by James and later fined $1,500 and threatened with disqualification from the tournament which he subsequently went on to win, beating Bjorn Borg in a nail-biting final and winning the first of three Men's Singles titles there in the next four years.

Interestingly, television replays actually show that McEnroe appears to have been right!

In 2007, a team of researchers at the University of California led by Dr David Whitney studied the phenomenon of erroneous line calls to see if they could shed any light on the issue. Their results take us back to the neurophysiology we looked at in an earlier chapter. They found that our brains struggle to keep pace with rapidly moving objects – our sluggish visual system can take around a tenth of a second to register an image landing on our retina so by the time we see a fast-moving object it has already moved on. Our brain tries to compensate for this error by projecting ahead to where it thinks the object probably is but is prone to over-estimation. It perceives that an object has travelled further than it actually has. A line judge watching a ball travelling rapidly towards the baseline is more likely to perceive a close line call as on the far side of the line ('out') than on the near side ('in'). It's not, strictly speaking, a misjudgement, it's what the line judge genuinely perceives. But they are in error!

Here Comes Hawk-Eye

The researchers looked at 4,000 randomly selected shots from Wimbledon. They found 83 incorrect calls in their sample and 84 per cent of those were incorrectly called 'out'! Their brains had incorrectly 'seen' the ball land beyond the baseline when it was actually in. A 2008 study from the University of Sussex confirmed this view analysing data from the recently introduced Hawk-Eye system and noted that baseline calls tended to be more likely to be called incorrectly than calls on lines running lengthwise on the court such as the centreline or perimeters. The study showed that both line judges and players could determine ball position to within about 40 millimetres – remarkably accurate given the speed of the ball and the distance from the viewer.

However, the human perceptual variation throws up discrepancies (and disputes). The same image produces slightly different perceptions each time it is reviewed. This perceptual error is in addition to normal lapses in concentration or possible gamesmanship by the player disputing the call. The Hawk-Eye system is accurate to within 3.7 millimetres. The study looked at disputed calls within 100 millimetres of the line (less than the width of two tennis balls). It showed around 40 per cent of umpires' calls to be incorrect – enough to have an impact on the outcome of a close match.

To mitigate this problem, many sports now employ electronic help, probably the best known being the 'Hawk-Eye' system mentioned above which was developed in 2001 in the UK by Paul Hawkins and David Sherry. It was first used in cricket for analysing 'leg before wicket' decisions before being adopted by tennis in 2006. It works by placing six (occasionally seven) cameras high in the stands pointing at the court. The cameras track the ball and by triangulating a number of images can predict the trajectory to within 3.6 millimetres (5 per cent of the width of a tennis ball). It was introduced in soccer to the Premier League in the 2013/14 season as goal-line technology.

In tennis, players are entitled to a set number of disputed calls (usually three per set but this resets if they are proven correct and for tie-breaks or other more critical phases of the match). Sony, who now owns the Hawk-Eye company, are working on 'Hawk-Eye Live' which will use ten cameras and will call borderline decisions 'in' or 'out' in real time using a synthesised human voice.

The Gaelic Athletic Association (GAA) in Ireland adopted the technology in June 2013 after it was installed in the GAA's showpiece stadium, Croke Park in Dublin. It was suspended temporarily in August of that year after an issue during the Minor Hurling Semi-final between Limerick and Galway. The Hawk-Eye system ruled a point by Limerick as wide despite the graphic showing it clearly was between the posts making it a valid score. The referee disqualified the score as per the Hawk-Eye call but the system was stood down for the subsequent Senior game which followed. Post-match analysis by Hawk-Eye revealed Human Error on the part of one of their staff which generated the incorrect display, showing that regardless of how advanced our technology becomes error will always find a way through!

CYCLING

My own sport, cycling, isn't immune either. Riding stage 14 of the 1988 Tour de France for the Fagor team of Stephen Roche, Scottish rider Robert Millar was clear with Frenchman Phillipe Bouvatier and looking good for another Tour stage win. On the ascent to Guzet-Neige in the Pyrenees, the two broke clear of the peloton with Italian rider Massimo Ghirotto following close behind. With 200 metres remaining after four and a half hours of racing, there was a sharp left turn to the finish line. The lead motorcycle missed the turn and rode straight past the frantically waving gendarme marshalling the junction into the race vehicles' car park with Millar and Bouvatier following. Millar immediately realised his error and did an about turn but Ghirotto had taken the correct route (not having the motorbike misleading him) and claimed an unexpected victory.

Millar explained later that he had raced this climb in the previous month's Route de Sud but the finish line and parking area were reversed in the Tour. The episode summed up what was a relatively unsuccessful Tour for the 1984 King of the Mountains classification winner and he retired from the race three days later on Stage 17.

Going the wrong way isn't an uncommon event in top level cycling. Stage 5 of the 2015 Tour of Alberta threw up a surprise winner also. Danish rider Lasse-Norman Hansen had broken clear of the bunch and was being chased by Norwegian rider Sven Erik Bystrøm with the peloton close behind. With less than 10 kilometres remaining, Bystrøm took a wrong turn, again despite a flag waving official (who, in fairness to Bystrøm, wasn't very prominently positioned) and was then followed by the whole bunch. By the time the police outriders told him what had happened and the error was rectified, Hansen had gained an unassailable lead and won the stage. Second place went to a rider who had been dropped by the bunch but had taken the correct route on reaching the turn. Hansen said after the race that he hadn't actually intended to win the stage but had simply broken away as he was cold and wanted to warm himself up!

In the 1991 Tour de France, Irish superstar Stephen Roche made an unfortunate slip-up on Stage 2, a team time-trial stage. Leader of the French TonTon Tapis team, Roche was finishing his warm-up for the race alone and arrived at the start line to discover he had got his timings wrong and had missed the start. The rest of his team were already on the road. Roche, the Tour winner in 1987, then raced the 36.5 kilometres alone but finished outside the time limit leading to an automatic exit from the race. Race commissaires dismissed an appeal from Roche and his Tour was unfortunately over before it had properly begun. I had raced against Roche a few weeks earlier in Ireland in the Ever Ready East Coast Classic so maybe he was distracted by the memory … I may be wrong of course!

Four-time Tour winner Chris Froome had an embarrassing time-trialling error too in the 2006 World Championships in Salzburg whilst still riding for Kenya, the country of his birth, before he declared for Great Britain in 2008 when Kenya failed to qualify a team for the Olympic Games in Beijing. Only metres from the start ramp the route veered to the right. There was also a road to the left although there was a race official there to indicate the correct direction.

Froome got a little confused and failed to turn either way and rode straight into the official leaving them both lying on the tarmac! Froome is also remembered for a memorable incident on the Mont Ventoux climb on Stage 12 of the 2016 Tour when he, Richie Porte and Bauke Mollema crashed into the back of a lead motorcycle which got obstructed by the spectators trying to get a better view. While waiting for his team car to reach him with a replacement bike, Froome starting running up the climb, no easy feat when wearing cycling shoes! The race jury later awarded all three riders the same finish time, negating the effects of the accident.

Cycling and Safety

One of the biggest concerns however in cycling currently is rider safety. Errors have been all too common over the last decade jeopardising riders and creating negative publicity for the sport which is still recovering from the drug scandals of recent decades.

Suze Clemitson of *The Guardian* wrote in 2016 that 25-year-old Antoine Demoitié's death in the Spring Classic,

Gent-Wevelgem, 'should be a wake-up call for cycling's crowded races'. Outspoken BMC team manager Jim Ochowicz demanded in 2015 for 'someone to please step forward' from the Union Cycliste Internationale Safety Committee, criticising their lack of action following a number of high profile incidents involving his riders. 'Safety problems at races continue to accelerate and are now a nearly everyday issue'. Ochowicz proposed a series of safety measures including reducing the number of riders, improving course design and addressing the number and driving standards of the vehicles involved with a race.

Slovakian legend Peter Sagan was knocked off his bike on Stage 8 of the Vuelta a España that year by a Shimano service team motorcycle, but luckily avoided serious injury. The motorbike pilot was excluded from the race and Sagan was fined 200 Swiss francs for making 'threats and insults' to him. His Tinkoff-SaxoBank team threatened to sue the organisers saying, 'Such accidents caused by reckless human error are unacceptable at the top level of the sport of cycling'. Ochowicz repeated his call in February 2016. The UCI support legislation such as the 'A metre matters' campaign for us civilian riders on our streets but its approach seems to fall short when we turn to the professional peloton. For instance, race regulations state that race organisers are solely responsible for the safety of the event but they can only limit the numbers of vehicles in the cavalcade with the express permission of the UCI.

Only weeks after Ochowicz's call for safety to be addressed, Demoitié crashed in the Gent-Wevelgem and was then hit by a Commissaire's (a race referee) motorbike. He died a few hours later of his injuries. Riders such as German sprinter, Marcel Kittel spoke out saying:

> There is a difference between riders crashing in the last hectic kilometres of a race, fighting for the right wheel before the sprint and riders crashing because of unsafe road furniture, reckless driving of motorbikes or cars, extreme weather conditions and unsafe race routes.

Riders have supported Kittel's comments but, as Clemitson pointed out, Rule 1.2.063 states that 'In no case can the UCI be held responsible for defects in the course or installations or for any accidents that may occur' giving them little incentive to get involved with safety while recent initiatives they have implemented include the length of a rider's socks in relation to their leg length!

UCI President at the time, Britain's Brian Cookson, declared that 'complex problems require complex solutions' although many riders and team managers have suggested remarkably simple solutions which would be a good start.

The first stage of the 2020 Tour de France saw riders again take things into their own hands after a number of crashes on slippy roads around Nice led to dozens of riders injured and Bahrain-McLaren rider Rafael Valls sustaining a broken femur. Germany's Tony Martin went to the front of the bunch and persuaded riders to neutralise the final descent after requests to the Commissaires for intervention were refused, only starting racing again with 25 kilometres to go on the flat run in to the finish on the Promenade des Anglais. An appeal by the Lotto-Soudal team after their rider, John Degenkolb, finished outside the time limit after one of the crashes was refused by the race jury, spelling the end of his three week race on Day 1.

Some riders have complained that their own representative body, the Cyclistes Professionnels Associés (CPA), haven't been forceful enough, but apparently a group of about 30 senior, influential riders have formed an informal group sharing ideas so we may see some progress on this in the near future. The recent spate of crashes have led to riders becoming more vocal and taking control of their own safety. In the past, an influential rider or 'patron' such as Bernard Hinault had the authority to call the shots in circumstances such as these, but this new development is allowing all teams to have an influence on decisions. Early the following week, the CPA issued a statement calling on the race organisers to step up and do more for rider safety. The joint approach will hopefully mitigate against teams trying to manipulate events for their own benefit and keep a united front on one of the most important issues in cycling.

Despite what the UCI has said, many of these issues are actually remarkably simple. Unfortunately their focus seems to be misplaced. In April 2021, new anti-littering rules came in banning riders from throwing used team branded drink bottles to the side of the road, a practice which has delighted generations of fans who keep them as souvenirs. This rule has been implemented mercilessly from day one with fines sometimes exceeding the prize money available to riders. Meanwhile, with three kilometres to go in Stage 2 of the Tour des Alpes in late April 2021, riders were racing along a side-street lined on both sides with parked cars, an extremely dangerous situation which the UCI appear to have little interest in. Efforts by the riders' union to highlight this danger have so far had little effect unfortunately.

So, error is ubiquitous in sport too and has become a subject which sports psychologists often focus on. The most successful sportspeople aren't the ones with the fewest errors, they are the ones who deal with them best and move on quickly without losing focus. Again, it's all down to good Error Management. That applies equally to participants as well as event organisers. Let's turn now to a sport which, unlike cycling, has taken a serious and proactive approach to error and its consequences for several decades now with spectacular results.

FORMULA ONE

Formula One motor racing is the highest level of open wheel motor racing overseen by the the Fédération Internationale d'Automobile (FIA). There is both a Driver's Championship and Constructor's Championship which run simultaneously with events over three days – practice sessions on the Friday of a Grand Prix weekend, followed by qualifying on the Saturday and the race on the Sunday where points are awarded for the top ten finishers as well as for the fastest lap. Drivers must hold the FIA's highest level licence to compete, namely a Super Licence. As in the history of aviation, error was always an issue and, again like aviation, the speed involved meant errors could be deadly.

Attempts were made to improve safety prompted by a better understanding of errors. Again though, like aviation, Formula One needed a 'Tenerife' event to kick-start dramatic change which transformed the sport into the model of safety it is now. That event was the death of reigning World Champion, Ayrton Senna, live on TV at the Italian Grand Prix at Imola in 1994. Let's trace the history of Formula One to see how Error Management evolved and how it has transformed the sport.

The first Formula One race was held in 1948, while the inaugural World Championship was launched at the British Grand Prix at Silverstone in 1950, consisting of only seven races. The 2022 season comprised twenty-two races.

Driving a car at speeds of up to 200 miles per hour is, unsurprisingly, quite a risky endeavour. In the 1950s, however, this was simply accepted as part of the deal and neither car manufacturers nor racing circuits paid much attention to improving safety.

Despite the smaller number of events, fifteen drivers lost their lives at the wheel of a Formula One car in the 1950s. This improved a little in the 1960s. Cars had safety belts improved whilst fuel tanks were given some protection. Roll bars were added to protect the driver in the event of the car turning over. Helmets (rudimentary though they were) and fire-resistant overalls became mandatory. However, thirteen drivers still lost their lives in that decade.

The 1970s saw the beginning of the drivers' campaign for improved safety, led by Jackie Stewart. It gathered momentum near the end of the decade with the death of Ronnie Peterson in 1978 at the Italian Grand Prix in Monza. Peterson was a ten-time GP winner and had been runner-up to Stewart in the 1971 World Championship. He was involved in a multiple car pile-up on the first lap in Monza due partly, it is alleged, to an error involving the green start light being lit unexpectedly early which meant the field bunched up going into the early corners. Peterson was shunted off the track and his car caught fire. Other drivers managed to extricate him from the car with only minor burns but he had sustained 27 fractures to his legs and feet. He was transferred to intensive care but died of complications the following day.

This decade saw the improvement of safety at races with long circuits removed (which had made rapid access for medical cover problematic) and the first modern day F1 cars introduced with aerofoil spoilers creating huge down force thus improving road holding. In 1979 the FIA appointed a professional, full-time race starter, partly in response to the previous year's incident in Monza, and improved fire safety was also incorporated into the cars. Nonetheless, F1 still suffered twelve fatalities during this decade.

The most significant development in its approach to safety occurred in 1978 with the appointment of Professor Sid Watkins as official Race Doctor to F1. Watkins had been involved with motor sport from the 1950s, including during his time as a neurosurgeon in Syracuse, New York. He returned to London in 1970 and a chance meeting with Bernie Ecclestone saw him being offered the F1 post. Safety at the time was very much an after-thought with a medical tent and a local volunteer ambulance team. After Peterson's crash Watkins insisted that many safety changes be implemented before the next race, including improved equipment and facilities, provision of a Medevac helicopter and an anaesthetist, as well as a high powered safety car which followed the race for the first lap, statistically the time most major accidents occur. All requests were accepted and F1 moved into a new era.

These improvements contributed to the greater safety of the drivers and only four deaths occurred in the 1980s, significantly fewer than in previous decades despite more drivers, races and higher speeds. The sport moved onto a more serious business footing with Ecclestone and Max Mosley setting up the Formula 1 Management group which standardised the race meetings, track design, cars, drivers' licences and so on. The 1980s saw the introduction of carbon fibre technology, while turbo charging was limited initially then completely outlawed from the 1989 season to reduce the speed of the cars.

F1 then enjoyed a period of twelve years without a fatality in a race meeting since the death of Gilles Villeneuve in 1982 in Belgium with drivers surviving crashes that previously had been fatal. Unfortunately, 1994 saw the removal of many of the in-car safety devices the drivers had got used to plus an increase in the speed and power of the cars. Several drivers (ironically, including Senna) predicted that in 1994 there would be an increase in the number of fatal accidents. This prediction came to pass during a horrific weekend for the sport at the Italian Grand Prix at Imola.

The race weekend started badly at pre-race testing on the Friday as Brazilian Rubens Barrichello suffered serious injuries when his car hit a kerb and got airborne. Professor Watkins has been credited with saving his life by clearing Barrichello's airway after he swallowed his tongue on impact. Senna actually stopped his own car to attend the scene of the accident of his friend and countryman. The following day during qualifying, another serious crash occurred which cost the life of Austrian driver Roland Ratzenberger after a front wing failure caused him to crash into a concrete wall. Senna was again involved when he commandeered an official car to rush to scene of the accident and on to the medical centre where he learned of Ratzenberger's death. Professor Watkins was said to be so concerned at Senna's mental state following the serious accident of his compatriot, Barrichello, and the death of his friend Ratzenberger that he tried to persuade Senna not to race and to go fishing with him instead!

On the morning of the race, 1 May 1994, Senna set the fastest time at the warm up session by almost a second. Following this he had a thirty minute meeting with recently retired driver Alain Prost where he discussed the need to improve safety and agreed to meet up before the following race in Monaco. Following the drivers' briefing before the race, Senna discussed with the other drivers the need to re-establish the Grand Prix Drivers Association in order to address safety concerns and, as the most senior driver, agreed to lead it.

An accident on the first lap of the race threw debris into the crowd and onto the track and led to the safety car being deployed. The race restarted at the end of Lap 5 with Senna leading Michael Schumacher. Schumacher later commented that Senna appeared nervous going into the high speed Tamburello corner. On the next lap, Senna lost control on the corner but managed to reduce his speed from 192 miles per hour before hitting a concrete barrier at 131 miles per hour. Senna suffered multiple, unsurvivable head injuries. Watkins supervised his removal from the car and performed an emergency tracheotomy before having him air-lifted to Bologna Hospital where he died of his injuries hours later. A further error at the track led to a race car being released prematurely from the pit-lane and almost colliding with the helicopter on the track.

Legal arguments ensued for years afterwards on the cause of the accident (driver error, rear wheel puncture and the failure of a hastily lengthened steering column have all been blamed) as well as the time of death. Italian law decrees death as the time of a severe brain injury, regardless of whether the heart is still beating. This would have involved declaring the accident a crime scene and cancellation of the race. The same argument held for Ratzenberger's crash the day before as some felt that qualifying and the actual race should both have been abandoned, an event which would have cost the insurers $6.5 million.

Examination of Senna's car after the crash found that he had an Austrian flag which he planned to unfurl at the end of the race in honour of Ratzenberger. The following race at Monaco left the first two grid positions empty and painted one with the Brazilian flag and the other with the Austrian flag.

The Drivers Association was set up before that next race and was headed by Niki Lauda and Michael Schumacher. Many safety changes were demanded. Circuits were redesigned including the fatal Tamburello turn becoming a chicane to slow traffic down; Imola was subsequently withdrawn from F1 altogether. Pit-lanes saw speed limits enforced, perimeter walls were moved back and adjusted such that cars would hit at an oblique angle to reduce impact and circuits were redesigned. Cars were lengthened to allow more room, power reduced and more head support built in. Safety became F1's number one priority with the result that the sport wouldn't suffer another race fatality for over twenty years until the accident involving Jules Bianchi in 2014 which would lead to his death nine months later from his injuries.

Formula One has become an example to other Safety Critical industries on how to transform performance and culture by addressing error. It changed from a high-risk sport where it was simply accepted that things could go seriously wrong to one where errors were actively sought out and mitigated such that safety would be maximised. The most important aspect of this is that Formula 1 changed its culture. It decided that risking drivers' and spectators' lives simply wasn't acceptable any more which became the over-arching factor in decisions involving track design, car design and so on. It was a living culture so that when Formula 2 driver Henry Surtees died in 2009 after being hit by a loose wheel, F1 started looking for a solution. This eventually resulted in the introduction of the controversial Halo device which protects the driver from flying debris though some drivers had objections on aesthetic grounds.

The increased reliance on radio communication, live telemetry and team involvement in decision making also leads to more public errors such as the very costly decision by Mercedes AMG's Head of Strategy, James Vowles, in the 2018 Austrian GP not to take advantage of the race being slowed by the Virtual Safety Car to bring leader Lewis Hamilton in for fresh tyres (unlike his main competitors who all did so). The resulting loss of places cost Hamilton a clear chance of a win and also his lead in the Drivers' Championship. Vowles was forced to apologise to a furious Hamilton on live radio, acknowledging that the error was his:

'Lewis, this is James,' he said on the radio. 'We understand. It's my mistake.'

A seething Hamilton said: 'I want to say something, but just leave me to it.'

Moments later, Hamilton was back on the radio again. 'I don't get it,' he yelled. 'I am not going to be able to pass these guys. We have thrown away the win.'

After the race, Hamilton apparently paid tribute to the team but used the episode to force a rethink on strategy and the need to anticipate and manage errors. He recovered to win his fifth World Championship and Mercedes won their fifth consecutive Constructors' Championship. It's not about whether you make errors, it's about what you learn from them!

The F1 response to Senna's death is a testament to what can be done when error is accepted as inevitable but its consequences aren't. Circuit design, car design and enhanced medical cover have all contributed to the huge improvements in safety. A similar change in mindset and expectations can transform the outcomes in industry and society and is perhaps the main theme of this book.

There was a notable overlap between F1 and healthcare in the early twenty-first century which we will discuss in our healthcare chapter as well as McLaren's divergence into designing and producing respiratory support devices during the Covid-19 pandemic in 2020. Formula 1's most significant development though continues to be the cultural change brought about after the death of Senna in 1994 – F1's Tenerife moment. This change of attitude to risk and error meant that the industry was free to seek out potential errors and learn from near misses in order to make changes which improved safety. The Just Culture allowed reviews of the sport's systems and continuous improvements to be made with results as spectacular as those seen in aviation.

This pattern will be evident in other industries as we shall see, although some have implemented it more enthusiastically than others which may explain the inconsistency of results.

So how do you approach error in your life? Are you forgiving when someone gets your order wrong in a takeaway or does it cause a meltdown? Are you forgiving of yourself when you make a mistake or do you beat yourself up for hours over it? By simply changing our attitude to the inevitability of error, we can greatly reduce the stress in our lives (and in the lives of others). Once we accept that error is often not our fault or, in most cases, not that big a deal, life becomes that little bit easier. So, cut yourself some slack and read on to meet some people where error usually is a big deal – our emergency services and legal system.

Chapter 4

Blues and Twos and
Justice for All

When we are in difficulty, we call for help. When we are in big trouble, we call the emergency services, who arrive promptly by deploying their blue lights and two-tone sirens – 'Blues and Twos'. Let's have a look at how error is dealt with in some of these high-stakes services, namely firefighting, security and then in the justice system.

FIREFIGHTING

Dr Sabrina Cohen-Hatton, the Chief Fire Officer in the West Sussex Fire and Rescue Service, describes the thought processes of senior firefighters in her excellent 2019 book *The Heat of the Moment*. Firefighting is another Safety Critical industry – errors occur as in every walk of life but outcomes are often life threatening. Sabrina completed a PhD in Behavioural Neuroscience in 2013 and has been instrumental in changing the Fire Service's approach to error.

In an interview with *Marie Claire* magazine, Sabrina credits a very personal experience as the instigator of the change she has brought to the service. She was part of a crew responding to a fire which was already being fought by another crew which included her then fiancé, Mike. On the way to the scene, Sabrina was aware that a firefighter had been seriously injured at the blaze but didn't know who it was. It transpired that Mike was safe but another colleague had been hurt due to errors in decision-making at the incident. Subsequent research shocked her by showing that around 70 to 80 per cent of industrial accidents were due to error yet this wasn't being systematically addressed. This prompted her to study psychology, eventually leading to her Doctorate and her interest in the management of error in the fire service.

Sabrina's research for the National Fire Chiefs Council included fitting cameras to Incident Commanders' helmets and studying the decisions made and subsequent outcomes. She identified that only 20 per cent of decisions were made using an analytical approach, the other 80 per cent were simply on gut feeling with 'decision traps' being a major risk factor. Her research led to a structured decision control process which encourages commanders to consider goals, risks and consequences of their decisions taken under often extreme pressure. The system is the Decision Control Process, a three-stage method where commanders ask themselves:

1. What do I want to achieve?

2. What do I expect to happen as a result?

3. Do the risks outweigh the benefits?

The system was incorporated into National Operational Guidelines for Decision Making. This goal-orientated training has been shown to increase Situational Awareness fivefold. Sabrina has initiated various training techniques such as simulation/virtual reality, firehouse training and 'live burn' practice fires. She co-supervises a research group in Cardiff University studying decision-making in the emergency services environment.

In her book, Sabrina Cohen-Hatton also outlines another crucial aspect of Error Management – practice. She describes an incident where she was in command of a team of fire-fighters responding to an explosion in the Blackhall Tunnel in London resulting in structural damage and thirty civilians being trapped inside. By the time she arrives and takes charge, the officer who had initial control has deployed twenty crew into the tunnel and 115 civilians have already been successfully evacuated. Her decisions will be based on information as to exactly how many civilians are left in the tunnel, their location and a report on its structural integrity by an engineer. None of this information is available at this early stage. She first contacts her police counterpart, their commanding officer, to be briefed on the situation from the policing aspect. She is now informed of a telephoned threat of a second bigger device expected to detonate in 15 to 20 minutes, a threat deemed from a credible source. It appears that the small device was to lure emergency services to the scene before targeting them with a bigger one.

So, decision time! She estimates it'll take 90 minutes to evacuate everyone based on what she knows at the moment given that there are thirty civilians including young children and twenty crew in there and a credible belief that a bomb will explode in minutes. She's the boss, so what's the plan? While she's thinking, let's have a look at one of the most high profile fires in recent UK history.

GRENFELL TOWER

An event in 2017 showed that however much progress we've made, errors will still occur and learning must be continuous and life-long. In June of that year, a tower block of flats in London caught fire. The subsequent report into the incident praised the individual firefighters but felt the organisational system they were operating in had let them and the public down. Many of the problems raised in the report related to failures of Error Management and the principles have relevance to anyone working in Safety Critical industries, not just the Fire Service.

Many of the issues here will be familiar to us from our study of Crew Resource Management. They arose in the very critical Phase 1 report released in October 2019 investigating the June 2017 Grenfell Tower fire in West London which resulted in the death of 72 people and included serious criticism of the London Fire Brigade (LFB) response to the disaster. As in almost all serious incidents the underlying causes were many fold. There were, however, many failures which could possibly have been mitigated through Threat and Error Management analysis before the event. The most obvious was the refurbishment of the tower using aluminium composite cladding with a flammable polyethylene core, a major error, as was the electrical fault in the fridge-freezer in a fourth-floor flat which led to the fire. This started a chain of events, the outcome of which would be determined by the resources available and the choices made by emergency services. Hindsight has not been kind.

Sir Martin Moore-Bick's report praised the courage of individual firefighters on the night but found institutional failures in the LFB, concluding that their planning and preparation for this type of incident was 'gravely inadequate'. He said control room staff fielding the 999 calls 'undoubtedly saved lives' but he found shortcomings in 'practice, policy and training'. Senior control room staff had not been trained in handling large-scale incidents where so many people would be asking for fire survival guidance. He said that mistakes made in a 2009 fire in Camberwell which took the lives of three women and three children were repeated. A lack of training in knowing when to call for an evacuation and how to manage it was highlighted after residents were told to stay in their flats for almost two hours when the evacuation should have commenced perhaps an hour earlier. Communication from the control room to firefighters on the ground was 'improvised, uncertain and prone to error' whilst Incident Commanders seemed unwilling to change tack when their initial approach wasn't working. Crews at the scene had also never received training on the techniques needed to fight a cladding fire.

The LFB Fire Chief, Dany Cotton, was criticised for her opinion that training for fighting a cladding fire was akin to training for the likelihood of the 'Space Shuttle landing on The Shard' and that, even in hindsight, she wouldn't change anything about the response to the disaster, prompting fears that the service would fail to learn the lessons necessary to deal with a similar event in the future. Cotton took early retirement shortly after the report was published and was replaced by her deputy, Andy Rowe.

Perhaps Cotton's biggest mistake was her seeming inability to accept error as inevitable, and that we can always improve our performance by reviewing major events and finding possible weaknesses. We saw in our study of decision-making that the most crucial part was reviewing the result and running the process again to try to improve it. Grenfell can be assessed from all the CRM angles and shows that there is always room for improvement.

Previous disasters have often led to a clamouring for people to blame and demands for retribution such as sackings or disciplinary action, but we need to change this approach. We are all fallible and must be accountable for our actions, however can we afford to dismiss people who have put their hands up and acknowledged their error and shown a determination to learn from the event? We will be left with fewer capable people and will have given others an incentive to cover up mistakes rather than learning from them. We need to move on from the 'name, blame and shame' approach to one that will be to our benefit in the long term. This is applicable to all industries, indeed life generally, and we will come back to it regularly over the following chapters.

Phase 2 of the Grenfell Public Inquiry, which began in September 2017, reported that the company who supplied the controversial cladding, Harley Facades, has permanently lost many design documents after allegedly storing all this information on a single employee's laptop which was 'wiped' after that employee left the company. There was no backup made onto any company server or copies linked to another e-mail account despite the importance of the information. This is a major impediment to uncovering the truth of what happened. Given that I make seven backups of this manuscript every night before signing off suggests either a grossly short-sighted error by the company or a deep-seated fear of being held responsible for major failures such as Grenfell. Either way, it shows a dysfunctional relationship with error which stands in the way of investigating what factors led to the disaster and therefore affording us the opportunity of correcting them. I fear we still have a long road ahead of us.

So, how is Sabrina getting on with her conundrum? The good news is that, like my own example earlier, this is a simulation, not a real event. It is the cheapest, simplest version of this type of recreation in that it is a mental exercise in a bar over a bottle of wine with a colleague who specialises in this type of scenario. They have been at a training conference in Scotland and her friend, Professor Jonathan Crego, is testing her decision-making thought process.

Remember that Cohen-Hatton's research showed that in 80 per cent of events such as this tunnel scenario, decisions were being made by a 'seat of the pants' process rather than a formalised structured framework. Not very reassuring given the level of error inherent in the information generally available and the seriousness of the potential outcomes. One of the issues she found in her studies was 'decision inertia', a delay in making crucial decisions for fear of making the wrong one. It is sub-divided into two groups, 'decision deferral', putting off making the call or passing it onto someone else, and 'decision omission', not making any decision at all. This is understandable in that people don't want to be responsible for having ordered what turned out to be a catastrophe. We also live in a society where people are very intolerant of failure (in others, mainly) and when something goes wrong, they want someone to blame.

Cohen-Hatton's work focuses on improved decision-making. It trains a systematic approach to the discipline as opposed to the previous 'seat of the pants' version. Her approach is similar to the '6 As' technique.

1. Aware that there is a problem – the emergency call.

2. Assign control of the situation so someone is always alert to developments (for instance, just after her arrival while she assesses the situation before taking control from a less senior officer).

3. Assess in detail – take input from a selection of stakeholders.

4. Agree a course of action amongst the team – solo runs generally don't end well in Safety Critical industries!

5. Act – implement the agreed plan.

6. Assess again. Has the plan improved things? If yes, great. If not, go back to the start of the cycle.

In this case, she has been presented with a 'wicked problem', that is, one which is constantly evolving, is based on incomplete information, often has contradictory requirements and has no right answer in that someone is going to get hurt by your decisions regardless of how well you perform. Performance is improved by practice so rehearsing scenarios such as this improves a leader's ability to make the best call (not the 'right' call – there isn't always one of those) in such a scenario. We can see from our previous exploration of Crew Resource Management principles that the same issues are addressed in Sabrina's scenario as would be on my flight-deck or indeed in any Safety Critical industry in the event of a major failure. The crucial point is that the problems encountered and the framework we apply in addressing them are universal.

This only dawned on me when I passed my command checks to qualify as a captain in my airline back in 2010. I had been expecting the focus to be on knowing the aeroplane inside out and knowing the content of the many manuals covering technical information about the plane – procedural manuals on company guidelines for almost every topic, legal manuals for every country we fly to and so on. These were important and a good working knowledge was expected, but the critical issues were rarely to do with the plane. They were always regarding people management, decision-making under tight time constraints and constantly trying to plan ahead to anticipate and manage errors – and errors did occur, every day. I have been obsessed with how we address error ever since. I realise that we must have a good idea what's in all the manuals but it's expected that we know where to find stuff, not to recite it from memory. Indeed, we get criticised (rightly) if we perform a common checklist from memory rather than reading it to avoid errors through complacency.

I always felt that our aviation approach could be beneficial to my former colleagues in healthcare and recruited a team from my airline to help me share our learning. The more I read, the more I recognised similarities in thinking across the various 'risky' industries and realised that we are all trying to solve essentially the same problems. These diverse groups are now learning from one another in an attempt to improve outcomes in all industries. Oh, and Sabrina's tunnel incident – how did it turn out in the end? Was there a second bomb? Did anyone get hurt? You'll have to check out her book, *The Heat of the Moment*, to find out!

THE SECURITY INDUSTRY

Emergency services such as our police force can't be expected to handle routine issues such as crowd control at venues or to protect our belongings. Instead, we rely on security companies and devices as an adjunct to our police force and justice system, which might include, for example, physical security for a venue, cash delivery vans, product security for vehicles, or online security at work or at home. All these systems are designed and operated by humans at some level so is it safe to assume that some errors are inevitable? Let's have a look.

Security Staff

It's 14 September 1989 and The New York Stock Exchange is preparing for a protest by a group called ACT UP (AIDS Coalition To Unleash Power) at midday, timed to coincide with other protests in San Francisco and London. ACT UP was formed in 1987 by a group of Gay and Lesbian activists in New York at the height of the AIDS epidemic which was having a particularly severe effect on the city. They were protesting against the apathy of the public and inaction by the government to support those involved. They adopted the slogan 'Silence = Death' with writer Larry Kramer being one the highest profile members. Their main target was the American pharmaceutical company Burroughs-Wellcome who manufactured Azothioprine (AZT), the only drug known at that time to slow down the effects of the HIV virus. They accused the company of profiteering by charging around $10,000 for a year's supply of the drug, beyond the reach of most of the AIDS victims who needed it. They also accused the industry of showing little interest in researching cheaper or better alternatives.

Demonstrations had been held in 1987 and 1988 in New York on the junction of Wall Street and Broadway and at the drug company's offices as well as at the offices of the Food and Drug Administration (FDA) who approved drugs for use, but the 1989 demo was planned to take place in front of the NYSE itself. However, a small group of activists had a different plan. Two of their number were traders at the exchange and had valuable information which allowed an alternative protest. The exchange is formally opened for business at 9.30 am by the ringing of the iconic bell. Many traders would nip outside for a smoke before business and move back in just in time for trading to open. Security staff were used to this pattern and although traders had photographic ID cards, being in a shirt and tie and in possession of a large trader's badge was enough to slip past them.

Five ACT UP members walked onto the trading floor along with their two colleagues who actually worked there just before 9.30 am. The five targeted a small VIP balcony overlooking the floor and slipped discretely up the stairs while their friends stayed with the other traders. Ten seconds before the bell, the five unfurled a banner with 'Sell Burroughs-Wellcome' printed on it, dropped fake $100 bills onto the floor and started sounding foghorns, delaying the opening of trading for the first time in the Stock Exchange's history. Their colleagues were ready with cameras to record the disturbance. Security staff overpowered the five who had by now chained themselves to the balcony whilst the other two slipped out and transported the cameras to the nearby Associated Press who released the pictures.

Burroughs-Wellcome reduced the price of AZT four days later by around 20 per cent initially, with a further drop bringing it to around $6,500. Competition brought better and cheaper drugs and within a short while, a year's suppression therapy cost around $2,000 which brought it within reach of a much larger group of patients. The FDA gradually changed the system for approving drugs from small, lengthy trials to large, short trials when appropriate, and also allowed access to experimental drugs, dramatically changing the landscape and credited with bringing forward the eventual discovery of an effective treatment.

The group that day used a number of Human Factors approaches to exploit the errors they were expecting. Security were anticipating a demo at midday so their Situational Awareness would be focused on that. The group also knew that Workload Management meant that the usual large group rushing in from their smoke break at the last minute weren't formally checked as security didn't want to be seen to disrupt trading, and when the team were dressed like everyone else the security staff exhibited confirmation bias by seeing what they expected to see. It brings to mind the phrase, 'Where do you hide a lie? In a forest of lies!' Its effectiveness also highlighted that businesses don't like to look bad and, if it's detrimental to their share price, can be persuaded into action.

Vehicle Security

How secure are our vehicles? Figures for the UK covering 2017/18 show over 112,000 vehicles stolen in a year, that's one every five minutes. These rates have been increasing in England for the last five years, decreasing in Scotland while Northern Ireland has stayed the same. In short, that's a lot of vehicles stolen in the UK. So, what errors are we making that are contributing to this?

Police in Stevenage appealed to motorists to lock their cars after an unbelievable 50 per cent of thefts from vehicles were from unlocked cars! Items stolen included phones, laptops, sat-navs, designer sunglasses, bank cards and so on. They re-emphasised the standard advice not to leave valuable items on display (and at least lock your car). Other simple advice is to park somewhere secure and not to leave the keys in the vehicle while nipping into a shop or to pay for fuel, and when at home not to leave keys on display or near a door where thieves can access them easily. Whilst in the past people often used mechanical devices such as steering wheel locks or wheel clamps, most cars built since 1998 have electronic locking, alarms and immobilisers. Apart from accidentally pressing the wrong button on the fob or the locks not actually activating, thieves can now intercept the code transmitted to the car from up to 100 metres away allowing them access once you are safely out of the way. Similar electronics allow them to over-ride immobilisers. They even work at your home. One thief stands at your door with a relay box which tricks your fob into emitting its signal which the relay then boosts and sends to a second thief standing by the car which they can then use to open and start the vehicle.

What happens to your car next? Cars are sold on the black market for astonishingly low prices. Vehicles retailing at £40,000 to 50,000 are worth only £1,000 to 2,000 to the thieves stealing them with vehicles worth up to £100,000 selling for little more, around £3,000! Improved security by manufacturers include a 'sleep' mode when fobs that haven't moved for a length of time can't be activated until physically moved stopping thieves using the relay technology. Tracking devices which usually plug in to a car's USB vehicle maintenance port are simply discarded rendering them useless. The final destination for vehicles is obviously difficult to gauge but cars stolen in the UK have turned up in Spain, Greece and the Middle East. Figures from Manchester police show that around 25 per cent are never traced and a large proportion of them are thought to end up broken up for parts in so-called 'chop shops'.

Internet Security

We are all spending increasing amounts of time online nowadays and it's likely to increase. We shop, bank, communicate and socialise online and the fall-out from the pandemic has made access more important than ever. Businesses try to protect our information by implementing intricate security systems and multi-stage identity verification, and access to most sites requires using a password. So that should be pretty secure then, right? No! Errors abound!

Studies show that 21 per cent of us forget the password we've picked within a fortnight and 25 per cent forget a password at least daily. Website designers have a number of options to address this – they don't want us locked out of their site. A past favourite was to ask us a security question. Unfortunately, it was often easier to answer (where did you grow up?) than to guess the password itself so this actually became the weakest point of the whole process. The most common approach now is to send an e-mail to the address registered to the user (security firms recommend that an e-mail address is used as the username for a number of reasons) with a link to a password reset function. A previous programming error was to post a message outlining when a valid e-mail address was not found. This was exploited by software which could fire a huge number of e-mail addresses at a system and have it verify valid ones which could then be sold on to advertisers or worse. A common approach now is to inform the user that an e-mail has been sent to their registered address with a reminder to check their junk mail folder – another common source of errors when looking for mail. A follow-up e-mail informing them of the change of password is another safety-net so the user is aware.

So, what are our options? One is to use a password manager program which can generate much more complicated passwords than we can remember and sign us into websites by remembering them across our devices. The obvious flaw here is that we sign into them using, guess what, a password!

One that we need to remember and that will give anyone getting past that step access to all our information. Only 1 per cent of us use password managers. Other options are using phrases as passwords such as 'IUseAPhraseAsAPassword!'. A more complex version is abbreviations or acronyms. For instance '20wtyIwmfb!' (20 was the year I wrote my first book!). Using an easily guessed password such as a child's name but typing the letter to the left on the keyboard works and apparently becomes second nature (maybe I didn't try it for long enough!). Easily spotted letter substitutions such as 'Ch33rs' are easily searched for by algorithms so are best avoided. Adding mathematical symbols is a good move as they're rarely used '2020+5=2025!'. Some passwords allow brackets or spaces which break up word patterns 'use a space' or 'use a (space)'. If we want different passwords for different sites, we could add the site to the password 'bubbles-amazon' or 'bubbles-bt'. Many work sites insist on regular password changes so changing them on the first of the month and including that month helps in remembering, for example, 'memory.april20' and so on.

So, what are the guys on the other side (the ones trying to steal our details) doing? Trying to log into a website by using a computer to guess our password doesn't work well since most lock after a number of failed attempts or have Captcha checks like selecting pictures with traffic lights to eliminate bots. Captcha is an acronym for 'Completely Automated Public Turing test to tell Computers and Humans Apart' and is also known as a reverse Turing test since it is administered by a computer, not a human. Incidentally, the information generated is also used to help train computers in Artificial Intelligence so it's doubly useful!

Instead, the bad guys either steal or buy stolen lists of passwords (as when you hear of companies being hacked for customer details). Your password isn't stored as your password but as a password 'hash', a scrambled version using an algorithm to juggle the components. The brute force method tries every possible option until one works (computers can test billions of options per second). There are several well-known hash algorithms and if the criminal can manage to access one, it speeds up their work immensely. It also tries obvious options first such as 'password!' or 'qwerty'. Common towns and countries as well as names are tested early on too before turning to more complex options. The brute force method can be defended against by increasing complexity. The numbers are frighteningly convincing. The BeCyberSafe.com website has worked these out for us. If a computer can take 20 million guesses per second, a six-letter combination of lower-case letters has 308,915,776 combinations (26 options per character) and takes only up to 15 seconds to break. Adding only two letters increases the time needed nearly 700 (26 x 26) fold to 2.9 hours. Adding capital letters and numbers into the equation means each character now has 26 x 26 x 10 possible solutions.

Even staying with a total of eight characters, the time needed now increases to anything up to four months! There is, of course, the possibility that the computer will get lucky and hit the combination within two minutes, but there you go! There are no guarantees, it's all about tipping the odds in your favour. The figures quoted are for a typical home PC. Unfortunately, the big criminal gangs have computers which could guess billions of passwords per second. The complex password above can now be broken in minutes. Gangs can also buy the hash algorithms for passwords up to 10 characters so very secure passwords need to be at least 12 characters long as well as having capitals, numbers, symbols and so on.

Banking security is usually a multi-stage process requesting a different part of a password or sequence each time and often involves using an extra code texted to a different device such as a mobile phone (two factor authentication) and which is only valid for around 30 seconds making it much harder for criminals. They often resort to fairly crude methods to trick vulnerable people into revealing their details such as bogus phone calls pretending to be from the bank and asking for PIN numbers, security numbers from the back of cards and so on. This electronic version of this type of approach is called 'phishing' and is unfortunately quite common. Human Factors show repeatedly that we humans are the weakest link in the chain so it's often easier to focus on that than the higher tech options! For example, phishing scams commonly involve sending us an e-mail directing us to a fake bank website and tricking us into divulging security details which the criminals can then use to transfer money out of our account.

More sophisticated versions of this include 'spear phishing', which involves building a relationship with a target to improve chances of success before stinging them. This is the technique used by the 'Fancy Bears' group (a Russian cyber espionage group) against 1,800 accounts linked to Hillary Clinton's 2016 US Presidential election campaign and other government agencies including in Europe. 'Whaling' is a similar approach but aimed at a senior member of an organisation. 'Cat-phishing' involves building a relationship with the aim of tricking the target into allowing the criminal access to information or resources under the target's control. Malicious software (malware) is often used in conjunction with this type of approach to give the criminal access to or some control over the target's computer. We can be tricked by copycat programs (Trojan Horse), worms, spyware and keystroke loggers. Malware can also affect mobile devices and can allow criminals to access a phone's camera, microphone or GPS tracker. Clues that this has happened are changes such as increased data usage or faster battery charge depletion. Android devices tend to be affected more often as Apple tend to keep tighter control of apps available for their iOS operating system.

Malware is not new with the first example being the 'Creeper' virus introduced in 1971 as an experiment by engineer Robert Thomas for BBN Technologies which crept through mainframes displaying the message, 'I'm the creeper, catch me if you can' but causing no damage. It was later modified by computer scientist Ray Tomlinson to enable it to reproduce, thereby inventing the first worm. Its development has increased exponentially since the development of the World Wide Web which increased the opportunities for criminals to monetise the technology.

The common denominator in all these security industry examples are the intent to steal by provoking Human Error. An understanding of Human Factors gives an advantage to whichever side exploits it. If our 'team' wins, we generally give it no further thought. If the criminals win, we turn to our justice system for help. It, unfortunately, is as error-prone as the other examples we are studying in this book. Let's dig a little deeper.

THE JUSTICE SYSTEM

Another, slightly less obvious, Safety Critical industry which our cyber-criminals (and criminals generally) hopefully have to deal with is our justice system. Errors here can see murderers walk free to kill again, rapists free to target more victims and, equally scary, innocent men and women incarcerated for decades, their lives destroyed and reputations torn asunder. In countries with the death penalty, it can even cost innocent people their lives. So, it would clearly be of benefit to our legal system to have a clear understanding of the sources of error and a robust Error Management Strategy. I fear this isn't the case. Our system includes Threat and Error Management which is an umbrella term incorporating several of our Crew Resource Management tools and which can be summarized by 'Where can this go wrong?' The most relevant issue here though, are the errors due to bias, either conscious or subconscious. Our brains like simple, tidy solutions and will often accept the first plausible explanation (and ignore confounding factors, thus applying confirmation bias) and being misled by heuristics such as framing, availability and anchoring. We will discuss some examples of these errors shortly. So, where can this go wrong?

An alleged offence in the UK's justice system goes through a clear pathway looking something like this:

1. The complaint is made to the police who investigate it by looking at all reasonable lines of enquiry, speaking to the complainant, the accused (usually under caution with a legal representative alongside) and assessing any other evidence.

-   They now apply a two-stage test (with the help of the Crown Prosecution Service (CPS) in serious cases):

(a) Is there a reasonable chance of conviction?

(b) Is it in the public interest to prosecute?

2. The suspect is charged.

3. Using information provided by the police, the CPS prepares a file for the first hearing at a Magistrate's Court.

4. More serious cases progress to the Crown Court where a CPS lawyer deals with the legal preparations while a CPS caseworker helps with the administrative details. They liaise with the police to present the case to a barrister who will argue the case in court.

5. This culminates in a trial where all relevant information is presented and a jury, under the guidance of a judge, consider the evidence and return a verdict on whether the allegation is proved beyond reasonable doubt.

Simple, sure what could possibly go wrong? An exposé of the 'justice' system in the 2018 book, *The Secret Barrister: Stories of the Law and How It's Broken,* would suggest that a lot can go wrong with little evidence of an Error Management framework to counterbalance it. A combination of an over-stretched, under-funded system and some good old-fashioned Human Factors leaves ample room for error.

Starting at the beginning, the complainant, who has genuinely suffered an indisputable injustice (assault victim, for example), can inadvertently identify a suspect in every good faith but be mistaken – more of this anon.

Next, the charging decision. An inspection by the CPS Inspectorate in 2015 found that nearly 20 per cent of the police charging decisions and 10 per cent of the CPS decisions were fundamentally wrong on basic points of law. It read, 'These are offences and issues that lawyers deal with on a daily basis and should rarely result in errors'. A later review in 2017 found that around half of pre-charge CPS advice was still below the standard expected. Fifteen per cent of cases brought to court had never been assessed by a CPS lawyer so, in summary, if you are accused of an offence and are brought in front of the Magistrate, there's a 50 per cent chance the prosecution haven't fully prepared the case against you.

Moving on to the trial, the CPS produce a brief setting out the charges, the evidence, witness statements and so on, including a Schedule of Unused Material, information discovered in the course of the investigation which isn't actually used as evidence. This is reviewed after the Magistrate's hearing before going to trial and any information which may benefit the defence is legally obliged to be disclosed to them to ensure fairness. This document provides a road-map to guide the barrister. Our Secret Barrister tells us that the information, including findings that may potentially exonerate the defendant, is actually handed over only in approximately 25 per cent of cases. The fact that the CPS staff numbers have been depleted by around a third in the last eight years may be a contributory factor increasing the risk of error quite considerably.

Apparently, the evidence the prosecution rely on to secure a conviction is often missing as well, necessitating delays in rescheduling cases while waiting for information from the police or the CPS. The defence may seek to dismiss the charges if they feel the evidence served is poor before their defendant is even arraigned, and if the judge agrees the case can be dismissed there and then or an extension may be given to allow time to come up with some evidence. This reflects poorly on the CPS so they may occasionally sub-contract cases out to an independent counsel so that they take the flack in the event of a dismissal.

For all this to happen, we rely on many staff over various sections of our judicial system to produce the goods in an agreed timeframe and for the IT system to function adequately to transport the information and allow it to be accessed by the relevant people. Given that the police force in England and Wales has been reduced by over 20,000 officers, that's 14 per cent on average over the last decade (or, accounting for population growth, 19 per cent per person) and the CPS lost 25 per cent of their prosecutors in 2010, many of them experienced, senior staff, it is probably little surprise that errors are prevalent. A CPS employee interviewed for a BBC News report said:

> There will be miscarriages of justice down the road from here because there are some cases that are going through the system and people have not looked at disclosure properly and have not looked at what is going on behind the scenes. Things we simply would not have had ten years ago.

In 2020 fifteen sex offenders in Northern Ireland had their convictions rescinded due to an error in how updated legislation was drafted eleven years earlier. In 2009, before the devolution of justice powers to the Northern Ireland Assembly, Westminster drafted legislation which unintentionally removed the ability of certain sexual offences to be tried in a Magistrates Court, meaning they had to be tried in the higher-level Crown Court. When the error was spotted, a review of cases found the fifteen defendants who had been convicted of seventeen offences, eleven of them against children including fifteen counts of Indecent Assault and two of Unlawful Carnal Knowledge. The cases had been tried in the Magistrates Court which, due to the error, no longer had the authority to hear the cases, rendering the convictions invalid. Assistant Director of the Public Prosecution Service stated he was 'truly sorry to have to inform all affected by this unforeseen and undetected error in the law'. He said a decision on whether to retry the cases would be taken as quickly as possible in consultation with the victims who faced having to testify all over again. Errors in our legal system have real and important consequences to both individuals and society.

We have only now reached the stage of actually holding a trial and already we seem to have navigated a minefield! How confident are we that justice is being done in a fair and transparent manner?

Is Justice Being Served?

Let's assume we have selected the correct level of court for the case and fast forward through the jury selection, although that in itself is an error-prone judgment call for legal teams deciding who they want to select or reject, depending on the case and which side they're on. Let's just call the first witness, the victim of the alleged crime. We will be relying on their first-hand testimony of what happened, say, two or three years ago. Dip into the memory banks and retrieve the file marked 'My Assault' and reproduce its contents. Easy, right? Unfortunately not. Memory is an unreliable, constantly evolving thing, not a saved computer file, so what the victim (or any other witness) reproduces may stray quite a bit from what they saw, or more correctly what they think they saw, at the time of the alleged offence. Let's move across the Atlantic to look at a horrific case which happened on the shores of Lake Michigan in 1985 and was described very well in Kathryn Schulz's book, *Being Wrong,* and was also the subject of a 2016 Netflix original, *Making a Murderer.*

Penny Beerntsen had gone to a beach on the shores of Lake Michigan in late July 1985 along with her husband, Tom, and their 11-year-old daughter. During the afternoon, Penny went for a run and headed three miles north before turning and heading back to her family. With about a mile left, she glanced at her watch and checked the time at 3.50 pm. When she looked back up, she saw a man emerging from the sand dunes moving towards her. She immediately realised she was in danger and tried to get away but the man caught up with her and grabbed her in a choke hold. She said later that she had two thoughts, firstly, that she needed to stay calm, and secondly, 'I need to get a real good look at this guy, so that if I survive this, I can identify him'. The man dragged her into the dunes where she put up whatever resistance she could, trying to talk the man down and then trying to scratch his face in order to leave an identifying mark. He knocked her unconscious and then physically and sexually assaulted her. When she came round, she was naked and bleeding. She managed to crawl back to the beach where she was helped by a young couple and found by her husband who had come looking for her. She was taken to hospital and interviewed by the police who asked if she had got a look at the attacker. 'Yes,' she said, 'I sure did.'

The word 'witness' derives from the Old English meaning 'attestation of fact or event from personal knowledge'. Eye witness testimony is one of the oldest forms of legal evidence and often the most compelling. In the last twenty years, DNA evidence has emerged to augment (or challenge) it and, although this can be prone to procedural errors, when carried out correctly is as close to a silver bullet as we can get. DNA can be matched to a given individual within a very tight margin of error. A local sheriff spoke to Penny on the ward and showed her the pictures of nine men. She picked out the man she recognised and by that night Steven Avery was in custody.

Late the following night, after being discharged home, Penny received an obscene phone call from someone who seemed to know more of the details of the attack than he could have gleaned from the newspaper reports. The sheriff's department decided to hold a lineup to make sure they had the right man. She described looking carefully at each man but 'when I came to Steve, I had a real visceral reaction. I started to shake, I could feel the colour drain from my face. I could feel the hair stand up on the back of my neck.' Penny identified Avery and confirmed this again at the trial where she declared herself 'absolutely sure' that he was her assailant. At the end of a week-long trial, 23-year-old Steven Avery was convicted of sexual assault and attempted murder and sentenced to thirty-two years in jail.

Two years later, Penny attended a talk on Restorative Justice which focuses on the impact of crime on the individual or community rather than the rather impersonal approach of the state. She became interested, trained in victim/offender mediation and began working as a volunteer with Wisconsin prison communities. She worked in high security prisons and emphasised to prisoners that although they can't change the past, they can choose to do something positive with their futures. She talked to them about the importance of acknowledging their errors and moving on.

In the meantime, Avery fought to overturn his conviction but failed repeatedly. Finally, in 2001 the Wisconsin Innocence Project, part of a nationwide organisation who used the relatively new technique of DNA evidence to overturn wrongful convictions, took on his case. After more delays, Penny learnt in 2003 that Avery couldn't have been her attacker.

Many victims in cases like this refuse to accept the new reality. It's difficult to criticize such people. They have been victims of sometimes heinous crimes and have spent years trying to deal with that. To then suddenly discover that you have been a major player in a life-changing miscarriage of justice may be beyond the emotional capabilities of many. The mind responds by holding tight to its original narrative, the replacement being too traumatic to be processed. In Penny's case, her guilt was doubled in that not only had she sent Steven Avery to prison for eighteen years for a crime he had no part in, she felt she had missed the chance to stop the real assailant (a man named Gregory Allen) from carrying out further attacks, including a particularly brutal rape of another woman for which he was sentenced to sixty years.

Reviewing the case afterwards, Penny uncovered several Human Factors issues which conspired for her to misidentify Avery. Memory is a fickle thing and research has shown that once we select a photo of an assailant, that picture becomes the brain's default for our attacker, not the original view which allowed Penny to misidentify him repeatedly. In other words, the picture of Steven Avery became associated in her mind as her attacker. The Sheriff's Department reinforced her initial decision telling her that Avery (a man with learning disabilities, an IQ of around 70 and previous convictions for burglary, animal cruelty and firearms offences) was indeed the suspect they had in mind – confirmation bias. In the week following the attack, the police contacted Penny to tell her they had another suspect in mind, one who looked like Steven Avery and had been showing signs of increasingly erratic and disturbing behaviour. They had been tracking him but not on the day of the assault. The Sheriff's Department told her not to engage with the Police Department and when the police contacted the Sheriff's Department directly, they dismissed the new suspect saying, 'We've got our guy'. The other man turned out to be Gregory Allen.

Shortly after Avery's release, Penny Beerntsen contacted him to apologise. She wrote:

> When I testified in court, I honestly believed you were my assailant. I was wrong. I cannot ask for, nor do I deserve, your forgiveness. I can only say to you in deepest humility, how sorry I am.

Penny met with Avery five months later along with their lawyers. At the end of the meeting they hugged and she said, 'Steve, I'm so sorry'. Avery replied, 'It's okay Penny, it's over.'

This case exposes a multitude of errors which Human Factors thinking could have addressed. Penny's initial mistake was compounded when several chances of revisiting it were denied to her by the law enforcement agencies. The sheriff's office turned down several opportunities to consider other alternatives before proceeding, and at the trial the jury dismissed sixteen eye witnesses and a time-stamped shop receipt placing Avery forty miles away shortly after the attack. They had made their decision and only accepted evidence which backed this up and dismissed anything which contradicted it – a clear example of confirmation bias.

Pressures to meet targets and reduced police numbers all contribute to a system which may be too focused on getting results and not enough on getting justice.

Following Avery's release in 2003, he filed a civil suit for wrongful conviction and for $36 million in compensation. The Wisconsin Assembly Judiciary Committee recommended improvements to the legal system to reduce the chance of a recurrence which were eventually drafted into legislation in 2005, known as the Avery Bill, which was renamed the Criminal Justice Reform Bill a month later after Avery was charged with murder in another case involving the death of a photographer, Teresa Halbach. Avery and his nephew, Brendan Dassey, were both convicted of the murder which Avery protested was a 'frame up' to distract from his upcoming wrongful conviction case. Both men dispute their conviction and there has been considerable legal activity to try to exonerate them, but they remain in prison. The suit was settled in February 2006 for $400,000 following the murder indictment.

But let's get back to the legal system in general. Let's assume that everyone has done their job and all evidence produced is beyond reproach. Now let's meet the decision makers – the judge and jury.

Justice and the Human Factors

The word jury originates from the Anglo-Norman word *juré* meaning sworn. Juries are generally part of the Common Law legal system such as exists in the UK, USA and Australia. Jury trials have existed from around 500 BCE in Ancient Greece. Around 1200 CE, jury trials started to replace the 'trial by ordeal' (when, for example, an alleged thief would have molten metal poured over their hands – if it healed well, they were deemed innocent as it was assumed God had intervened). Early juries were people who were expected to make a decision without a trial as such – they were locals who would be expected to know the 'facts' of a case and the people involved and could make a decision based on that. By the 1700s in Britain, lists of citizens considered to be eligible as jurors were published and jurors were picked at random with local authorities having some say as to who could be used. Women were only considered as jurors in 1919, although they had to meet the same requirements as men in each jurisdiction such as property ownership. Local authorities had discretion to designate rules such as this until the English Justice system standardised the selection process which only happened in the 1980s.

Twelve is often thought to be the specified number of jurors but this actually varies. Scotland for instance has fifteen, the Republic of Ireland has twelve but can select up to fifteen if a trial is expected to last over two months. Alternate jurors are also sometimes selected – these are not on the panel but are required to be in court in case any juror needs to be excused for any reason, for example, illness. A study by the University of Glasgow showed that seven is actually the optimum number to stop overbearing members exerting too much influence over their colleagues.

A jury is intended to be an impartial panel capable of reaching a verdict. It is picked at random, but in the US system lawyers have some scope to reject members at the selection stage if they consider them to be biased or predisposed against their client (challenge for cause) or even without a specified reason (peremptory challenge). A Head Juror or foreperson is selected as spokesperson for the jury. The integrity of the jury is paramount so they are generally instructed not to follow media coverage of the case or conduct their own investigation either on-line or by visiting the crime scene, talking to people about the case and so on. Easier said than done! Another obvious risk is jury tampering or intimidation.

The jury's function is to determine the 'question of fact' whereas the judge's role is to determine the 'question of law'. In cases where intimidation is considered likely, cases may be heard without a jury. Northern Ireland instituted the 'Diplock Court' system in 1973 by the Northern Ireland (Emergency Provisions) Act to try terrorist cases related to the Troubles, which was reversed in 2007 by the Justice and Security (Northern Ireland) Act. The option is still available in certain cases as it is in Great Britain with the 2003 Criminal Justice Act, and first used in 2009 against four men accused of an armed robbery at Heathrow Airport. A similar system exists in the Republic of Ireland – the Special Criminal Court consisting of three judges hears cases related to gangland crime or terrorism.

The verdict reached by this group of people will obviously vary according to a huge body of Human Factors aspects and the fact we pick a random selection of people is an attempt to minimise errors. One huge influence on the jury is the prosecution and defence teams, the solicitors and/or barristers. We have already had a glimpse of the less than optimum system they operate in with barristers possibly only briefed in the case they are about to 'passionately argue' minutes beforehand. In the event of a barrister being delayed in another court, the new case may be handled by one of their junior, less experienced members.

The judge is also an important component, but being human they are influenced by Human Factors too. A study by Professor Shai Danziger at Tel Aviv University looked at the decisions made by judges in parole hearings. It studied the decisions of eight judges over the day showing that results dropped from 65 per cent petitions granted early in the session to almost 0 per cent before rising back up to 65 per cent again after they'd had lunch. It then steadily dropped again until their next break!

So, we're ready to start – feeling confident? Let's fast forward a bit. You've had your trial and everything appears to have progressed as well as could be expected. We have a verdict! Now, what are the chances of the verdict (which is, after all, simply the opinion of a group of your peers based on whatever has been presented to them) being wrong?

Miscarriages of Justice

Research suggests that the chance of an incorrect decision, a miscarriage of justice (also known as a failure of justice) is between 2.3 and 5 per cent! That amounts to around 10,000 wrongful convictions per year in the USA alone. A 2014 study there suggested that around 4 per cent of prisoners on death row are likely to be innocent and that up to 340 innocent people have been executed since 1973! This can of course cut both ways – an innocent person may be found guilty but a guilty person may also be found innocent!

Misidentification of the accused is the problem in 70 per cent of miscarriages of justice. Other causes are evidence not being disclosed (whether deliberately or through inefficiency), confirmation bias, incorrect forensic test results, possibly due to contaminated evidence, coerced statements, perjury by witnesses and so on.

In the UK, a series of high profile cases were prosecuted during the 1970s and 1980s by the West Midlands Serious

Crime Squad (which was subsequently disbanded in 1989). When cases began to collapse regularly as the decade progressed due to evidence tampering and so on, an investigation showed the unreliability of the team's prosecutions. As of 2017, over 100 of their cases had collapsed or been overturned on appeal with 60 convictions being exonerated including the high-profile Birmingham Six.

A group in the USA called the Innocence Project takes on cases it feels have been miscarriages of justice, but most of those falsely convicted have to fight alone and have generally spent a sizable length of time in jail before proving their innocence. In the UK, compensation of up to £500,000 is payable if you have been incarcerated for up to 10 years and up to £1,000,000 if imprisoned for longer, and payments in the USA can be even higher. Richard Phillips, the longest serving victim, spent 45 years in a Michigan jail before being exonerated from his conviction for murder and received $1.5 million. He was convicted in 1972, but in 2010 another man, Richard Polombo, admitted the shooting. Justice grinds slowly and it took until 2017 before Phillips was granted a retrial leading to his release in March 2018.

These cases all show how that simple question – 'where can this go wrong?' – if asked at an early stage would have resulted in life-changing errors being avoided and a better chance of achieving justice. A miscarriage of justice has huge implications for the wrongly convicted person, but equally means the real criminal is still at large and likely perpetrating further crimes which would have been avoided had a proper Error Management strategy been applied.

In April 2021, the UK faced what could be the most widespread Miscarriage of Justice in British history. Between

2000 and 2014, 736 Post Office staff, mainly sub-postmasters and sub-postmistresses, were convicted of theft, fraud and false accounting with several serving prison sentences. Many were then shunned by their communities and struggled to secure jobs due to their criminal convictions. Some lost their homes over the scandal. However, the underlying issue turns out not to have been greed and dishonesty, but computer programming errors.

In 1999, the Post Office installed a new computer system known as Horizon. From an early stage, the system appeared to have significant bugs causing misreporting, sometimes involving substantial sums. After years of campaigning, the affected staff are starting to see the fruits of their labour. In December 2020, 500 won a civil case on the issue and six had their convictions quashed, followed in April 2021 by 39 more, among them Janet Skinner who ran a post office in Hull. In 2007, Janet was imprisoned for nine months due to a shortfall of £59,000 in her accounts. She said her conviction 'destroyed everything'. Others like Harjinder Butoy were jailed for longer – in his case over three years. Neil Hudgell, a solicitor representing many of the group, said the Post Office:

> . . . has been found to have been an organization that not only turned a blind eye to the failings in its hugely expensive IT system, but positively promoted a culture of cover-up and subterfuge in the pursuit of reputation and profit. . . . they readily accepted that loss of life, liberty and sanity for many ordinary people as a price worth paying in that pursuit.

Much of the attention now is focusing on Paula Vennells, CEO of the Post Office between 2012 and 2019, who repeatedly defended the IT system, even to parliamentary committees long after glitches in the system had been widely reported. She insisted the system was 'robust', a word which I often hear in management presentations and which generally causes me to tune out everything that follows as unsubstantiated and overly optimistic.

At the Court of Appeal, Lord Justice Holroyd said the Post Office 'knew there were serious issues' and 'had a clear duty to investigate' but that the Post Office 'consistently asserted that Horizon was robust and reliable' and 'effectively steamrollered over any sub-postmaster who sought to challenge its accuracy.' As CEO, Vennells chose to fight lengthy, expensive legal battles against her former staff seeking redress and the judge who found in the favour of staff in the civil case in December 2020 said that under Vennells' leadership, the actions of the Post Office had been 'both cruel and incompetent'. In 2019, Vennells was honoured with a CBE for 'services to the Post Office'.

A further 22 cases are now under review by the Criminal Cases Review Commission and they have asked anyone else who feels their conviction to be unsafe to come forward. Given that there were 736 convictions, that is likely to be quite a group!

The case flags up many of the issues we have touched on already in the book, the main one being the apparent refusal to accept the very possibility that an error may have been made! Acceptance of even this basic concept may have transformed the trajectory of this case before it gathered so much momentum that the people involved were unable to back down without losing face – the second big message being that since error is ubiquitous in everything we do, there should be no embarrassment in acknowledging its existence. Indeed, the embarrassment is evident now in the calls of why wasn't it obvious this was a disaster in progress? An investigation of the IT system may have flagged up 'what went wrong' rather than the easy option of blaming staff and focusing on 'who went wrong'. Accepting that most people go to work to do a good job, rather than to cheat and steal, would have been a good starting point for any investigation.

Looking at all the evidence, instead of allowing confirmation bias to creep in leading to the dismissal of evidence which doesn't fit our prejudicial view, could have nipped this whole affair in the bud. Even with only a limited understanding of our aviation Safety Management System approach, we can see that this case fell at almost every possible hurdle resulting in a huge human (and financial) cost. This whole debacle was completely avoidable.

I think given what we have found on this quick exploration of error in the criminal justice system, we should finish with a quote by the author William Gaddis from his book *A Frolic of his Own* which is quite apt:

> Justice? You get justice in the next world, in this world you have the law.

Chapter 5

Where There's Muck,
There's Money!

There would appear to be little linking the seemingly very different industries of agriculture and finance. However, they both share a fairly cavalier approach to error which has a huge impact at a family and community level in one and on a global geopolitical level in the other. It seems to be a combination of poor situational awareness leading to equally poor decision-making. In both industries, there is a lack of awareness of the risks they are exposed to followed by a 'get it done' attitude. Let's start in Hillsborough, Northern Ireland, just up the road from where I live.

AGRICULTURE

Nevin Spence was a rising star in Irish rugby. The County Down man joined the Ulster Academy system before making the senior squad at the age of 19. He made 42 appearances over the following two years and in 2011, the Irish Rugby Union Players' Association named him Young Player of the Year, beating off some strong competition such as Conor Murray and Rhys Ruddock. In short, Nevin was an up and coming star, highly respected by his colleagues and teammates. He also helped out around his family's farm in Hillsborough, County Down, alongside his father Noel and elder brother Graham. On Saturday, 14 September 2012, tragedy struck when Nevin, Graham and Noel all died in a farm accident.

Emergency services were called around 6.00 pm after Noel fell into an underground slurry pit, possibly while trying to rescue an animal which had strayed into the pit. Graham, Nevin and their sister Emma all tried to rescue their father but were overcome by toxic fumes from the slurry. The three men died, but Emma thankfully survived after a time in intensive care. Nevin was only 22 years old. After their deaths, teammates from Nevin's Ballynahinch club (Noel and Graham had both played for the club as well) worked on a rota to help run the farm.

So how common an event is a farm accident? A 2015 study suggested that approximately 100 accidents per month resulting in the need for hospital treatment occur in Northern Ireland alone. In 2011 and 2012 there were 12 deaths in the industry with an average of about 8 per year since. With 27,000 working in agriculture in the province that's a rate of almost 30 per 100,000 employees. The small population can skew the figures a little so let's look at a bigger sample.

A total of 360,000 people in the UK work in agriculture, which is around 1 per cent of the workforce. The industry accounts for around 20 per cent of workplace deaths, however, showing something's not right! Farming accounts for around 10 deaths per 100,000 workers compared to 0.45 per 100,000 across all industries. Figures for the UK in 2019 recorded 39 deaths and a five year average of 33 deaths per year, 20 times higher than the average proportionately.

What about the Republic of Ireland? Figures for 2019 show 18 deaths with around 265,000 working in farming giving a rate of about 7 per 100,000.

So, it seems fairly clear that farming has a problem. It is another Safety Critical industry but doesn't seem to see itself in that light, and doesn't appear to be addressing the issue effectively. Although the figures have actually improved somewhat since the early 2000s, they have plateaued at an unacceptably high level in the last number of years.

Let's dig a little deeper into the figures to locate the danger areas and where the errors leading to the deaths and injuries are happening.

UK figures for 2018/19 show 35 per cent of the 39 deaths were caused by farm workers being struck by a moving vehicle (tractor, tele-porter, all terrain vehicles and so on). Almost 25 per cent were caused by livestock, usually cattle. Almost 20 per cent were caused by falling (from fragile roofs, ladders, combine harvesters and so on) with the last 20 per cent being a mixture of machinery incidents, drownings and being struck by objects such as a bale or a tree branch. This pattern is generally representative of other years although contact with electrical cables has also been a cause.

Almost half of those killed were 60 years old or over. Over the last five years, 20 members of the public have died, one-quarter of them children.

A 2013 study in Ireland by the Economic and Social Research Institute (ESRI) asked farmers about their personal experience over the previous 10 years – 12 per cent had been involved in an accident, 27 per cent had experienced a 'near miss' and 8 per cent reported an accident involving a colleague on their farm. About half of the accidents involved four or more days off work. Two of the biggest examples of risky behaviour were not asking for help when necessary and not checking machinery for defects. Younger farmers were more likely to take risks so the report suggested more focus on this in the training colleges. The report also showed a 50 per cent higher level of injuries compared to industry generally. The Teagasc Farm Safety Survey shows that trips and falls account for 42 per cent of non-fatal accidents with another 33 per cent caused by livestock and 11 per cent by machinery. Other studies have shown very young and relatively older farmers to be at most risk with the older group more likely to suffer a fatal accident. This Irish study also showed dairy farms to be particularly at risk, accounting for 58 per cent of deaths between 2000 and 2007 despite making up only 11 per cent of farms in the country. Larger farms were more likely to skip the use of safety gear, possibly because of a higher pace of work or because staff needed to go further to access the equipment.

Malcolm Downey is the recently retired Principal Inspector of the Health and Safety Executive of Northern Ireland. In 2019 he stated:

> Farming and food production plays a crucial role in the life and economy of Northern Ireland. But every year we have to reluctantly report that agriculture has the poorest safety record of any occupation here.

He also pointed out that 'All too often accidents happen on our farms which are preventable'. A UK-based charity, 'Yellow Wellies' agrees and focuses on farm safety training, advice and support.

The continuing high level of risky behaviour and the consistent patterns of the numbers and type of incidents would suggest that agriculture has a cultural issue similar to that of aviation in the 1970s and 1980s before a decision

Detailed cause of fatal injury over 5 years (2017/18–2021/22(p))

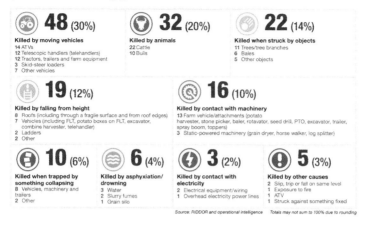

48 (30%)

Killed by moving vehicles
14 ATVs
12 Telescopic handlers (telehandlers)
12 Tractors, trailers and farm equipment
3 Skid-steer loaders
7 Other vehicles

32 (20%)

Killed by animals
22 Cattle
10 Bulls

22 (14%)

Killed when struck by objects
11 Trees/tree branches
6 Bales
5 Other objects

19 (12%)

Killed by falling from height
8 Roofs (including through a fragile surface and from roof edges)
7 Vehicles (including FLT, potato boxes on FLT, excavator, combine harvester, telehandler)
2 Ladders
2 Other

16 (10%)

Killed by contact with machinery
13 Farm vehicle/attachments (potato harvester, stone picker, baler, rotavator, seed drill, PTO, excavator, trailer, spray boom, toppers)
3 Static-powered machinery (grain dryer, horse walker, log splitter)

10 (6%)

Killed when trapped by something collapsing
8 Vehicles, machinery and trailers
2 Other

6 (4%)

Killed by asphyxiation/drowning
3 Water
2 Slurry fumes
1 Grain silo

3 (2%)

Killed by contact with electricity
2 Electrical equipment/wiring
1 Overhead electricity power lines

5 (3%)

Killed by other causes
2 Slip, trip or fall on same level
1 Exposure to fire
1 ATV
1 Struck against something fixed

Source: RIDDOR and operational intelligence   Totals may not sum to 100% due to rounding

Worker fatalities over time

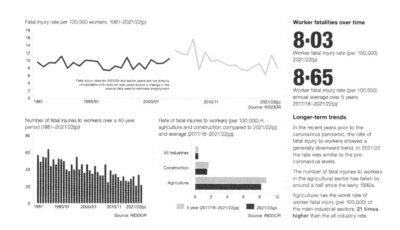

Fatal injury rate per 100,000 workers, 1981–2021/22(p)

Fatal injury rates for 2003/04 and earlier years are not directly comparable with rates for later years due to a change in the source data used to estimate employment

Worker fatalities over time

8·03
Worker fatal injury rate (per 100,000)
2021/22(p)

8·65
Worker fatal injury rate (per 100,000)
annual average over 5 years
2017/18–2021/22(p)

Longer-term trends

In the recent years prior to the coronavirus pandemic, the rate of fatal injury to workers showed a generally downward trend. In 2021/22 the rate was similar to the pre-coronavirus levels.

The number of fatal injuries to workers in the agricultural sector has fallen by around a half since the early 1980s.

Agriculture has the worst rate of worker fatal injury (per 100,000) of the main industrial sectors: **21 times higher** than the all industry rate.

Number of fatal injuries to workers over a 40-year period (1981–2021/22(p))

Source: RIDDOR

Rate of fatal injuries to workers (per 100,000) in agriculture and construction compared to 2021/22(p) and average (2017/18–2021/22(p))

All industries
Construction
Agriculture

5 year (2017/18–2021/22(p))   2021/22(p)

Source: RIDDOR

Source: UK Health and Safety Executive

was made to change behaviours to focus on eliminating risk wherever possible, and otherwise to mitigate it to avoid catastrophe. Farm workers appear to have a blind-spot to the Situational Awareness which would alert them to the level of risk they are exposed to while the need to get things done often leads to risky decision making. If farmers could be convinced that this problem is addressable rather than simply an occupational hazard, we could begin to transform the industry in the way that aviation changed and continues to learn from its errors.

Simple approaches start with awareness of the risks among farm workers and a decision to do something about it. High-Viz jackets could reduce the number of vehicle injuries. Better design of work practices would help to avoid having staff near vehicles in the first place. Animal injuries could be addressed by ensuring adequate staff numbers when handling cattle, suitable facilities such as the use of a well-constructed crush and even an awareness of when not to approach beasts at all, for instance, cows with young calves. Better securing of equipment such as ladders and a simple awareness of the risk of falls from poorly secured surfaces such as fragile roofs are also simple first steps.

Above all, an acceptance of the need to improve safety is the essential starting point. Are our farmers ready?

FINANCE

At 5.46 am local time on 17 January 1995, the city of Kobe in Japan was rocked by the worst earthquake Japan had experienced in 70 years. Almost 6,500 people died, 400,000 buildings were destroyed and 120 of the port's 150 quays were damaged. The quake led to improvements in the country's disaster response plans with a special focus on protecting transport infrastructure which had hampered the response to the Kobe event.

The earthquake also triggered a shockwave which changed the life of English financial derivatives trader Nick Leeson, 830 miles away in Shanghai and, within five weeks, toppled Baring's Bank, the world's second oldest merchant bank. The underlying cause, as ever, was human error!

Nick Leeson left school in Watford in 1985 with two A-levels in English Literature and History – he failed the third, Mathematics! He joined Coutts Private Bank as a clerk, moving to Morgan Stanley in 1987 working in their back office clearing and settling derivative transactions. Leeson joined Baring's in 1990 at the age of 23 after spending a number of years learning his trade in Coutts Bank and Morgan Stanley. He rose through the ranks to become a spectacularly successful trader and by the age of 25 was heading up the bank's operation on the Singapore International Money Exchange (SIMEX). He was denied a trader's licence in the UK for having committed fraud on his application form – he omitted to mention a judgment against him lodged by National Westminster Bank. Neither he nor Baring's mentioned this 'error' on his Singapore application!

Leeson had made enormous profits for the bank through some unauthorised trades in 1992, which accounted for 10 per cent of the bank's total profits that year. His salary of £50,000 was topped up with a bonus of £130,000. He wasn't quite so lucky in the following year but hid his losses in an 'Error Account' created to park losses due to mistakes such as when a colleague accidentally sold futures contracts for Fuji Bank when she was supposed to have bought them, costing Baring's £20,000. He started using this account to hide his own 'errors' which were accumulating. Leeson says he crossed a line when he chose not to reconcile a trade losing Baring's $1.7 million. He thought this was the only way to keep his job but losses steadily accumulated. He was seen as a major mover in Singapore and given a lot of freedom by London as he appeared to be producing the goods. He cleared a £6 million loss in 1993 using a 'doubling strategy' where he would trade double the loss to recoup his position. He could have reigned in his ambition at that point, probably without his losses ever being detected, but the temptation to gamble to keep up with his swash-buckling reputation was too strong.

Baring's management had made a big error too in making Leeson both General Manager and Chief Trader, whilst also allowing him to be the one to reconcile trades, normally positions held by two different people to act as a check against this very situation. His stellar 1992 results made him appear to be a genius and earned him unwavering trust. He hid documents from the bank's auditors who don't appear to have noticed any discrepancy, raising serious questions about the bank's internal accounting oversight too. The bank appeared totally unaware of the risks being taken on their behalf. Leeson also lied to regulators about losses which should have sent up a red flag, but again no discrepancy was spotted. Baring's also had a special dispensation from the Bank of England allowing them to lend more than 25 per cent of their total capital to one entity. This litany of errors gradually accumulated.

By the end of 1992, losses were at £2 million. A year later, they had reached £23 million and had ballooned to £208 million by 1994 as Leeson tried to trade his way out of his predicament. On 16 January 1995, Leeson took a conservative position called a 'short straddle', basically betting that there would be very little movement overnight between the Singapore and Tokyo exchanges which would produce a small profit while he waited for the next big move which would dig him out of his hole. At 5.46 am the next morning, the tectonic plates near Kobe moved down 1.2 metres and across 2.0 metres. The financial tectonic plates followed suit as the Asian markets opened and went into a tailspin. The

Nikkei lost 7 per cent in a single week. Leeson made ever more risky positions in a vain attempt to recover the losses and finally threw in the towel on 23 February leaving a note saying simply 'I'm sorry' and fled first to Thailand then to Germany. Baring's had by now discovered that 'they' had racked up losses of £827 million, more than twice their total capital, and was declared insolvent on 26 February after 223 years of existence.

Leeson was arrested in Germany on 2 March and extradited back to Singapore where he was sentenced to 6.5 years in jail although he was released in 1999 after being diagnosed with bowel cancer. He wrote his autobiography, *Rogue Trader*, in prison and it was subsequently made into a movie starring Ewan McGregor and Anna Friel. Leeson now lives in Barna in County Galway where he again rose to prominence due to his involvement with the Galway United soccer team where he eventually became CEO for a time.

The fallout from the scandal has led to increased regulation of banks and the creation of 'compliance officers' to strengthen risk control. However, never underestimate the human ability to find ways of making mistakes! Meet Jerome Kerviel.

Jerome joined French securities firm Société Générale in 2000 at the age of 23. In 2005 he became a junior trader where his job was to capitalise on the discrepancy between the price of derivatives (a financial vehicle grouping shares together) and the price of the underlying shares themselves. To minimise risk, traders generally make two bets, one in each direction, but in different areas such as in currencies or markets. In late 2006, Kerviel starting gambling on one-sided bets but created false trades in the company's computer system so that this riskier approach wouldn't attract attention within the company. Initially, he was so successful that he actually deliberately made some losing trades, again to prevent the false trades being noticed.

In January 2008, the group spotted Kerviel's deception and immediately closed off his trades. When they totalled up the damage, they discovered that Kerviel had lost the company €4.9 billion! Although he hadn't benefitted personally, he was convicted in 2010 of breach of trust and other offences and sentenced to three years in prison and, somewhat optimistically, ordered to repay the €4.9 billion in restitution. He served only five months and in 2016 an appeal court agreed with his argument that the bank knowingly colluded by looking the other way as he appeared to be making profits for them. The judge said it was not 'occasional negligence' that allowed Kerviel to get in as deep as he did, but 'managerial choices'. His fine was reduced to a more manageable (relatively speaking) €1 million.

Whether the errors were in management failing to spot what was going on or colluding in what they erroneously thought was going on, the international banking system was again caught out by human error, showing that the learning from the Baring's crash was perhaps not quite as extensive as it could have been. And these are only the traders who got caught – we don't really know how deep the errors run.

It's clear then that human error in finance can escalate sufficiently to crash a bank – repeatedly, since we seem to be slow learners! Is error sufficiently powerful to crash an entire global banking system? Let's turn our attention to perhaps the biggest set of financial errors in history – the banking crash of 2008 which led to a global financial crisis.

GLOBAL FINANCIAL CRISIS, 2008

When I was growing up, one of my father's best friends was a bank manager who lived in the next street to us. The principle of banking back then appeared reasonably straight forward. The bank had access to money (whether from other customers who placed their savings in the bank or from Central Banks) and loaned it out at a profit to people or commercial enterprises who bought cars, houses or expanded their businesses with it. The manager's job was to work out the odds like a bookmaker and gauge whether the bank was likely to get its money back and, if so, what interest rate reflected the risk involved for the bank. Factoring in human error (the man wasn't infallible), he had to allow a big enough margin that the bank could afford to lose some 'bets' but still turn a profit at the end of the year. If he succeeded, he kept his job (or even got promoted); if he failed, someone else got a go at his job instead. Simple!

Like many others, however, the banking industry grew greedy. If this year's profits were 5 per cent, then next year's had to be 7.5 per cent and the year after 10 per cent. Staff were encouraged to expand the business and squeeze more and more profit out of it. The more successful they were, the more they were emboldened to keep pushing, forming what they and their superiors saw as a virtuous circle.

Unfortunately, there is only so much profit that can realistically be made so things gradually morphed into something a little more creative.

In the USA, banks loaned money for property, like elsewhere. If they are not lending, they don't make profits so there is a clear incentive. There are, however, only so many houses out there so a couple of other factors evolved. If there are an excess of bidders competing for a house, the price goes up. This encourages people to buy now rather than next year before they might be priced out of the market. They will stretch a little further to buy. Unchecked, this builds into a housing bubble unless someone steps in. To continue increasing profits, banks must keep lending but the 'good bets' have all already been taken up, so they must start targeting slightly riskier buyers and accept the risk that these buyers may not be able to repay the loan. Ater all, they can always repossess the house which is the collateral which secures the debt. All the same, to mitigate the risk they invented financial instruments called CDOs (Collateralised Debt Obligations) or alternatively MBSs (Mortgage Backed Securities).

These new products had two benefits: they bundled a number of mortgages together and sold the package on to another investor who gambled that if some of them failed, the successful ones would balance it out leaving them with a profit, and they allowed the original lender to 'insure' against bad debts leaving them confident that they now had the capacity to sell more mortgages. In effect, in the absence of enough mortgages to gamble on, Lender B got to gamble on Lender A's gamble, each side making a cut of the profit. This premise worked as long as more mortgages were sold. This led to mortgages eventually being sold to customers without checking whether they had any capacity to repay the loan, what their previous credit history was and so on. Welcome to the sub-prime mortgage market!

By 2006, almost 30 per cent of new mortgage approvals were based on little or no documentation, two-thirds of these were sub-prime loans. The risks were again mitigated by packaging a bundle of good mortgages with riskier ones and selling the package on the financial markets as CDOs.

The virtuous circle had now disintegrated into a vicious one spiraling downwards. The financial regulators were discouraged from intervening – no one wants to spoil a party – and the government was earning taxes from each transaction so there was little incentive for anyone to shout 'stop'!

A similar situation was playing out in Europe. Irish economist David McWilliams' excellent 2010 book, *Follow the Money*, outlines a very simple explanation of how the 'boom and bust' cycle played out in Ireland – simple enough that even I could follow the logic.

McWilliams traces the problem back to Ireland joining the Euro, the new currency linking the financial systems of the European Union and replacing the previous system of countries having their own currencies which they could devalue and revalue as necessary. The Euro was launched as an 'invisible' currency on 1 January 1999, used electronically for accountancy purposes and then launched as an actual physical currency of notes and coins three years later on 1 January 2002 when the biggest cash changeover in history took place in the 12 EU countries. This led to Ireland having access to vast amounts of money which they could borrow from Europe at much lower rates than previously available, since countries such as Germany had an older population with a very strong saving culture and needed to lend this money out to generate a return. In 2005, Germans were saving €130 billion more each year than they were spending. By 2009, this figure was €250 billion. This money needed to be loaned out to make a profit – Ireland was happy to oblige. The 'Celtic Tiger' was born.

Houses prices in Ireland rocketed by 17 per cent in the 12 months from May 2000 to May 2001. By 2006, prices had more than doubled, similar to the American experience.

In 2004, Irish banks had a loan book of €256 billion. Within four years, this had doubled to €591 billion. Like in the US, Irish banks had to keep lending money to sustain the ever-increasing profits so they funded builders to construct estates in more and more unlikely areas and then loaned money to ordinary customers like you and me to buy, thus scoring a profit twice on the same property. Taxes from each transaction bolstered the economy and the government had more money in the coffers than ever dreamt of. Again, there was no incentive for anyone to shout 'stop' so the cycle continued. The party in government at the time, Fianna Fáil, hosted a tent at the legendary Galway Races festival each year where they lavishly entertained the builders who were making the profits which were bankrolling the country.

Why did nobody speak up? Some actually did despite it not being popular to pour cold water on a party where everybody's quality of life seemed to be improving after years of austerity. In the USA, the most high profile was Nassim Nicholas Taleb, stock trader and financial risk engineer (probably best known for his 2007 book, *The Black Swan*) who spent years warning of the inherent unsustainability of the prevailing system and the risk of a breakdown in the banking system and the economy in general. He highlighted the poor risk models and the fragility of the premise on which the banking system was now built. Taleb put his money where his mouth was and took a gamble on the collapse of bank stocks which paid off handsomely when the crash came. 'They didn't listen, so I took their money.'

In Ireland, while cheerleaders of the boom predicted a 'soft landing' for prices, that is, that they would stabilise and stay there, economists such as McWilliams, Morgan Kelly

116

and Eddie Hobbs gave a slightly more realistic view. They were ridiculed for their negative opinions when the country was obviously booming and enjoying unprecedented prosperity. The Irish Taoiseach (Prime Minister) at the time, Bertie Ahern, called them 'nay-sayers' and 'merchants of doom' and uttered the now legendary quip, 'I don't know how people who (talk down the economy) don't commit suicide'. The finance minister, Brian Lenihan, accused McWilliams of 'dangerous talk', but eventually realised he needed an alternative opinion to that which his government advisors were giving him. He famously turned up at McWilliams' front door in Dublin the night after the Lehman's crash in September 2008 to solicit his advice off the record.

So, when did it unravel? Prices peaked in 2006 and started slipping as 2007 began. In April 2007, New Century, a lender specialising in sub-prime loans, filed for bankruptcy protection, thus setting off the sub-prime mortgage crisis. By June, Bear Stearns, one of the big global investors headquartered in New York, bailed out two of its CDO-exposed funds to the tune of $20 billion. The following month it liquidated them. Shortly afterwards, it became clear that banks were now refusing to do business with each other as they feared each others' exposure. By September the crisis had spread to Europe with a run on the English bank, Northern Rock, after it was bailed out by the Bank of England. Over the next six months, institutions steadily went bust or were taken over by bigger players.

By March, Bear Stearns was taken over by JP Morgan for $10 per share (down from a high of $133 before the crisis). By early September 2008, it was clear that Fannie Mae and Freddie Mac, the two big US Government-backed institutions created to buy and repackage mortgages, thus creating liquidity for banks and stabilising the housing market, were in trouble and likely to become insolvent very soon. They received $190 billion of bailout funding after a federal takeover. A tipping point came on 15 September when the Federal Reserve declined to bail out Lehman Brothers bank. The following day, the Federal Reserve took over American International Group (AIG), the huge investment and insurance broker which was sinking under $85 billion of debt. As panic set in, investors withdrew $144 billion from the US money markets on 17 September, causing the short-term lending market to freeze, threatening the supply of money that many overseas governments rely on for the day-to-day running of their countries. By October, the International Monetary Fund (IMF) was warning that the world financial system was teetering on the 'brink of systemic meltdown'. Stock markets across the world dropped further and bottomed out in March 2009, over 50 per cent lower than the Autumn 2007 high point.

Over in Europe, countries with the biggest exposure to debt started to struggle with the collapse of the Icelandic banking system in 2008 before spreading to the group known as the PIIGS (Portugal, Ireland, Italy, Greece and Spain) in 2009. In 2012, the IMF estimated that Ireland's debt was 650 per cent of its GDP! The European Union, fearful of a systemic collapse of the Euro, partnered with the IMF and the countries were bailed out over subsequent years before regaining some financial independence in time.

Economists such as Charles Kindleberger, active as far back as the 1940s and 1950s, and more recently Tim Harford and McWilliams, have repeatedly emphasised that real-world economics doesn't work rationally like in textbooks. People are irrational and make decisions as herds. We influence each other and get swept up by fads and bubbles – we make errors! McWilliams says:

> . . . most people are what is known in financial markets as 'momentum investors' – they follow the crowd, buoyed up by the excitement of it all, rather than 'value investors' who constantly ask themselves whether prices reflect real value or something else.

If we are at least aware of this, we can try to intervene before reaching the level of a crash. Realistically, of course, we probably won't and will repeatedly make the same mistakes generation after generation 'because it's different this time!' Human Factors should be an essential component of study for bankers and economists, as should Error Management, although it will always be difficult to convince people to rain on a parade!

The lessons we learn in our study of Crew Resource Management all apply in finance too. The ability to speak up if we aren't happy about a decision or direction of travel without being humiliated or ostracised (or disciplined!) is badly needed. A system structured in such a way that actually prevents a dangerous move (an effective regulator with safeguards that can't be circumvented) as well as the six CRM pillars, especially Decision Making and Threat and Error Management. If the financial authorities had accepted that error is a given and made plans to deal with it, we could hopefully have avoided the worst of the recent excursions from economic stability. In the meantime, though, as Bette Davis said in the 1950 classic, *All about Eve*, 'Fasten your seatbelts, it's going to be a bumpy night!'

Chapter 6

Your Good Health!

'Oh shit! Shit, shit, shit!'

I was sitting at the nurses' station on my General Surgery ward in a major Belfast hospital. The bed closest to me in the bay opposite the desk had the curtains pulled. The 'crash' team had just left and behind the curtains was an elderly lady I had been looking after who had been admitted via the Accident & Emergency Department a few days previously. The curtains were pulled because the lady had just died from irrecoverable cardiac failure and cardiac arrest, precipitated by me prescribing her more intravenous fluids than her ailing heart was apparently able to handle. I had just killed my first patient!

I felt gutted. I had been entrusted with this lady's care and I had failed utterly. 'What am I going to tell the family? The nurses must think I'm useless! How am I going to explain this to my consultant?'

I finished writing up the notes and steeled myself to call my boss and confess that I had just killed one of our patients. I explained to him what had happened and the actions I had taken which precipitated her crash and waited to be berated for my incompetence. I was taken aback by his kind and considerate response. 'She was very unwell, Niall, and had co-morbidities that made her unsuitable for transfer to Intensive Care. You did your best for her. Thanks for letting me know. Hope the rest of your night is a bit quieter. See you tomorrow.' And he was gone.

I sat at the desk digesting what had just happened. No one seemed overly perturbed. She was a sick patient who had the odds stacked against her but I had given her the final nudge over the edge. Her husband was so gracious and accepting whilst the nurses prepared her for transfer to the mortuary before moving on to the next task in their unending list of jobs. Inside, I was beating myself up about how I could have given her less fluid or given it more slowly or monitored her more closely or … or …

This episode happened over a quarter of a century ago but I still recall it clearly. I had been a doctor for two and a half years by then so when I say I had killed my first patient, it is possibly more accurate to say this was the first patient who had died in front of me as a result of my mismanagement. Looking back, surely there must have been others. I couldn't have been that lucky! I don't know. Healthcare doesn't really talk about these sorts of errors. It doesn't fit the macho, arrogant, unshakeable image we are expected to portray, especially in surgery where many of us used our personalities as a contraceptive! Management weren't keen on us admitting to any errors either as the lawyers would get upset. We were usually on six-month or maximum twelve-month contracts so there wasn't much incentive for advertising errors – we hoped to progress and have a career.

So, we kept quiet.

It is such a common event that healthcare even has a technical term for it – iatrogenesis (derived from the two

Greek words, *iatros,* meaning healer, and *genesis,* meaning origin – in other words, caused by the healer). It is defined as 'the causation of a disease, a harmful complication, or other ill-effect by any medical activity, including diagnosis, intervention, error or negligence'. The management term used for it is an 'adverse event', an 'unintended event causing harm resulting from the medical management of the patient rather than the illness'.

As time progressed, I saw colleagues make errors at least as egregious as mine and some much worse. It seemed normal – complications, the families were told. And nobody really questioned it, neither the families nor the staff. We were too busy, we closed the chest and sent for the next patient. With the constant grind of long days, longer on-call shifts (we did an unbroken 56-hour shift once a month on top of a one in four rota covering three wards, a High Dependency Unit, an Intensive Care Unit, cardiac theatres, Accident and Emergency referrals and tertiary referrals from most of the country). We tried to publish papers and attend meetings and conferences to further our careers. I gave up my cycling career (such as it was) but stayed as Medical Officer to both the Ulster and Irish national cycling federations. I volunteered as one of the two race doctors alongside the incomparable Dr. Phil Brady on the FBD Milk Rás, Ireland's premier cycling event, a 9-day international cycle race round the country and a race I had ridden twice earlier in the decade when I had fewer commitments. We had little time to ruminate on failures since the next patient was always already waiting and errors were stored away by colleagues to be brought up as ammunition when promotions were being contested.

After six years working as a doctor, and despite achieving my Fellowship of the Royal College of Surgeons in Ireland (FRCSI) at the first attempt, publishing a few papers and now hoping for one of the scarce training posts in cardio-thoracic surgery which would lead eventually to a consultant job, I joined the dots and realised that I wasn't going to get that post. In cardiac surgery at that time, the medium to long term alternative to a training post was … well, actually there wasn't an alternative! You would work on six month contracts as a Registrar (non-training post) alongside the Specialist Registrar (training post) in exactly the same capacity and pay but without long-term prospects until, eventually, your contract wouldn't be renewed and your career stalled irrevocably. One week in March 1999, the realisation – which had been slowly developing in the back of my mind – abruptly crystallised that having tried unsuccessfully to get a training post in Ireland, the UK, Australia and the USA, I didn't have any long-term prospects in cardiac surgery. After twelve years of seemingly endless study, training and exams, I was at a dead end.

CAREER CHANGE

A couple of days after this bombshell realisation, Aer Lingus, Ireland's national airline, placed a half page advertisement in the *Sunday Independent* newspaper seeking cadet pilots to join them. An 18 month, fully funded programme leading to a steady, pensionable job for one of the country's most sought after employers flying jets worth up to $260 million (2018 prices) and carrying over 300 passengers. As I looked at the ad, an escape route materialised in front of me, despite having no previous interest in or experience of flying (other than as a passenger). I lifted the phone and dialed the number in the paper and after answering a few basic questions checking my eligibility for the scheme, I was given a date ten days hence to sit an aptitude test in a hotel near Dublin Airport. Within minutes, my focus had pivoted from learning all I could about cardio-thoracic surgery to learning all I could about aviation. This was my escape tunnel to a long-term career structure, something which surgery no longer offered me. I had one chance in my eyes and couldn't afford to blow it.

As it turns out, around 4,500 people made the same call that week and after eight rounds of assessments (all done without my consultants' knowledge as I was still working in the cardiac surgery unit in Dublin), I made the cut and was the 11th of 38 new cadet pilots employed in that intake. I served out the rest of my six-month contract, then spent a few weeks doing agency work in A&E units in Northern Ireland before heading off in August 1999 to train in Oxford and Arizona before coming back to Dublin to train on Airbus A321 jets and start the next stage of my life.

Aviation was a revelation compared to healthcare. I spent the next few years learning the ropes of my new career and embracing a refreshingly different mindset. I spent seven years as a co-pilot on our European Airbus A321 fleet before spending two years on our transatlantic A330 fleet. I came back onto the A321 and studied for my command checks (the exams to qualify as a captain) which I passed in November 2010. I went back onto the A330 for another 18 months while waiting my turn in the queue to take up a European command which I did in our Belfast base in April 2013. The following years have been spent as a captain between Belfast, the Virgin Atlantic Little Red operation, which was staffed by Aer Lingus pilots, our transatlantic

Boeing 757 fleet, our Dublin A320 and A321neo fleet and finally, in 2023, our A330 long haul fleet.

Early in my flight training, a concept known as Crew Resource Management (CRM) was emphasized, which we have looked at length in an earlier chapter. This was a major part of the company's Safety Management System (SMS) and comprised the expectation that we would speak up if we made an error or spotted a potential error without fear of disciplinary action or any form of retribution (known as a Just Culture approach). Similarly, it was a management system that helped us spot and deal with issues that arose so they could be processed before causing an accident. I realised early on that some of these were concepts I had suggested whilst still in healthcare (and had been dismissed by my superiors).

For example, simple ideas like running through a checklist before establishing a patient on cardio-pulmonary bypass during cardiac surgery. I vividly recall the response in theatre when I proposed this – 'if you don't feel up to assisting this case Niall, we can get one of the other lads in to replace you'. Still, I knew that this was a concept which could greatly benefit healthcare but I was too busy learning my new job, raising my young family, project-managing the building of our new home and so on to develop it at the time.

A few years later, whilst working through the command process (a several month long programme of training both academically and practically, culminating in a two week long exam flying in the left seat of the plane acting as the captain with a Line Standards Check Captain acting as a 'competent co-pilot' assessing me) I realised how little of being a captain involved technical knowledge and ability.

A certain standard was expected naturally, but the difference between being a good co-pilot and being a captain was managing the overall operation which largely revolved around application of Human Factors, a term I still had never heard of at that stage. After successfully negotiating my command checks and whilst waiting my turn in the queue to be formally upgraded to the rank of captain, I started looking a bit deeper into the idea of applying what I had learnt in aviation to my previous field of healthcare. I started researching what sort of problems were occurring and what sort of numbers were involved. What I found was mind-blowing.

INTRODUCING ERROR MANAGEMENT

The incidence of iatrogenesis – harm caused by the healthcare system, not the disease – was so staggering I assumed the figures I had found must be incorrect. I cross referenced them from a different angle and got the same results. I tried a different approach, but again got similar results. Every study I read showed that around 10 per cent of patients admitted to hospital suffered some sort of adverse event causing harm. About 30 per cent of these suffered serious harm, and around 3 to 5 per cent of them died due to the error. There were studies from all over the world going back decades and right up to the present, all saying essentially the same thing. Why was no one doing something about this? I realised that I had found something valuable that I could contribute back to healthcare, combining my knowledge of that industry with the new skills I had learnt in my aviation career. I set up Frameworkhealth Limited in May 2011 (with the intention of sharing our Aviation Error Management Framework with healthcare – hence the name). It was such an obvious fit between the two industries that I naively expected to embed our approach quickly and to start to transform the landscape right away. How wrong I was!

First, let's crunch some numbers to see just how big a problem we are dealing with. Let's start with the UK.

The population of the UK is around 66 million. In 2018, figures from the Office for National Statistics showed total healthcare spending for the year to be £214 billion in total (10 per cent of GDP) with government financed expenditure totaling £167 billion of this. Half of this went into hospital care, approximately £83 billion. If we look only at hospital admissions, figures for NHS England show around 15 million admissions per year, around half being day-cases who are discharged the same day. If 10 per cent have an adverse event, that's 1.5 million per year. International figures put the average cost of extra treatment, increased length of stay and so on in an adverse event at around £5,000 giving a total increased cost of £7.5 billion in NHS England alone. Extrapolating to the whole UK gives around £8.25 billion. This is uncannily consistent with statistics quoting adverse events as costing 10 per cent of a country's healthcare budget (which we showed at around £83 billion for hospitals).

UK figures for 2017/18 show 16,000 compensation claims, 5,000 of which led to legal proceedings with approximately 150 going to trial and over 200 being settled by mediation. The total compensation cost for clinical claims was £2.3 billion. International figures show total costs as usually totaling 3 to 4 times the compensation pay-outs once extra treatment costs, legal costs and so on are factored in, giving a total of between £6.9 billion and £9.2 billion, again consistent with our estimate of £8.25 billion! Interestingly, Obstetrics accounts for 10 per cent of claims but 50 per cent of costs.

A breakdown of adverse events in NHS England published in 2018 shows medication errors to be the most common event with around 237 million occurrences (incidentally, that is not a mis-print – 237,000,000) per year in the UK, and while 75 per cent are thought to cause no harm to the patient, 25 per cent do cause harm – 59 million events! UK researchers estimated that there are at least 700 deaths from avoidable drug errors and they could possibly contribute in up to 22,000 deaths.

In second place is Hospital Acquired Infections (HAIs) with around 300,000 incidences. The other parameter considered as a canary in the coalmine for issues is the Never Event. This is a serious adverse event considered avoidable using standard procedures/checklists. The figures for the 10-month period April 2018 to January 2019 recorded 423 events. These included 165 incidences of wrong site surgery, examples including biopsy of the wrong breast, cystoscopy on the wrong patient, circumcision performed instead of cystoscopy and chest drains inserted into the wrong side of the chest.

The costs incurred by these are estimated at £1.6 billion for drug errors and £1 billion per year for HAIs, almost a third of the annual bill of approximately £8 billion.

Let's cross the water to look at the Republic of Ireland's figures for comparison.

The Republic of Ireland (ROI) has a population of about 4.9 million and is served by a two-tier healthcare system with 47 public hospitals divided into 7 groups regionally and approximately 19 private hospitals. The public system has around 11,400 beds and the private system, 2,000. Healthcare employs 127,000 staff including 3,450 consultant posts (up to 900 of which are vacant due to recruitment issues) and 7,400 Non-Consultant Hospital Doctors (NCHDs), a catch-all term for all other hospital doctors, also known, somewhat inaccurately, as 'junior doctors' since some may have been qualified for 10 years or more and have several post-graduate qualifications. Around 47,000 nurses fill 40,000 Whole-Time Equivalent posts and primary care is provided by 4,250 General Practitioners, many of whom are self-employed and supply both state-funded care as well as private care for those ineligible for a Medical Card (around 55 per cent of the population). Forty per cent of the population have private health insurance, much higher than most other EU countries, with the average annual premium around €2,000.

Seven per cent of GDP is spent by the government on healthcare, with recent figures showing around €18 billion per year and a further €4 billion spent on private healthcare. Public hospitals have around 635,000 admissions per year with a further 1,000,000 day cases (60 per cent of patients) whilst the private system account for 100,000 admissions annually and 300,000 day cases (75 per cent of their total).

How much impact does error have on the Irish system? Reporting programmes introduced over the last ten years or so are acknowledged to only collect a proportion of the actual events due to poor reporting culture, fear of disciplinary action and staff simply not having time to fill in lengthy forms. In addition, there is often no sense of the forms having been seen by anyone, much less providing feedback on any outcomes or proposed changes.

The first published study looking at adverse events in the Irish system was in 2016 in the *BMJ Quality and Safety* journal by Dr. Natasha Rafter and a team from the Royal College of Surgeons in Ireland (RCSI). The findings were consistent with studies published worldwide in various countries. They showed that over 12 per cent of admissions suffer an adverse event (some patients have more than one!), 10 per cent of these suffer a permanent disability and in around 7 per cent of them it causes or contributes to their death. Applying this to total hospital in-patient admissions gives an adverse event rate of 73,500 per year with around 7,350 left with a permanent disability and over 5,000 deaths. Remember, this is only applying the data to in-patients, not the other 60 per cent of patients managed as day cases. Nor does it look at Accident and Emergency cases, Psychiatry or Primary Care, which includes 3.7 million GP visits and care supplied to our nursing homes or to the private hospital system so the actual figure is likely to be much higher.

The study had reviewed cases from 2009 and assessed costs due to error at around €194 million or 4 per cent of total government health spend. Applying this to today's numbers, 4 per cent would amount to €720 million, not including compensation payments (over €265 million in the first 9 months of 2019 alone including legal fees of around €50 million and €4.6 million on expert witnesses) and medical inflation compared to 10 years previously bringing the total to well over €1 billion for 9 months alone, leaving a full year total comfortably in the region of 10 per cent of total government spend as in other countries. A follow up study published in 2021 in the same journal by many of the same team using identical methods looking at cases from 2015 showed no change in the figures, suggesting that healthcare needs to try a different approach if it hopes to make progress in this critically important field.

What about the USA? Surely things are better in the land of the free? In 1999, the seminal 'To Err is Human' paper was published by Dr. Lucian Leape and his team from the Institute of Medicine which claimed that up to 98,000 lives per year were lost in the US from adverse events (human error effectively). This stirred quite a bit of activity and the formation of the government sponsored Agency for Healthcare Research and Quality (AHRQ). Despite a lot of effort, the results showed little or no change. A study published in the *British Medical Journal* in 2016 by Professor Marty Makary of Johns Hopkins University reviewed a collection of papers and drew the conclusion that the USA's hospital system had around 300,000 deaths per year due to adverse events – generally due ultimately to human error in design and/or execution of the healthcare system.

SAFER PATIENTS AND CHECKLIST MANIFESTOS

Paediatric cardiac surgeon Mark DeLaval and Ken Catchpole of London's Great Ormond Street Hospital realized that they needed help with how they handed over a critically ill post-op patient to the Intensive Care staff, and in 2006 turned to the Ferrari Formula 1 team for assistance. A trip to Ferrari HQ in Maranello with a video of their current procedure led to input on how to co-ordinate a complex, risky operation like a pitstop and apply it to the ICU setting. On return to London and with the input of two British Airways pilots, a new four-stage procedure was developed. Improvements were noted across all 27 parameters measured and training across the entire unit was carried out successfully. This was an early example of cross-over between two complex, high risk industries (aviation and F1) and healthcare, and the successful introduction of a checklist.

Another two doctors who managed to effect change were Johns Hopkins anaesthetist (or anaesthesiologist as they say in the States) Professor Peter Pronovost and Boston surgeon Dr. Atul Gawande.

Pronovost was stirred early in his career by the death of his father in the late 1980s from a misdiagnosed cancer which meant he missed the curative treatment window and was left only with the option of palliative care. Allied to this were further errors in his care leading to his father's premature death at the age of only 50 years.

Pronovost explains in his fascinating 2011 book *Safe Patients, Smart Hospitals* how he has dedicated his career to improving the system for others. Working in the world famous Johns Hopkins Hospital in Baltimore, he had seen other patient safety incidents but the death of an 18 month old named Josie King in 2001 due to a Hospital Acquired Infection from a central venous line, allied again with Human Factors failures in teamwork and communication, proved a turning point for the hospital. Pronovost drove changes in standardisation of central line management including using one standard technique, using a pre-prepared kit with everything necessary included, a simple checklist to ensure steps were completed in sequence and, crucially, empowering nurses to question the doctor directly if they didn't follow the new protocol.

The unit eventually reduced its infection rate from 19 per 1,000 catheter days to essentially zero, saving an estimated 8 lives and $2 million annually. The concept has been exported widely and many Intensive Therapy Units have transformed their infection rates. Pronovost also developed similar strategies improving outcomes in Ventilator Acquired Pneumonias (VAPs) and Surgical Site Infections (SSIs). He had established the value of checklists in healthcare.

In his best-selling book, *The Checklist Manifesto*, published in 2011, Atul Gawande describes how Pronovost's concept was expanded to a globally mandated Surgical Safety Checklist. In 2006, Dr. Gawande received a phone call from a lady in the World Health Organisation in Geneva asking him to be involved in a programme which planned to improve surgical safety worldwide. Early in 2007, he attended the first meeting which convened in Switzerland and was held over two days to address the problem. Present were clinicians from leading institutions in the US, Canada and Europe, as well as a doctor working single-handedly in a remote area of Ghana, the lead surgeon for the International Red Cross, a Russian bio-engineer, an Irish nurse and a patient representative, a father from Zambia whose daughter had inadvertently suffocated from lack of oxygen during treatment. In other words, the sort of diverse team research such as that discussed in a 2016 *Harvard Business Review* article by David Rock and Heidi Grant has shown to improve both performance and objective outcomes in diverse industries.

The checklist idea came up when the experience of Columbus Children's Hospital was discussed. They had an issue with SSIs related to failure to administer antibiotics at the correct time before incision. The hospital's surgical director, a paediatric cardiac surgeon, also happened to be a pilot and was familiar with checklists. He introduced a 'Cleared for Take-off' concept involving a checklist which prompted the administration along with some other basic details ('correct patient, correct operation' – don't laugh, remember the Never Event statistics above). Initially just over 60 per cent of appendectomy patients received antibiotics at the correct time. Within three months, this had risen to 89 per cent and by ten months it was 100 per cent.

Richard Reznick, head of surgery in the University of Toronto, then outlined how his hospital had trialed a checklist and team briefing approach. Professor Marty Makary, a pancreatic surgeon also based at Hopkins, and a group from Southern California shared that they had tried something similar. The group realised that the underlying theme was changing surgery from a virtuoso performance by the star performer, the surgeon, to a team effort focused on everyone contributing to reduce the inevitable errors which were occurring worldwide. It was decided to trial the checklist at a selection of sites around the world.

Initial results weren't encouraging but Dr Gawande then brought in one extra bit of diversity to the team – a pilot! He travelled to Seattle and met with Daniel Boorman, a 51-year-old pilot with many years of experience flying and working for Boeing who had produced checklists for both the 747 and Boeing's new 787 Dreamliner. He introduced Dr Gawande to the way pilots use both normal checklists and also more extensive Quick Reference Handbooks, essentially a collection of checklists to be followed in the event of a failure of a piece of equipment. He explained how checklists are living things which get regularly updated when real world events show failings which hadn't been considered.

An example would be the addition of a new checklist at the very back of an A320 QRH on what to do if you lose both engines at low altitude (introduced after Captain Chesley Sullenberger's 'Miracle on the Hudson' incident). Crucially, Boorman emphasised that a checklist is simply a tool at the pilot's disposal – it can't fly the aeroplane! The pilots must first fly the plane to buy enough time to get to use the checklist. They must employ the Human Factors approach outlined previously, prioritising decisions, using clear communications and maintaining Situational Awareness at all times. Checklists can be in a 'challenge and response' format, or they can be 'read and do'. Aviation is also very clear on who does what, making it easier for crews who have never met before (an almost everyday occurrence in any reasonably sized airline) to work safely and efficiently together.

The two-person crew is divided into 'pilot flying' (the one operating the controls) and 'pilot monitoring' the other one checking that the first one isn't making a mistake (which we frequently do – we're human beings operating a highly technical bit of kit in a very complex, dynamic and potentially dangerous environment). Boorman took Dr Gawande for a spin in the 777-200 ER simulator and reproduced a cargo door failure event which he had discussed earlier to demonstrate in real time how the system works.

Dr Gawande took these new ideas back to Boston and started redesigning his checklist. They adopted the 'do and confirm' format so ensuring critical steps weren't overlooked. They decided that the circulating nurse would initiate the check as per the pilot monitoring's responsibility for it in aviation. It was agreed that the check wouldn't be signed or recorded, it would simply be done and it was tweaked to keep each of the three sections to a usable one minute maximum duration.

The final iteration was then trialed in eight diverse hospital environments around the world. A three month period pre-checklist was studied to provide a baseline which showed the extent of the problem. Of almost 4,000 cases studied, more than 400 developed major complications with 56 deaths. The complication rate over the locations ranged from 6 per cent to 21 per cent of cases. In Spring 2008, the checklist was introduced with the inevitable hiccups but initial results started arriving in October 2008. The results were staggering. There were substantial improvements in all eight locations with a drop in complications from 11 per cent overall to 7 per cent and a reduction in deaths from 1.5 per cent to 0.7 per cent overall.

The results were published in January 2009 in the prestigious *New England Journal of Medicine*. Although the checklist is now mandatory in many countries worldwide, it hasn't been plain sailing. There was some opposition to the idea from staff who felt it was an imposition dictating to them what they needed to do. Surgeons argued that there was no statistically significant improvement in mortality rates in the high-income countries studied. It was agreed that there weren't enough patients in the sample to prove the case and subsequent studies addressed this.

Many studies have assessed the long-term change since 2009 and results have been mixed. Some were poorly designed or had insufficient numbers to be statistically relevant. Although most still show improvements, it's difficult to attribute these specifically to the checklist due to the variations and weaknesses in the design of the studies quoted. So the checklist is used extensively and improvements have been seen, but it is still often viewed as another chore to be carried out, not a safety net to protect the patient and staff. There has been little implementation of an overall Human Factors approach in which the checklist is only one small part. The number of Human Factor experts in the NHS (an organisation of over 1.3 million staff) is still around single figures. The cultural shift which this will need still hasn't happened.

Aviation had a test pilot culture in the 1950s when airplanes were very different to nowadays. These pilots lived by the seat of their pants, helping to develop the aircraft which eventually led to our modern fleets. They had amazing skill, courage and an ability to improvise quickly. They also had a 25 per cent mortality rate! As safety benefits accumulated and modern innovations such as simulators became standard, their 'rock star' status waned and they were replaced by conservative, boring, sensible heads like me! Dr Gawande proposes that surgery still has many who feel their expertise in handling complexity is what makes them who they are – they have Chuck Yeager's 'right stuff'.

Checklists and the acknowledgment of inevitable errors are difficult concepts to sell. For checklists to work, surgeons need to focus on the team rather than individual skill. They need to delegate authority to junior staff and be willing to be pulled up by them when they err – again, a difficult sell to someone who has spent decades getting to a position of authority. This may be why checklists have only made limited progress in healthcare. They need to be seen as only a part of an overall Human Factors-based approach to managing error. The inevitability of error needs to be accepted by both staff and patients alike so that errors aren't immediately seen as evidence of incompetence demanding disciplinary action and compensation. This will also involve a culture shift for the public and the legal system so that alternatives to litigation such as mediation are considered. Doctors need to feel safe in reporting errors or else the old system of cover-up and obfuscation will persist.

AVIATION SKILLS APPLIED TO HEALTHCARE – WILL THEY FLY?

Doctors often tell me that the aviation approach won't work in healthcare because patients are more complex than aeroplanes. They are correct – patients are much more complex. However, that misses the point. The inevitability of error is just the same in both industries. Indeed, that very complexity makes error in healthcare even more likely so a system which hunts out errors and manages them before serious harm ensues is just as critical if not more so.

So, how does aviation perform compared to healthcare? Putting those 5,000 plus deaths in the Irish system (consistent, remember with almost every other study – Ireland is not a poorly performing outlier) into context, let's compare with another industry which contributes hugely to Ireland's economy. Worldwide, aviation has over 4 billion passenger movements per year (pre-Covid 19 figures) yet generally has less than 1,000 deaths annually in commercial passenger jet accidents. In 2017, there were none at all! In 1977, aviation saw around 3,000 deaths, following a steadily increasing trend – if the trend had continued allowing for the almost 10-fold increase in passengers flown, we would have around 30,000 deaths per year yet we generally have less than 1,000, a 97 per cent reduction. Probably the most significant reason for the improvement is aviation's acceptance of error and its focus on a Human Factors approach to all aspects of the industry.

In short, healthcare needs to accept the value of a Just Culture where staff feel free to highlight where errors have occurred without fear of humiliation or disciplinary action. I explained previously that this is an underlying foundation of aviation's Error Management strategy and is the jumping off point for all other improvements to occur.

Some courageous individuals have put their heads above the parapet in an attempt to do the right thing and to improve the flawed system they work in. To their credit, most people in healthcare accept the need for change but are up against an embedded culture, hierarchy and unwillingness to speak up as staff see very clearly how healthcare treats 'whistleblowers'. Even the term is pejorative whereas these brave people should be lauded as having the courage to acknowledge the failings in the system and for trying to improve it. How has healthcare dealt with those who have tried to drive such change?

Whistleblowing

In August 2013, Dr. Chris Day started a placement in the Intensive Care Unit of Queen Elizabeth Hospital, Woolwich in London as part of his training programme in Emergency Medicine. Having no previous experience of Intensive Care or anaesthetics, he was alarmed to discover that, when on call, his new role involved being the only doctor responsible for up to 18 ICU patients as well as any 'outliers' (patients under their care but who were on other wards due to a lack of beds). Four of his new colleagues were apparently similarly inexperienced. Day raised his concern with management that this situation was unsafe but was told 'the system has worked well for years'.

In November of that year, core standards for ICUs were published stating that there should be no more than eight patients per doctor and there must be immediate availability of a doctor skilled in advanced airway techniques. In Woolwich, this function was covered by the on call anaesthetist. Unfortunately, if they were in theatre with a case, they would not be 'immediately available', leaving the ICU junior on their own. In November and December, two patients under the care of on call ICU junior doctors died in 'Serious Untoward Incidents' – one where a chest drain was inserted incorrectly puncturing the patient's liver causing them to bleed to death, and a second where a failure to admit a hypotensive patient to ICU in a timely manner led to their death. In January 2014, two locum doctors failed to turn up leaving Day covering ICU as well as four other wards. He formalised his concerns about this shortage of staff by making a protected disclosure to his employers, Lewisham and Greenwich NHS Trust, and also Health Education England (HEE) who are the body supervising training posts in England. The HEE agreed with Day and said that a GMC survey had seen others raise similar worries. There was little progress so Day raised his concerns again at his end-of-year appraisal meeting in June 2014.

In August, the British Medical Association (BMA), the doctors' trade union, agreed to take on his case. Things started changing quite quickly then. Within weeks, the HEE had withdrawn Day's training number, effectively removing him from the consultant training programme he had been on and thus seriously jeopardising his long-term career prospects. The following month, October 2014, his union, the BMA, suddenly withdrew from his case. When his case finally reached an Employment Tribunal in February 2015, the HEE changed tack, arguing that they had no concerns over staffing levels and, moreover, that they weren't Day's employer so had no part in the case and had the case struck out without being heard. The HEE asserted that junior doctors were not entitled to protection under the statutory whistleblowing protection. That June, Day was refused permission to appeal the decision but subsequently had this overturned in August.

The case was finally heard in March of the following year, 2016, but Day was refused the right to an Employment

Tribunal and was again denied the right to appeal the decision to the Court of Appeal, a decision the Court itself overturned and indeed expedited on the basis of the public interest. At this hearing in March 2017, Day finally had his case heard and the judgment delivered in May 2017 found in his favour and called for the HEE position to be clarified. In 2018, the HEE were forced to acknowledge that they were indeed responsible for the country's junior doctors and that the doctors were covered under whistleblowing law when a contract they had failed to disclose revealed the influence they had on junior doctors' terms of engagement, which clearly demonstrated their responsibility. Lady Justice Gloster and Mr Justice Moylan also queried why the BMA had sought to obstruct and undermine the case which was to benefit 54,000 junior doctors and their patients. They also extended the judgment to clarify the status of agency-type workers in other industries working in triangular-type arrangements between the agency, worker and workplace.

After over four years of obstructions to the case, it finally went to a hearing in October 2018, scheduled for 21 days. After six days of cross-examination the Trust indicated to Day that in the event of him losing the case, they now intended to pursue him for the full costs which at that point were around £500,000. He appears essentially to have been backed into a corner and was left with the option of either withdrawing the allegations or face financial ruin and the loss of his home.

Day chose to withdraw and the Trust and HEE issued a statement agreeing that he had acted in good faith and had performed a public service in winning whistleblower protection for junior doctors. After almost five years of obstructing the case and spending £700,000 of taxpayers' money on it, the Trust and HEE were off the hook while Chris Day's career lay in tatters. Day has since challenged the circumstances of his withdrawal from the case and has sought to get the findings set aside in order for the case to be heard fully. In March 2020, the Court of Appeal granted him leave to appeal with cost protection but then weeks later claimed that the signed and sealed judgment of the court was actually a clerical error. Unbelievably, the case is still working its way through our legal system in 2023. Although we have yet to hear the final outcome, it is clear that that healthcare still hasn't fully come to terms with the Just Culture concept, despite the establishment in 2017 of designated staff to whom others can raise safety concerns without worrying about disciplinary action or retribution.

Sir Robert Francis QC

Sir Robert Francis QC, a senior barrister and Deputy High Court Judge, has been one of the major players in trans-forming patient safety over the last decade and more. He is hugely experienced in medico-legal cases including the Organ Retention scandal at AlderHey Children's Hospital in Liverpool and the Bristol Babies Heart Surgery scandal, both reporting in 2001. He has chaired several independent inquiries, three of which are particularly relevant to our study of error and how it should be managed.

Two reports investigated the failings uncovered in Mid Staffordshire NHS Foundation Trust. It looked at failings in care between 2005 and 2009 after locals and family members raised repeated concerns regarding the treatment of family members at the hospital. Francis had published an initial report in 2010 based on an independent inquiry held behind closed doors which focused on failings at the

Trust. The poor standards of care uncovered made national headlines and horrific reading. The local community led by family members of patients who had suffered and died felt this report was insufficient in both scope and transparency, and called repeatedly for a public inquiry into events at the Trust and in the wider context of the NHS generally. They formed a campaign group, Cure the NHS, which eventually managed to secure a public inquiry into the allegations. The Healthcare Commission (forerunner of the Care Quality Commission (CQC)) had exposed appalling patient care and higher than expected mortality rates at the hospital. The commission didn't publish figures but it is widely thought that between 400 and 1,200 patients died unnecessarily between 2005 and 2008 when, ironically, the hospital gained its coveted Foundation Trust status. Francis' first inquiry estimated around 500 deaths.

The public inquiry exposed a litany of poor care including patients left in their own urine and excrement, unable to reach the food left for them, call bells unanswered, falls concealed and triage in A&E carried out by receptionists instead of clinical staff. It also exposed a pattern of callousness by nursing staff. What happened? Were these bad people? The answer is more likely rooted in Human Factors leading to many avoidable errors.

Francis' first report, published in 2010, highlighted a long history of understaffing of nurses as well as a bullying culture in the Trust, and said that senior management were in denial as to the extent of the problems at the hospital. Managers seemed to be primarily focused on attaining Foundation Trust status and meeting targets rather than on patient care and listening to staff concerns. This inquiry revealed an organisation which was inward-looking with few new staff coming from elsewhere so became entrenched in its negative culture. The South Staffordshire Primary Care trust, which was responsible for the hospital, appeared to be more focused on the financial problems facing its bigger teaching hospital, the University Hospital of North Staffordshire. The regional body in charge, the NHS West Midlands, was said to have put the high mortality rates down to data errors – a clear case of confirmation bias, seeing what they wanted to see.

The second report, the public inquiry which reported in 2013, widened its net well beyond the poor nursing care at the hospital and looked at the whole structure of the health and social care system in England and how it was poorly designed to support staff. The report ran to 1,782 pages and made 290 recommendations. Specifically, it highlighted the toxic culture which hinders staff from reporting issues of concern for fear of bullying and adverse career progression. It recommended the introduction of legal protections for 'whistleblowers', the very same protection incorrectly denied to Dr Chris Day shortly after its introduction. It said a 'duty of candour' should be enshrined in law ensuring that staff would speak up when they see something they weren't happy with. They should inform a patient and their family if harm has occurred and answer questions truthfully. The same requirement was made of the Trusts. He also recommended that nursing assistants should be trained and regulated like other professionals. In his concluding statement, he called for 'a real change in culture, a refocusing and re-commitment of all who work in the NHS, about putting the patient first'. He essentially called for a Just Culture where staff can speak up without fear of retribution and where issues get addressed with a view to resolution and avoidance of recurrence, not to apportion blame. He advocated an Error Management strategy.

Freedom to Speak Up Report, 2015

Sir Robert was commissioned to write a third report, published in 2015, following on from his findings of bullying and fear of speaking up due to the repercussions it often prompted. This 'Freedom to Speak Up' report looked in huge detail at the issues and consulted widely both inside and outside healthcare, including with aviation, to get a view on how other industries have tackled the same problem.

The main thrust of the 2015 report was that staff should be able to speak up about any issue which they felt impacted patient care and safety. They should be able to do so without fear of repercussions and with a support structure to help them. This led to the establishment of the 'Freedom to Speak Up Guardian' system with each healthcare provider encouraged to appoint a staff member to facilitate the raising of safety issues by staff. Although they have very little authority to intervene in the actual processing of cases, they have a wide remit to highlight concerns and reports of problems both inside the organisation (with direct access to the CEO) and, if necessary, outside as well. They facilitate staff to get their concerns on the table and to ensure that the issues are adequately addressed and that the staff member is not penalised in any way for highlighting shortcomings.

Francis's plan was for the reporting of problems to be normalised and a regular event, rather than a rare occasion when things got so bad no other option seemed available. It essentially drove the view that other Safety Critical industries accepted long ago: that errors are inevitable and only by acknowledging them can they be either eliminated or mitigated.

This led to the establishment in 2016 of the National Guardian's Office led by Dr. Henrietta Hughes, a London GP and former Medical Director at NHS England. The Office aims to make speaking up a routine part of health-care and leads, trains and supports a network of over 500 Freedom to Speak Up Guardians (FTSUGs) as envisaged in Sir Robert's report. Organisations who provide services under the NHS Standard Contract (NHS Trusts, Foundation Trusts and others) must appoint a guardian although many other bodies now also appoint one.

The Office's remit is to challenge healthcare generally in its approach to patient safety issues. It is, however, not a regulatory or investigatory body and is not empowered to investigate individual cases. It cannot arbitrate on cases and does not replace existing legal processes such as those involving professional bodies or employment tribunals. They can, however, make recommendations in cases they feel haven't been handled satisfactorily. FTSUGs are appointed by the organisation they support and work for under a universal job description issued by the Guardians' Office to ensure standardisation across healthcare. They do this work alongside their current function but with pro-tected time allocated to it. An organisation can have more than one FTSUG. Larger organisations have also appointed Patient Safety Champions and Ambassadors who work alongside the Guardians. Their role is less defined and varies according to the needs of the organisation. Having spoken to some of the Guardians who have been in the role for a number of years now, they are happy that the role is taken seriously by management and that they have been effective in driving some change.

Another recommendation from the report was the encouragement of reflective practice, an established activity in healthcare for many years. In addition to long established Morbidity and Mortality meetings, and the more recent multi-disciplinary Schwarz rounds, Francis recommended that all NHS organisations provide opportunities for staff to engage in regular reflection and review of concerns in their workplace. He felt that this would result in staff feeling more valued and supported, thus improving the quality and safety of the service they provide. He felt staff should be encouraged and empowered to implement remedies themselves and to then communicate this to management who could share these with others, both inside the organisation and beyond. However, the issue of reflective practice, which was intended to be an activity used to help learning from mistakes in a timely way, took an ominous turn with a case involving a paediatric trainee, Dr. Hadiza Bawa-Garba, which caused much controversy in the second half of the decade.

The Bawa-Garba Case

The case centred around the errors in the care of a six-year-old child, Jack Adcock, who was admitted to the Leicester Royal Infirmary Children's Assessment Unit (CAU) in February 2011. Jack, who had Down's Syndrome and a heart condition, presented with diarrhoea, vomiting and difficulty breathing. Dr. Hadiza Bawa-Garba, a sixth year trainee in paediatrics, had just recently returned from maternity leave and this was her first acute shift in a hospital she was unfamiliar with, not having been given induction training. The doctor, who had a previously 'impeccable record', was the most senior doctor covering CAU, the ED and the ward since her consultant, Dr. Stephen O'Riordan, was in a different hospital that day (having been unaware he was on call, he had taken on teaching duties in Warwick) and the other registrar was on a training course with no substitute supplied.

Dr. Bawa-Garba saw Jack around 10.30 am, admitted him and ordered some blood tests and a chest x-ray, as well as prescribing intravenous fluids. His blood gas results showed an elevated lactate level. The chest x-ray was available around 12.30 pm but Dr. Bawa-Garba wasn't notified and due to her being busy seeing other patients, including performing a lumbar puncture on a baby, didn't see it until 3.00 pm when she diagnosed a chest infection and prescribed antibiotics. Due to a failure of the hospital's electronic computer system, her Senior House Officer was busy chasing results manually all day leaving her without crucial support and meaning she didn't see the blood results until six hours after they were taken.

At a review meeting with a consultant at 4.30 pm and again at 6.30 pm, Dr. Bawa-Garba raised no concerns about Jack. The hospital had a relatively unusual practice of allowing parents to administer a child's routine medications without them being prescribed for the current admission, so Jack's mother gave him his usual cardiac medication (Enalapril) around 7.00 pm which would have lowered his blood pressure. Jack's condition deteriorated suddenly around 8.00 pm and a 'crash call' went out to alert the on call team that he needed urgent resuscitation. Dr. Bawa-Garba was one of the team responding, and on entering

Jack's room mistook him for a different patient and called off the resuscitation.

The error was realised in less than two minutes and resuscitation resumed, but, tragically, Jack died at 9.20 pm. The cause of death was sepsis, a serious infection which had spread to the bloodstream and thereby led to failure of other organs. Mortality rates are very high (in the region of 40 per cent) and early aggressive treatment is critical.

At a reflective practice meeting the next day with her supervising consultant, Dr. Bawa-Garba discussed what had happened and how it could have been handled differently. She recorded her version of events and her thoughts on it in an ePortfolio used in the regular revalidation assessment system which was finally introduced in healthcare in 2012. Subsequent events were to have a seismic impact on healthcare in the UK.

In April 2012, the University of Leicester NHS Trust informed the General Medical Council (GMC) that a Serious Untoward Incident investigation had been held. It was found that there were serious systemic failures, including Dr. Bawa-Garba struggling to cover the roles of up to four doctors. The report made 23 recommendations and 79 actions to be undertaken. It stated that 'it has not been possible to identify a single root cause due to the systemic problems identified'.

Bawa-Garba was given three months supervised training and taken off the on call rota. The Crown Prosecution Service (CPS) decided not to prosecute. In June, Jack's parents contacted the GMC regarding the case who started a misconduct investigation but postponed any decision until after the inquest pending. This inquest was adjourned a year later in July 2013. The CPS began a review of its original decision not to prosecute, eventually resulting in Dr. Bawa-Garba and two nurses being charged with gross negligence manslaughter. She had continued to work throughout.

In January 2015, the Medical Practitioners' Tribunal Service (MPTS), which reports to the GMC board, suspended her for 18 months pending her investigation but Dr. Bawa-Garba successfully challenged this and continued to work until her trial in November 2015 when she was convicted as charged and received a two year suspended sentence. Whilst her 'reflections' weren't used in evidence, it appears that they were certainly available to the prosecution team given that they were written up in the hospital canteen on the morning after the event by Dr. Bawa-Garba's supervising consultant who subsequently became a witness for the prosecution. The jury were not made aware of the hospital's SUI investigation highlighting the many systemic failings contributing to Jack's death. From a Human Factors viewpoint, this gave a very skewed Situational Awareness and in the absence of this mitigating evidence, the availability heuristic allowed Dr. Bawa-Garba and Nurse Isabel Amaro to be blamed and convicted.

In June 2017, the MPTS suspended her for 12 months, rejecting a request from the GMC for her permanent disqualification, finding that she was a competent doctor who made mistakes in the context of serious systemic failures and recommended that she should be allowed to continue to practise medicine. The GMC appealed this and in January 2018 succeeded in having Dr. Bawa-Garba permanently struck off the register.

Within days, a crowdfunding initiative to mount a legal challenge was set up by concerned doctors and tens of thousands of pounds were raised on the first day. Within a month, in excess of £366,000 had been raised from over 11,000 donors. The erasure decision was successfully challenged and in August 2018, the Court of Appeal reversed the decision of the High Court to strike her off the register. The government carried out a rapid parliamentary review of the GMC (Williams Review) which recommended it be stripped of its right to appeal MPTS decisions. It rejected calls for 'reflective notes' to be given legal protection. Dr. Bawa-Garba's barrister, James Laddie QC, who was also involved in Dr. Chris Day's case, said the case had become 'something of a lightning rod for the dissatisfaction of doctors and medical staff in this country'. He also voiced the concerns of many doctors that the trial chose to disregard the 'systemic failings' which created the environment that she was working in. Most doctors could see the similarities in their own hospitals and felt 'there but for the grace of God, go I' and the case has had the unintended consequence of the drive to encourage the 'open disclosure' of untoward incidents being hampered.

Dr. Bawa-Garba was cleared to return to work in July 2019 under certain supervisory conditions for two years, although she opted to defer this due to being on maternity leave. She was admitted to the Specialist Register of the GMC in 2022 as a fully trained consultant paediatrician.

The handling of the case brought relations between the GMC and the profession it regulates to a new low point. In an interview with the Royal College of Physicians magazine, *Commentary*, the chair of the GMC at the time, Sir Terence Stephenson, acknowledged this:

> The relationship is at a low ebb. Did I think that was going to happen when I started in my role? No, because one of the reasons I stood as chair is that I

thought the GMC needed to improve its relation-ship with the profession, and I think there's a lot of evidence that we have done that over the past three years, until this case erupted.

We have reduced the number of investigations of doctors, and reduced the fees for doctors (especially trainees), for the first time in a long time. We have commissioned an independent review by Professor Louis Appleby, a leading UK mental health expert, to look at vulnerable doctors and accepted all of his rec-ommendations. These are all things we were doing to show that the best way to protect the public is to look after doctors, but of course this case has set that back hugely. It would be naïve to think otherwise.

Despite a few examples of commendable work, over-all we need a sea-change in the way error is thought of in healthcare. Generally, the concept of error is still not welcome and still seen as a failing. Staff who speak up are considered to have 'spat in the soup' to use a term used in cycling in the 1990s to describe those riders who spoke out against doping in the sport (and were, of course, eventually vindicated). Acceptance of a Just Culture and proof from management that they intend to 'walk the walk' by engag-ing constructively with 'whistleblowers' would send out a message to staff that the industry is prepared to change. Actually, a good start would be for the industry to stop call-ing them whistleblowers! That would open the door to the other two main legs of our framework, namely, review of how the error occurred from a systems mindset rather than to apportion blame, and finally, the adoption of the Crew Resource Management operating philosophy.

In October 2018, I was one of the organisers of a con-ference in Belfast bringing together the medical and legal professions to look at a better way of dealing with medical errors to the benefit of patients, staff and organisations. Sir Terence Stephenson kindly came over to speak at the event alongside our Lord Chief Justice, Sir Declan Morgan, as well as other senior representatives from both law and health-care. It was generally agreed that the current way of doing business was unsustainable and that an Error Management approach to reducing errors, followed by mediation as an alternative to litigation, was an attractive alternative. Progress is slow, but the concept of error as something to be addressed rather than ignored or covered up is certainly gaining traction in healthcare.

A similar collaborative approach to those who have 'sinned' against us in many areas of our own lives could pay dividends as opposed to the litigious, combative approach. There are mercifully few people out there 'trying to get us' so although it may sound a little Pollyannaish, attempting mediation first can actually achieve impressive results and can resolve problems much faster, cheaper and to the satis-faction of all parties instead of simply having a winner and a loser. Accepting error as inevitable, and not immediately assuming it was due to incompetence (although in some cases it will be), can reduce stress levels in all parties which usually leads to a better resolution.

None of this will bring Jack Adcock or the many other victims of unintentional error back, but it would be a fitting legacy if what we have learnt from these cases benefitted those coming after, both patients and staff.

Chapter 7

Political Blunders

Ulster Unionist Party MP Enoch Powell's best known quote was:

> All political lives, unless they are cut off in midstream at a happy juncture, end in failure, because that is the nature of politics and human affairs.

It was written in his 1977 biography of British statesman Joseph Chamberlain who, during his long career, managed to split not one but two political parties yet not achieve his ultimate goal of becoming Prime Minister. This would imply a certain degree of error somewhere along the line in political careers, and when we delve into that field that would certainly seem to be the case. From US Vice-President Dan Quayle's entertaining correction of 'potato' to 'potatoe' at a New Jersey school spelling bee in 1992 to the rather more serious error by Joseph's son, Neville Chamberlain, in his famous 'Peace for our Time' declaration in 1938 after negotiating with the German Führer, Adolf Hitler, less than a year before Hitler provoked World War II by invading Poland, politics is as littered by error as any of the other fields we have explored.

A common theme in many errors in both politics and science is in Situational Awareness. The difference, however, is that the scientist is generally aware that their work is incomplete but represents the best model available at that time, whereas the politician often speaks with supreme confidence on subjects of which they have no understanding, then proceeds to make critical policy decisions based on that misunderstanding. This lack of awareness is compounded by the common error of selecting a group of colleagues and advisors whose thinking is broadly in line with their own and conflicting views being discouraged. This distorted team working with a steep seniority gradient subsequently feeds through to sub-optimal decision making which can have global consequences. Ambitious politicians will also remember that contradicting the boss usually isn't rewarded with promotion! This scenario leads to the biases we will study in detail elsewhere, such as confirmation bias, anchoring and availability bias. An awareness of this risk goes a long way towards reducing the resulting errors and is a lesson from which we can all benefit.

So, now let's take a quick trip through the evolution of politics in our culture – we will find that error is a common thread throughout history, from the Greeks and the Romans into modern times.

GREEK EMPIRE

One of the first political systems was the Greek Empire of 2,500 years ago. After it's Golden Age of the fifth century BCE, it made a series of errors which turned it from a flourishing democracy to a dictatorship ruled by Demetrius who was hailed not only as a king but as a God. In his 2009 book *From Democrats to Kings*, Dr. Michael Scott of Cambridge University describes how the various city-states turned towards infighting and waging wars rather than focusing on the international trade that had driven its earlier success.

As Greece faced military defeat and submission to powerful Macedonia, democracy was eroded steadily into a more authoritarian rule. Scott offered this history as a warning to Britain at the time of the Economic Crash of 2008 to avoid the same decline. We haven't seen any God-like leaders yet but maybe it's too early for that development!

ROMAN EMPIRE

The Roman Empire originated in 27 BCE when Augustus Caesar became the first emperor of Rome. Joshua J. Mark's account of the sequence of events published in 2019 in *Ancient History Encyclopaedia* gives a clear timeline of its establishment with a storyline that could sustain a soap opera for many years!

When Octavian eventually achieved total control of the empire he was hailed as the saviour of Rome. In 27 BCE, the Senate granted him the title of Emperor along with the title Augustus (illustrious one) thus establishing the Roman Empire which was to flourish for 500 years with him, Augustus Caesar, its first emperor. He established the empire on a path to becoming one of the greatest political and cultural powers the world had seen and ruled until his death in 14 CE.

This would be a good time to clarify the terms BCE and CE which we have used in this timeline and those earlier in the book. This too derives partially from error. History has traditionally been divided into the time Before Christ, BC, and the time since the year of his birth, Anno Domini, AD. Historians, however, are fairly confident that the year of Christ's birth was miscalculated and that he was actually born around 4 BC. Add the fact that the term relates solely to Christianity, which represents only 29 per cent of the world's population, it was felt that dividing history into the two eras, 'Before the Common Era', BCE, and 'Common Era', CE, was more appropriate and is now in common usage.

The error which is felt to have spelt the eventual downfall of the empire was committed by Diocletian who divided it in 285 CE into two large sections, the Western Roman Empire and the Eastern Roman Empire (also known as the Byzantine Empire). The fortunes of the two sections diverged with the Eastern being much more successful so that on Diocletian's death in 311 CE, the empire was plunged into civil war again.

Theodosius ruled from 379-395 CE and proclaimed Christianity the state religion and outlawed paganism, closing the schools and converting pagan temples into churches. He doesn't appear to have considered Human Factors in his planning, however, which generally then pre-disposes to error. The people quite liked the idea of 'local' gods they could relate to and weren't keen on the idea of one remote god who had no special interest in Rome. This period is seen as the beginning of the end of the empire, not purely because of the adoption of Christianity but because of its unwieldy size causing instability and leaving it prone to attack from outside.

So, in the words of the Monty Python team, 'What have the Romans ever done for us?' Many things we take for granted derive from the Romans. Our Julian calendar, for instance, as well as the names of both the days of the week and the months. They also drove advances in road building, sanitation, security and a postal system. They transformed both the legal systems and healthcare where Latin terms are still in use. Their influence in church, government and the military is also still evident. Despite a few errors, the Roman Empire has certainly left an enduring legacy.

THE TWENTIETH CENTURY

The Treaty of Versailles

Fast forwarding to 1919, we can relocate to post-war Paris where the settlement negotiations between the Allied Forces who defeated Germany in World War I took place. Although the armistice was signed on 11 November 1918 to end the fighting, it took six months of haggling to conclude a peace treaty, the Treaty of Versailles, which was eventually signed on 28 June 1919. The Allies struggled to agree what they wanted from Germany with the eventual solutions leading to disquiet on many sides – some felt it too harsh, others too lenient.

One of the most controversial aspects was the insistence that Germany accept the 'War Guilt Clause'. This involved them disarming, making territorial concessions and paying reparations. This amounted to the equivalent of roughly £285 million in today's money. The British economist John Maynard Keynes felt the settlement was an error predicting a 'Carthaginian Peace' due to reparations being excessive and counter-productive. The terms were modified in time by the Locarno Treaties as well as the Dawes Plan and the Young Plan so that the impact was less severe than originally planned. The repayments were indefinitely postponed at the Lausanne Conference of 1932.

Although the actual impact was less than originally agreed, Human Factors meant that the resentment at their humiliation was already embedded in the German psyche and the severity of the Treaty is often considered by historians as being a major error which contributed to the rise of Nazi Germany in the 1930s and ultimately the death of around 85 million people (3 per cent of the world's population) in World War II between 1939-1945.

'Peace for Our Time'

Only a generation after WW I, the threat of war again hung over Britain in late 1938. The German Führer, Adolf Hitler, who had annexed Austria earlier in the year, had vowed to invade Czechoslovakia on 1 October to occupy the German speaking Sudetenland region. The British Prime Minister, Neville Chamberlain, had mobilised the Royal Navy and London was being prepared for war.

Two days before the deadline, Hitler agreed to meet Chamberlain along with Italian leader Benito Mussolini and French premier Edouard Daladier in Munich to discuss a resolution. It was agreed that the Sudetenland area of Czechoslovakia should be ceded to Germany (without any consultation with Czechoslovakia) and separately Hitler signed a non-aggression pact with Britain. As news of the diplomatic breakthrough reached London, jubilant scenes reminiscent of those celebrating the end of WWI swept the capital.

The error of Chamberlain's optimism was brutally exposed as Hitler invaded the rest of Czechoslovakia in March 1939 and then Poland on 1 September forcing Britain to declare war on Germany and thereby launching the Second World War. As with most errors, things aren't always as straight forward as they may seem. Some have argued that Britain and France weren't equipped for war in 1938 and the appeasement policy of the Munich Pact bought them time to strengthen their military power.

'We Begin Bombing in Five Minutes'

Moving across the Atlantic, one of the most famous political errors was given to us courtesy of US President Ronald Reagan in August 1984 at the height of the Cold War.

Reagan was preparing to give his weekly radio address from his ranch in Santa Barbara and many media stations were already recording the feed for use in their bulletins. Reagan, who had been known to inject a bit of levity into these checks, surpassed himself with the announcement, 'My fellow Americans, I'm pleased to tell you that I have signed legislation that will outlaw Russia forever. We begin bombing in five minutes.'

The administration had an agreement with the media outlets to keep unprepared, off the record comments under wraps but rumours of these remarks spread rapidly. Two days later, the Gannett newspaper corporation headquartered in Washington DC published the actual quotation. The White House Press Secretary refused to comment! By next day, the story was worldwide news. Although Soviet Foreign Affairs officials refused to be drawn into the controversy, state-controlled media outlets such as Pravda denounced the remarks as 'unprecedentedly hostile'. Whitehouse officials were forced to clarify that the remarks didn't reflect US policies or intentions. Reagan's presidential election opponent, the hapless Walter Mondale, failed to capitalise on the gaffe and Reagan was easily re-elected for a second term in November.

'Can You Hear Me Now?'

Live microphones have a habit of catching out remarks by politicians not intended for public consumption. During the General Election campaign of 2010, Labour Party Prime Minister Gordon Brown was confronted by a Labour supporter who took him to task on an issue she felt he wasn't addressing adequately. Brown was forced to grin and bear the attack as cameras recorded his discomfort.

Unfortunately, as he was driven away, one of his aides whose microphone was still on, captured his rant about this 'bigoted woman'. This became the story of the day and Brown was forced to return and apologise to the lady concerned. The incident has been credited as one of the decisive moments in Brown losing the election.

His successors, Prime Minister David Cameron and Deputy Prime Minister Nick Clegg, leading a Conservative/ Liberal Democrat coalition, were also caught out by a live mike after a televised Q&A session when Clegg commented that the difficulty separating party policies in a coalition would mean 'if we keep doing this, we won't find anything to bloody disagree on in the bloody TV debates!'

Cameron was also embarrassed by a less technological event in February 2020 when his close protection officer went for a 'comfort break' on a Trans-Atlantic flight and left both his gun and the former Prime Minister's passport in the bathroom. Another passenger handed the 9mm Glock 17 pistol and travel documents to a surprised cabin crew member. The officer was removed from operational duties.

Technology can catch out via Social Media too. In November 2017, Northern Ireland First Minister Arlene Foster tweeted her congratulations to the latest royal couple to announce their engagement. She unfortunately named the wrong prince and congratulated Prince Harry's brother, William, on his engagement to Meghan Markle! The error was quickly corrected although many felt Foster compounded the error by blaming a staff member saying that she had 'stopped tweeting personally a long time ago.'

Another politician tripped up by technology was Shane Ross, Irish Minister for Transport, who spent months pushing stringent drink-driving legislation through the

Oireachtas (the Irish parliament) then managed to vote against it. More worryingly, it wasn't even his vote! Members of Dáil Éireann had an unofficial system where some members would vote on each other's behalf if they happened to be out of the chamber at the time. This was facilitated by the electronic voting system whereby representatives simply push a button to vote either in favour or against. Ross placed his own vote before sliding over to the seat of his colleague, Katherine Zappone, and voting against his own legislation in error. On reporting his mistake, the Dáil record was changed but the practice of voting for an absent member was thrown into the spotlight and subsequently outlawed.

Ross had a history of gaffes in his role as Minister for both Transport and Sport. A favourite has to be his proposal to host the 2022 Commonwealth Games despite Ireland not having being a member of the Commonwealth since 1949. His jovial response was, 'I haven't a clue quite honestly whether it's a good or a bad idea . . . but sure let's explore it.' Voters' sense of humour ran out in the General Election of February 2020, however, when Ross lost his seat.

Leinster House, the home of the Irish parliament, had its own run in with technology when it transpired that the government had paid €808,000 for a new state-of-the-art printer but omitted to check that the room it was to be installed in had adequate height clearance. A 10 month delay ensued while a further €230,000 was spent to allow it to be fitted. Another delay ensued when staff refused to be trained on how to operate it until they were granted a pay-rise. The politicians who had produced over 25 million print copies the previous year, including over 270,000 personalised calendars, had to make other arrangements in the interim.

FOLLOW THE SCIENCE!

During the Covid 19 pandemic many senior politicians assured us that their policies were 'following the science'. That most senior politicians in the UK have no scientific training is clear from this statement. Our knowledge of this new, previously unheard of, virus was evolving constantly. Science is not categorical fact; it's a best guess based on what we know so far and is quite likely to change tomorrow. It's inherently error-prone.

Let's look at Covid 19 testing, for instance. There are two main types of test: detection of genetic material from the virus or detection of the body's immune response to an infection through antigen testing. There are pros and cons to both and the 'science' is continually evolving. No test is 100 per cent accurate but let's drill a little deeper.

The landscape in which tests exist also changes. The interpretation of tests before vaccination for Covid became widespread was different to the interpretation afterwards when the trajectory of the illness was much modified. Let's focus on the pre-vaccination phase when testing was most critical in society. Assuming the test has been produced, performed and transported correctly, the first issue is sensitivity – how good is the test at spotting someone with the virus? The Gold Standard test has been generally agreed to be the RT-PCR type test, performed in specialized laboratories with an average two to three days turnaround time. Sensitivity is agreed to be around 98 per cent accurate, which is pretty good as tests go. The UK government boasted about testing 100,000 patients daily at the height of the pandemic. During 2020 and 2021, the Covid positivity rate averaged 1-2 per cent, so for simplicity we'll say 1 per cent are actually carrying the virus, that's 1,000 patients.

Our 98 per cent accurate test will spot 980 of them but will miss 20 sick people and send them on their way to infect their family and friends. These are 'false negatives'. Not too bad you say!

Let's now look at the second parameter, specificity. This spots how good a test is at identifying only people who are actually sick. In this scenario, PCR was also accepted as being approximately 98 per cent accurate, which means that including our 99,000 virus-free patients, 2 per cent will be erroneously declared positive – 1,980 people. So, in total we have declared almost 3,000 people as having Covid (980 + 1,980) although only 1,000 are actually sick (and we missed 20 of them).

The second common test, Rapid Antigen Tests, caused some quite vitriolic opposition (such as Ireland's Professor Philip Nolan, Chair of the Government Advisory Body on Epidemiological Modelling, branding them as 'snake oil'). Sensitivity in these tests (correctly spotting illness) was quoted as between 30-80 per cent, depending on the stage of the illness the test was taken. Specificity (correctly ruling out illness) is accepted as around 98 per cent, similar to PCR tests.

As the pandemic developed, however, some scientists, most notably Professor Michael Mina of Harvard University's Department of Public Health, argued that there was a fundamental misunderstanding in what was being concluded from the two tests. His article in the *New England Journal of Medicine* in November 2020 included a graph, see below, which outlined his thinking.

His argument, which eventually found widespread acceptance, was that the PCR test, the benchmark against which other tests were measured, was indeed extremely

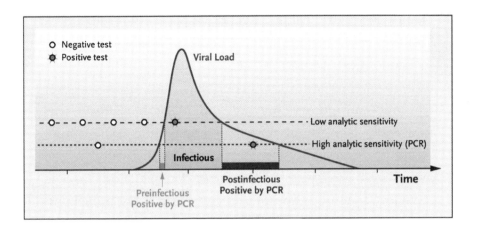

good at spotting any trace of the virus. However it remained positive for an average of 18 days (and a maximum of up to 82) while the virus loads were only high enough to be transmissible (and therefore rendering the person infectious) for about five days. This period, measured against the Gold Standard (five of the 18 days), gave the low sensitivity of around 30 per cent, but actually identified the more useful period needed to isolate carriers and break the chain of transmission. Since Rapid Antigen Tests gave a result in minutes as opposed to days, infectious people could be isolated much more quickly, and since tests were much less expensive they could be widely used picking up many more cases than had been possible previously. The result was that industries such as aviation were able to start to reopen although there was huge variation in how quickly this approach was accepted with Ireland being one of the last EU countries to implement widespread antigen testing.

Much research has now shown that the most successful teams are those with members from a wide range of educational and societal backgrounds. The team led by the UK Prime Minister Boris Johnson (with his degree in Classics), Foreign Secretary Dominic Raab (degree in Law),

Health Secretary Matt Hancock (degree in Philosophy, Politics and Economics), Home Secretary Priti Patel (degree in Economics), Chancellor of the Exchequer Rishi Sunak (Philosophy, Politics and Economics) and Chief Advisor Dominic Cummings (Ancient and Modern History) was noticeably lacking anyone with a scientific background. Scientific training teaches scepticism with results which are, at best, our current best guess. If none of our leaders have any scientific training, they are less likely to be comfortable questioning their scientific advisors, leaving many decisions quite one dimensional.

Matthew Syed's books have shown how important diversity is for seeing problems from various viewpoints; if all our politicians are from a similar educational background, this advantage is lost. Another problem with science is that data and its analysis constantly change so one needs to be ready to make frequent u-turns, something with which politicians are conspicuously uncomfortable. We, the public, are unfortunately complicit in this in that we tend to see a u-turn as a humiliating climb down at best or a sign of incompetence or cluelessness at worst. Of course, this lack of scientific understanding can lead to more obvious errors as well, such as when Boris Johnson, early in the pandemic, boasted about visiting a Covid hospital and 'shaking hands with everybody'.

Another issue with the science is that the dataset we are using is necessarily incomplete. We take a snapshot and use statistics to extrapolate to whole population estimates. This will always incur a margin of error as election night opinion polls often prove.

Politicians can manipulate numbers and frame findings in a way which is flattering to their side of the argument, as we will see in the next chapter on errors in statistics. Results are quoted with, for instance, a 95 per cent confidence limit, that is, we are 95 per cent sure we are correct depending on the size of our sample group, the expected incidence of what we are studying and so on. This all assumes that studies are well designed, have weeded out biases (like sponsorship by drug companies who stand to benefit from a specific outcome) and are carried out assiduously – and, unfortunately science shows that many aren't!

Much of the decision-making in the pandemic has actually been based on modelling, which isn't quite the same as science. In 1987, statistician George Box memorably said that 'all models are wrong but some are useful'. Peer review processes try to reduce the error but the urgency necessitated by Covid 19 meant many of the normal safety nets were bypassed. People were thus free to throw their hats into whichever extreme of the modelling results suited their agenda. And don't forget, correlation doesn't mean causation. Just because two parameters are heading in related directions doesn't mean there's necessarily a link between them. Media channels also sent their heavy hitting political correspondents to government press conferences when perhaps their less well-known science correspondents may have actually been a better choice.

Another scientific favourite of politicians is 'the target'. Targets make great headlines and are used for slogans at election time as proof of how successful that politician's policies have been. However, human nature will, naturally, encourage people to 'game' the system to achieve 'targets', but perhaps not for the overall outcome the target was designed to achieve.

Westminster's Crime and Justice Taskforce in August 2020 announced it was planning to impose targets on police and the Crown Prosecution Service (CPS) to reverse the decline in rape prosecutions over the past five years or so. Why the decline in the first place? It was to meet informal targets the CPS is alleged to have imposed internally to increase conviction rates for rape. They set 'levels of ambition' targets of 60 per cent (as opposed to the established legal norm of a 'realistic' chance of a conviction, that is, 50 per cent or more) in 2016 but dropped them again in 2018 when they realised they may have acted as a 'perverse incentive' by deterring the prosecution of less straight forward cases. These targets actually achieved the outcome of a 40 per cent drop in the number of referrals from the police and a 59 per cent drop in prosecutions to the lowest level since 2008 despite a more than 30 per cent increase in the number of reports of rape to the police. So what went wrong?

The CPS wanted to improve the conviction rate so police and prosecutors focused more on the cases they were most likely to win at the expense of the cases they probably most needed to win. They secured 1,439 convictions from a total of 2,102 prosecutions in England and Wales in 2019-20, an admirable success rate of 68 per cent. However, this was from a total of 55,130 reports of rape bringing the conviction rate of this total down to less than 3 per cent! Although there is no proof that all reports necessarily meet the criteria of rape, it is difficult to believe that such an enormous discrepancy can be genuine. If it is, that's an awful lot of false rape accusations. Winning 10 out of 10 cases prosecuted would give a success rate of 100 per cent, but it doesn't necessarily mean you've done a good job!

Similar targets on four-hour maximum waiting times in Accident & Emergency Departments in the past led to queues of ambulances being held outside the A&E entrance so that the clock wouldn't start running until staff had the resources to treat the patient inside the 'target' of four hours. Target met, but outcome achieved?

A final major problem for politicians is that as well as making policy decisions which will benefit society, a large part of their job involves ensuring they get re-elected so, being human beings, this will naturally bias their behaviour. Their decisions are often taken with a short timeframe in mind. Perhaps we need to look at our whole political representative system if we want to get a handle on long-term issues such as climate change?

In conclusion, when politicians call on us to buy into their policies because they are 'following the science', we should be sceptical since science is simply our current best but incomplete model. It also might be wrong. It can be distorted by biases, both known and unknown, and even at Gold Standard level has an inherent level of error which means the conclusions drawn may be incorrect. In short, caveat emptor!

Our whistlestop tour of errors in politics has shown us, among other things, that 'following the science' may not be the best policy. But let's have a closer look at science itself. Just how error-prone is it?

Chapter 8

Imperfect Science

Israeli-American astrophysicist Mario Livio describes in his book, *Brilliant Blunders*, some of the errors made by the greatest scientists of the last few hundred years and it's very refreshing to see how badly wrong these giants can be whilst still achieving world changing discoveries.

The DNA 'Triple' Helix Model

Let's look at two of these starting with Linus Pauling, the two-time Nobel prize winning chemist who is renowned as one of the fathers of quantum chemistry and molecular biology. As early as 1933, Pauling was studying nucleic acids, the building blocks of DNA. In 1951, he renewed this interest after hearing that Maurice Wilkins of King's College, London had produced some photographs of nucleic acids but Wilkins was unwilling to share the research. Pauling read research by Edward Ronwin later that year in November 1951 and although he decided that Ronwin's model was wrong, he drew on some of the ideas and decided, correctly, that DNA was helical in structure. He was due to visit England in May 1952 to attend a meeting of the Royal Society when he expected to meet with Rosalind Franklin, Wilkin's assistant, who had recently developed a very clear picture of DNA which would have been of great benefit to Pauling. However, his very public antiwar stance meant he was initially denied a passport but subsequently visited later in the summer and also visited France where he learned that DNA was the master molecule of genetics. He determined that he would solve the structure but on his return to California, he continued his work with proteins before finally turning his attention to the structure of DNA in November 1952. He had little data to work with but, knowing that others were also working on the problem and wanting to be the first, he rushed a triple helix model which had the phosphate bases in the core and the proteins pointing outwards.

The clumsy model didn't appear to be stable and violated some of the laws of chemistry Pauling himself had discovered. None the less, despite his reservations he submitted his paper to the 'Proceedings of the National Academy of Sciences' on New Year's Eve 1952 hoping that the details would somehow fall into place in time. The paper was published in February 1953 by which time it was looking even less likely to be correct. James Watson and Francis Crick produced a paper the following month and despite obtaining an advance copy of it, Pauling still clung to his idea. In April 1953, Pauling stopped off in England to visit Watson and Crick in Cambridge and examined their double helix model of DNA as well as finally seeing Franklin's photographs. He conceded defeat graciously and helped them tidy up loose ends in their model.

Pauling went on to win the Nobel Prize for Chemistry in 1954 whilst Watson, Crick and Wilkins won the Nobel Prize for Medicine in 1962 for their work on the structure of DNA which opened up the possibilities of gene therapy. Interestingly, Linus Pauling won the Nobel Peace prize that year making him the only person in history to win two unshared Nobel prizes in different disciplines. His error obviously didn't hold him back!

The Nobel Foundation

As a quick aside, the Nobel prizes themselves exist partly due to an error. Alfred Nobel made huge contributions to many fields and held 335 patents. He was, however, known mainly for his invention of an explosive, dynamite, which he created in 1867. It was much safer and more easily controlled than its predecessor, nitroglycerin, and was a huge commercial success, being used extensively in mining. It was also, however, used in warfare where it created destruction on a level previously never imagined.

When Alfred's brother Ludwig died in 1888, a French newspaper erroneously published Alfred's obituary. It read 'Le Marchand de la Mort est Mort' – The Merchant of Death is Dead! It continued, 'Dr. Alfred Nobel, who became rich by finding ways to kill more people faster than ever before, died yesterday'. Nobel was horrified that after a lifetime of inventing things, he would be remembered like this. He established a series of five prizes (physics, chemistry, medicine/physiology, literature and peace) for those who conferred the 'greatest benefit on mankind'. In 1895, the year before his death, he set aside 94 per cent of his estate (around £135 million in today's money) to establish the awards, first presented in 1901, which are still amongst the world's most sought after accolades.

The Steady State Theory of the Universe

Cambridge astrophysicist Sir Fred Hoyle was one of the best known and most influential scientists of the twentieth century and is possibly best remembered for a remark made on BBC Radio's *Third Programme* broadcast on 28 March 1949 when he described the alternative theory of the origin of the universe to his Steady State Theory, apparently derisively, as a 'Big Bang'.

Although he agreed with the Lemaître Theory that the universe is expanding, subsequently proved by Edwin Hubble's observations, he disagreed with the interpretation. Hoyle, an atheist, found the idea of the universe having a start point too close to the idea of a creator and thought it 'an irrational process, and can't be described in scientific terms'. Instead, Hoyle, along with colleagues Thomas Gold and Hermann Bondi, formulated a Steady State Theory which acknowledged that the universe is expanding but thought of this like a river which is flowing away from you but still remaining the same river. Galaxies are moving apart but the gaps are filled by newly created galaxies. Hoyle denied he was trying to be insulting when using the term 'Big Bang', and claimed he was simply trying to create a striking image which would explain the difference between the two theories. His opponents found the comments 'vain, one-sided, insulting, not worthy of the BBC'.

Evidence accumulated supporting the 'Big Bang' theory in the 1960s and further bolstered in the 1980s by the distribution of quasars and young galaxies indicating a more consistent age estimate for the universe. The Big Bang theory is now more or less universally accepted although Hoyle died in 2001 still refusing to accept he may have erred!

Incidentally, he also disagreed with Charles Darwin's Theory of Evolution, preferring to believe in 'panspermia' whereby life on Earth arrived from space by way of comets.

He believed that outbreaks of certain diseases such as the 1918 Influenza Pandemic had extra-terrestrial origins too.

Hoyle never won a Nobel Prize although William Fowler, who had co-authored a paper with Hoyle in 1957 on the synthesis of elements in stars, shared the prize with Subrahmanyan Chandrasekhar in 1983, even though it is accepted that Hoyle invented the theory of nucleosynthesis they described. It is felt this may be due to an earlier incident over the 1974 prize being awarded in part to Antony Hewish, another Cambridge astrophysicist, for his work in the discovery of pulsars when Hoyle made an off-the-cuff remark to a reporter that the actual discoverer was Hewish's research student, Northern Ireland woman Jocelyn Bell, who had been snubbed. Bell had made the discovery after noticing an anomaly in the data from the Interplanetary Scintillation Array she helped build. The regular pulse occurring every 1.3 seconds was dismissed by Hewitt as man-made interference, but after persistent persuasion by Bell was eventually shown to be caused by a rapidly rotating neutron star, later christened a pulsar.

Error is not simply an earth-bound phenomenon!

Humourism

Looking even further back than Livio's examples, we find errors in our understanding of anatomy and physiology. One of the most prolific errors was the idea of humours.

The concept of the body being controlled by various humours goes back 2,500 years to the time of Ancient Greece. A similar concept existed in Indian Ayurvedic medicine but the person best known for introducing the idea of humourism to medicine is Hippocrates around 2,400 years ago. Known as 'the father of medicine', Hippocrates is credited with developing a body of work named the 'corpus' although it is felt unlikely that he had direct input to much of it.

The most common version of humourism outlines four humours, namely black bile, blood, phlegm and yellow bile, which were thought to be the constituent parts of all liquids in the body, varying only in their proportions. These four constituents, each of which had its own characteristic temperament or mood were, according to Swedish physician Robin Fåhræus, possibly based on the observation of a quantity of blood in a clear container. After letting the blood settle for a time, we are left with four distinct layers. At the bottom, the heaviest part is the blood which has clotted into a dark, gelatinous mass, 'black bile'. Above this is a layer of red blood cells, 'blood' obviously. Next is a layer of white blood cells, 'phlegm', and on top, the clear, yellowish serum, 'yellow bile'.

From Ancient Greek times onwards, the four humours have been felt to represent the following temperaments:

- Black bile – lazy, sickly and fearful. Melancholy derives from an excess of black bile.

- Phlegm – low spirited and forgetful. Apathetic or phlegmatic.

- Blood – sanguine, enthusiastic and friendly, sociable nature.

- Yellow bile – bitter, short-tempered and daring.

The notion of humours persisted well into the sixteenth century before being challenged by Andreas Vesalius in 1543, although it stumbled on until William Harvey described circulation around 1628, and even as late as 1858 when Rudolf Virchow's descriptions of cellular pathology were established. Bleeding patients and the use of leeches persisted well into the eighteenth century with the aim of rebalancing these humours. President George Washington died at the age of 67 after an enthusiastic course of blood letting failed to cure his sore throat. Emetics and herbs inducing vomiting were also used to balance humours.

Remnants of the humour system persist to this day in modern healthcare. 'Humoural immunity' refers to circulating antibodies and 'humour regulation' describes the circulation of hormones. Blood disorders are still known as 'blood dycrasias' and terms such as 'sanguine' and 'melancholic' are still used in common parlance.

Sir Alexander Fleming

The discovery of one of the most important drugs of the twentieth century was partly due to a fortuitous error! Alexander Fleming was working in the lab of St. Mary's Hospital in London and was culturing Staphylococcus, a common Gram Positive bacteria (which causes illnesses such as pneumonia, meningitis, gonorrhoea and endocarditis, amongst others) for study. Fleming was apparently known to be a little careless with his housekeeping in the lab. He didn't get around to washing out the culture plates before going on holidays in August 1928 and left them near an open window where they remained until he returned.

On 3 September, he found the dishes contaminated with a fluffy white mould which had evidently blown in through the window while he was away and made itself at home on the plates. As well as the obvious mould, he noticed that there was a clear area around it where the bacteria had apparently been killed off. Luckily, Fleming realised that this was something that merited further investigation and over the next couple of years, he isolated the active agent in the mould whose spore-producing structures microscopically resembled a paintbrush, leading to it being named penicillin after the Latin for paintbrush – *penicillus*.

The mould was difficult to grow and extracting the active ingredient, penicillin, was notoriously tricky but Fleming managed to produce enough to confirm his findings and discovered that it was effective against a whole family of gram positive bacteria, offering huge potential for treating previously incurable infections. Having watched many die of sepsis in the First World War, Fleming realised the potential of the drug. He published his findings in 1929 and the drug was shown to work clinically in 1930 in *Ophthalmia Neonatorum*, a Gonococcal eye infection in infants. The difficulty lay in producing enough of the drug to be practical, and after failing to convince other doctors to share his optimism for penicillin, Fleming concluded his study of it in 1931 and moved on to other work.

After almost a decade, a group in Oxford led by Howard Florey and Ernst Chain managed to isolate greater quantities and proved it to be clinically useful. They still struggled to produce sufficient quantities in the lab and travelled to the USA in 1941 to try to convince drug companies of its potential. In 1942, a US-made penicillin was produced by Merck & Co but half of the total supply was used on only one patient, Anne Millar. By the following year, the US had enough penicillin to treat ten patients. The US War Production Board drew up plans to accelerate research into production to help with the war effort, and by 1945 over 646 billion units of the drug were being produced per year. It is estimated that penicillin improved the survival rate of soldiers with infected wounds by around 15 per cent.

In 1945, Fleming, Florey and Chain shared the Nobel Prize for medicine and development of the drug continued apace. Production methods improved and different types of penicillin with broader spectrum uses were developed. In 1957, John Sheehan of the Massachusetts Institute of Technology (MIT) managed to make the first synthetically made penicillin and, in time, many different variations of the drug were produced. Penicillin has been the most important antibiotic developed in the last century and in addition to his Nobel award Fleming was named one of the most important people of the twentieth century by *Time* magazine. And it all started with him forgetting to wash his dishes!

Even Albert Einstein ...

It's hard to believe that Einstein could possibly have got anything wrong but he had his fair share of errors too. Indeed, astrophysics generally has had a rocky history over the last 2,500 years. Around 400 BCE, the Greek philosopher Philolaus proposed a complicated model of the universe which saw the sun and the planets (including Earth and its moon) carry out perfectly circular orbits around a 'central fire'. The first heliocentric model (sun at the centre) was proposed around 270 CE by Aristarchus of Samos, but the more generally accepted model in the Western, Indian and Islamic worlds for at least the next 500-600 years was the geocentric model popularised by Ptolemy in the second century CE which placed the Earth at the centre of our universe.

This was the generally accepted view until Nicolaus Copernicus presented a heliocentric model in 1543 with astronomical observations which moved the concept from philosophical speculation to predictive, geometrical astronomy. Copernicus had actually spent 25 years writing his thesis, finishing in 1530, but didn't publish until 1543, the year before he died, probably so as not to lose his good standing with the church. The published version was dedicated to Pope Paul III and contained a preface arguing that it was useful for computation even if its main hypothesis was not necessarily true, thereby ensuring the book would cause little offence. Copernicus would have made an excellent diplomat!

Around 40 years later in the 1580s, Tycho Brahe resurrected the hybrid model but it was when Galileo Galilei came on the scene in 1610 that things started heating up. Galileo took the Augustinian view that the Bible is a book of poetry and songs, not a historically accurate document. Not every passage should be taken literally. In 1615, Galileo's writings were brought to the attention of the Inquisition where Cardinal Robert Bellarmine was called on to adjudicate. He found Galileo's description of heliocentrism to be 'a very dangerous thing' and to be harmful to 'the Holy Faith by rendering Holy Scripture as false'. The injunction issued by the Inquisition called on Galileo to completely abandon his theory and not to teach, discuss or defend it in any way. Books advocating the system were banned. Subsequently, Pope Urban VIII, well known as a patron of the arts and a friend to Galileo, asked him to write on the pros and cons of heliocentrism. The result, published in 1632, leaned a little too heavily towards the pros and Galileo had the character, Simplicio (simpleton in common parlance), advocate the pope's preferred viewpoint which didn't go down well. He was summoned to Rome and put on trial by the Inquisition again. He was forced to recant his theories once more calling them 'abjured, cursed and detested' and put under house arrest until his death eight years later at the age of 77 years.

Galileo's ideas spread despite the church's intervention and in 1667, Sir Isaac Newton elaborated on Kepler's work developing Newton's Laws of Motion which put heliocentrism on a secure theoretical footing. By the mid-1700s, the church's opposition was fading and in 1758 books advocating the heliocentric model were removed from the church's banned list, although it would be nearly 75 years before the writings of Copernicus and Galileo were uncensored! The church launched a review in 1979 into how Galileo was treated and a preliminary report five years later found that Galileo had been wrongfully condemned. The final report published in 1992 by the Pontifical Academy of Sciences (after 13 years of investigation) exonerated Galileo and finally brought to an end one of the church's most infamous errors. Such a formal acknowledgement of error is a rarity in an institution known to claim infallibility in matters of faith and society.

Which brings us to Albert Einstein! In 1916, Einstein published his seminal work, the General Theory of Relativity, which described in mathematical detail how everything in the universe moves under the influence of gravity. This theory has been proven to be stunningly accurate for a theory so ambitious in its aims. Most theories are roughly correct but need to be tweaked as more information becomes available – Copernicus's heliocentric model discussed above, for instance, assumed circular orbits which were subsequently modified to the elliptical orbits we know today. Einstein's Theory however has been incredibly accurate.

The prevailing view of the universe at that time was that it was essentially stable. Einstein reasoned that gravity would cause everything to collapse to a central point so something must be opposing gravity keeping the universe in balance, a very unstable, uneasy sort of equilibrium which didn't really fit our knowledge of complex systems. It was akin to a pencil being balanced on its sharp point but not falling over. To incorporate this concept into his calculations, Einstein came up with the idea of a 'cosmological constant' to which he assigned the Greek letter, lambda. This value kept the universe in balance, neither expanding nor contracting, in keeping with the prevailing belief of the time, by opposing the force of gravity.

Thirteen years later, in 1929, Edwin Hubble discovered that the universe is in fact not stable but is actually expanding at a huge rate, thus totally negating the need for lambda at all. Einstein's theory still worked by lambda being assigned the value zero, in that its presence is unnecessary. Einstein described his concept of the 'cosmological constant' as his life's 'greatest blunder'.

The story doesn't end there however. Sixty-nine years later in 1998, long after Einstein's death, two teams of astrophysicists (one led by Saul Perlmutter and another led by Brian Schmidt and Adam Reiss) published findings showing that certain stars were actually up to 15 per cent further away than previously predicted. The universe is expanding faster than we thought and the only thing that explained the phenomenon was none other than Einstein's 'cosmological constant'. This force which opposes gravity, an anti-gravity if you like, has been termed 'dark energy'. Perlmutter, Schmidt and Reiss shared the 2011 Nobel prize for Physics for their work. Subsequent work has actually shown this 'dark energy' to account for about 68 per cent of all mass-energy in the universe with 'dark matter' making up 27 per cent and 'regular matter' a paltry 5 per cent.

One of the best known Einstein quotes is, 'A person who never made a mistake never tried anything new.' Ironically, Einstein's biggest error was in declaring lambda to be his biggest error! He was right all along but his mental model of the time wouldn't allow him to see it.

Most of us strive to understand what is happening around us but the more successful are aware that our Situational Awareness is always incomplete and seek to improve it by seeking out contradictory evidence to test our position and, if necessary, revising our mental model. Failing to do this adequately leaves us prone to errors, the outcome of which depends on where on the safety critical spectrum we are at the time. We also need to question the mental model of others to assess their Situational Awareness before deciding whether to support their agendas.

LIES, DAMN LIES AND STATISTICS

Statistics is a field of mathematics which can seem impenetrable, but is critically important to our society. In essence, it gives us a measurement of an area of interest using an incomplete dataset and extrapolating or interpolating from the results obtained. It quantifies uncertainty. It gives us the odds if we want to bet on a sports event and it gives insurance companies the odds if they want to bet on road safety.

Statistics involves the merging of three disciplines, data analysis, probability and statistical inference, carried out in the business world by actuaries. Almost everything in life involves some degree of risk – driving home from work for instance. Statistics helps us quantify risk and allows road planners to design junctions, speed limits, traffic calming measures and so on to manage that risk. We assess risk when we decide whether or not it is safe to overtake. Insurance companies also assess whether we are high or low risk when setting premiums. Assessing previous outcomes allows them to take a calculated risk with the odds generally tipped in their favour. It takes a 'Black Swan' type event to upset this balance. Such an accumulation of events in the late 1980s, including Piper Alpha Disaster, Exxon Valdez oil spill and a number of hurricanes, very nearly caused the collapse of the iconic insurance group, Lloyd's of London. Calculation of these odds are often a blunt instrument which is why my daughters pay a higher premium on motor insurance than me simply due to their age profile. Recent 'black box' technology is giving young drivers the opportunity to reduce premiums, however, by monitoring their driving.

Statistics is a field which has an inherent level of error due to decisions being made from an incomplete picture (sampling error) or if the analysis used is inappropriate for the dataset collected (non-sampling error). Sampling error is simply picking an inappropriate group to study by only selecting from a very narrow, unrepresentative section of the population. If we want to find out what a group thinks about shortening school days to only three hours, we are likely to get a very different answer from a group of 8-year-olds than from their parents. This is a sampling error. The simplest way of exploring analytical errors would be to consider an 'average' result. That, of course, is not that simple!

Let's consider five children and count the number of books they have on their desk today. A quick count gives us 2, 2, 6, 8 and 100 (an over-achiever!). Average can be measured in four ways and the best way I've come across to remember them is a modified nursery rhyme.

Hey diddle diddle,
The median's the middle,
You add and divide for the mean.
The mode is the one that you see the most
And the range is the difference between.

Now let's see what our 'average' is. Written in order, we can see the middle result, the median, is 6. Adding the five results together and dividing by five gives a mean of 23.6 – hugely skewed by our outlier, the avid reader. The mode is the most common result, in this case 2. The range covers a huge span from 2 to 100. We can see our four 'averages' are wildly different and some are totally unrepresentative.

Good statisticans have techniques which can be applied to issues such as this to give us more representative and useful results whilst also quantifying the chance that they are wrong, the margin for error allowing us to decide whether or not we want to make a decision based on the information available. Some less scrupulous statisticians may give us the answer which best suits their (or their employer's) agenda. The small print at the bottom of an investment sales brochure, for example, quietly mentions that investments can go down as well as up. In other words, once again, caveat emptor!

We could go on and on about statistics and error, but I think it's time to move on and take a look at technology. Certainly the Big Tech companies have managed to remove error from their processes . . . ?

Chapter 9

'Move Fast and Break Things' – Will We Ever Learn?

In 2003, second year Harvard student Mark Zuckerberg created a website called FaceMash which was intended as a 'Hot or Not' comparison site for Harvard students. This fairly dubious premise allowed visitors to view two photographs of female students side by side and decide which was more attractive! He sourced the pictures from the database of the nine dorm houses on campus and within the first four hours had attracted 22,000 photo views by 450 visitors! While writing the software, Zuckerberg commented on his blog that he was both a little intoxicated and also unimpressed with some of the photos – 'I almost want to put some of these faces next to pictures of farm animals and have people vote on which is more attractive.' He followed this a few hours later with 'I'm not exactly sure how the farm animals are going to fit into this whole thing (you can't really ever be sure with farm animals) but I like the idea of comparing two people together.'

Apart from being a reminder of how anything you put online is up there forever, this gave an insight into the mindset that would predominate at the website's successor, Facebook.

FaceMash was closed down a few days later by the college's administration. Zuckerberg was charged with breach of security, violating copyrights and individual privacy and faced expulsion. Ultimately, the charges were dropped and he modified the project to a social study tool allowing students to view and comment on art images ahead of an Art History exam.

In February 2004, Zuckerberg launched a new site called The Facebook with fellow Harvard student Eduardo Saverin. They invested $1,000 each and within a month, half of the Harvard student population had signed up and they quickly expanded to the other Ivy League colleges. In June 2004, they moved their headquarters to Palo Alto in California and the following year changed the company name to Facebook. By the end of 2005, they had 6 million users.

The company's motto was 'Move Fast and Break Things!' emphasising the company's early acceptance that rapid progress could only be made with an acceptance of error. They launched tools and features which weren't glitch-free but this was considered acceptable to allow rapid progress. Bugs were ironed out as they went along or features could simply be dropped. Over time, however, Zuckerberg realised that they may have strayed too far across the boundary and changed tack. At the Facebook F8 conference in 2014, he said:

> We used to have this famous mantra ... and the idea here is that as developers, moving quickly is so important that we were even willing to tolerate a few bugs in order to do it. . . .What we realised over time is that it wasn't helping us to move faster because we had to slow down to fix these bugs and it wasn't improving our speed.

We must tolerate error to achieve anything useful in life, but Zuckerberg realised that he had strayed a little too far and launched a new slogan, the somewhat less sexy 'Move Fast with Stable Infra.' They planned to launch products which were more finished and to rectify bugs within 48 hours, giving a better experience of their infrastructure to users.

The company has made other mistakes such as missing out on the photo sharing market popularised by Snapchat but took steps to rectify this by spending $1 billion buying Instagram in 2012 which, as of 2020, had overtaken Snapchat by amassing a billion users globally versus Snapchat's 229 million. Snapchat's success is based on catering to the 15-25 year old market who enjoyed the app's premise that it mirrored real life by allowing photos and videos to be experienced, but that they would then self-destruct after as little as ten seconds. Just like real life, experiences are transitory. This reassured young people that, unlike Facebook, images and videos wouldn't be stored indefinitely on the web where they could come back to bite them in the future. In other words, they were free to make errors without worrying about long-term implications, which makes for a much less stressful experience. Indeed, 95 per cent of users say the app makes them happy and around 63 per cent of users visit the site daily, accessing their camera up to 20 times per day.

Facebook has made other mistakes such as investing heavily in the virtual reality headset company, Oculus Rift. The explosion in VR technology has yet to materialise although, like another highly publicised failure, Google Glass, it may just be a little ahead of its time. Virtual reality, after all, is how I learned to fly jets!

The first time I sat at the front of an Airbus A321 passenger jet back in 2001, I had a training captain take me for about ten circuits around Shannon Airport before letting me fly it back to Dublin. A few days later after finalizing the paperwork to receive my ATPL (Airline Transport Pilot's Licence), I had my second go and this time had a couple of hundred unsuspecting passengers along for the run. I had trained and been examined in a Full Motion simulator costing around $20 million which, as we saw earlier in the book, creates a pretty realistic VR experience as I proved by safely getting the plane to London Heathrow and back that day, despite having only about one and a half hours' experience in a real aeroplane!

VR is also making in-roads to healthcare where professional colleges are finally coming around to the idea that training surgeons and anaesthetists on real patients might be about as good an idea as letting me learn to fly a plane by getting straight into a real one with 300 passengers (although that's exactly how I learned surgery in the 1990s). As we have already seen, aviation and healthcare still have two very different relationships with error!

Facebook has grown its membership to 2.7 billion as of mid-2020 and also owns dozens of other companies, meaning that it has access to phenomenal amounts of data which it can mine for information, sell to third parties and, most worryingly, use to target information in ways that can manipulate world events, which is exactly what the Cambridge Analytica scandal revealed. In 2012, Zuckerberg wrote to his Director of Product Development who was concerned about the practice of allowing third party apps to access data on Facebook users' friends without their knowledge. Zuckerberg wrote:

> I'm generally sceptical that there is as much data leak strategic risk as you think. I just can't think of any instances where that data has leaked from developer to developer and caused a real issue for us.

Indeed, this cavalier approach to users' privacy is possibly Facebook's biggest error and has led to huge societal changes, many of which will play out for years to come.

Facebook is not alone in this quest to learn about us and dominate our attention. It is one of four global behemoths known as 'The Four Horsemen', namely Google, Apple, Facebook and Amazon. They make up four of the top five companies by market capitalization, the fifth being Microsoft when it is included in discussions. 'The Four Horsemen' have a combined market capitalisation of around $6 trillion as of late 2020, amounting to roughly 12 per cent of the entire US Stock Market (or 15 per cent when Microsoft is included). They have revolutionized how we interact with the world. Apple has transformed the hardware we use to access information and is offering to store all that information on iCloud servers linked easily to all our devices. Google is revolutionizing how we access information and prioritizing what it feels we should be shown with its Search Engine Optimisation (SEO) system. Facebook likewise directs us towards information it prioritises and Amazon directs us towards the products it wants us to buy. These companies have totally changed our relationship with information.

THE IMPACT ON EDUCATION

I'm old enough to remember going to the library and ordering books to access information; now it's at my fingertips. But we need to be skeptical regarding the veracity and completeness of the information we are being offered. These companies have the power to manipulate our Situational Awareness into a limited and incomplete view, or even to a completely false one. The knowledge and information landscape is irrevocably altered.

Why then does our education system still focus largely on memorizing information which can be accessed more accurately on our smart phones? If education exists to prepare us for the world we live in, our schools are now decades out of date. It makes little sense having a twentieth century attitude to twenty-first century issues. We need to teach young people how to access information and, more importantly, to critically assess its veracity and completeness. In an era of Fake News and media manipulation, this is becoming ever more important so we can build a complete and accurate model of Situational Awareness and thereby make better decisions at both a personal and societal level.

Let's dig deeper into how we are going to address the gulf in 'education as is' versus 'education as now needed'. Let's have a look at a few of the different learning approaches that educationalists have devised. Education could be said to be the process of reducing the blind spots in our knowledge and experience to minimise the amount of error swilling around our everyday lives. Different approaches to this problem will necessarily be needed, dependent on who is doing the learning, what style best suits them and the skill or information to be learnt. One of the classifications of learning theory subdivides theory into three styles, as described below

The Behaviourist Approach

This old-style approach of 'I'll teach, you shut up and listen' will remind many of us of our schooldays. Also known as pedagogy, from the Greek word for child, it involved some-one with knowledge (the teacher) repeating this knowledge so others can assimilate it. It is essentially the 'classical con-ditioning' approach that Pavlov taught his dogs.

I ring a bell, you salivate!

I ask for the causes of the First World War, you recite them back to me!

This is the type of learning which passes from one individual to another without necessarily being processed or understood by either. Retention of the information was rewarded and errors were punished, creating a mindset that would play it safe to avoid any risk of failure – an innocuous approach but one that is unlikely to create any revolutionary ideas. The benefits of this type of learning are limited, espe-cially now in the information age when the answer to almost any question can be found using your phone and Google.

The Cognitive Approach

This can be summarised by:

I've done something like this before. Come on and we'll work it out together.

This approach was popularised by John Dewey back around 1938 when he described it as 'learning to think'. Dewey disliked the passive nature of the Behaviourist model suggesting that it led only to superficial learning. He felt that the learner should play a more active part in the process – experiential learning in other words. Benjamin Bloom expanded this theory in 1965 considering learning to be both 'cognitive', that is, associated with memory and understanding, as well as 'affective', that is, provoking an emotional response to learning. This involved someone who is much more proactive and willing to try to solve problems rather than waiting for someone else to do it for them. It was also more tolerant of error being an inevitable part of the process.

The Humanistic Approach

This approach is the more recent development common in adult learning scenarios where it is expected that there is a body of core knowledge which can be leveraged and built upon. It is known as andragogy from the Greek for 'man', emphasising the more mature or adult-learning approach used. It is more self-directed and self-motivated and is compatible with our modern view of life-long learning. Leaving school or college is now considered a starting point, not a finishing point. It is driven by what the learner feels they need, rather than being simply subject-orientated, and is conducive to being assisted by a coach, rather than by a teacher, which has led to a new industry of executive coaching in the last number of years.

Fixed Mindset versus Growth Mindset

Another classification was the two-step system devised by New York-born psychologist Carol Dweck. Her 2006 book, *Mindset: The New Psychology of Success*, argued that people can be placed on a continuum depending on their implicit views of ability. At one end of the scale are people who believe their ability, intelligence and talents are fixed traits – that's your lot so get on with it. They possess a 'Fixed Mindset'. She feels these people focus on not looking stupid so don't leave their comfort zones, thus limiting what they achieve with the talent they have.

At the other end of the spectrum are those who believe that their talents and abilities can be nurtured and improved with work. They have a 'Growth Mindset'. These individuals are more accepting of error and are better equipped to cope with it. Dweck's work suggests that praise such as, 'Well done, you worked really hard at that' will produce more successful students than, 'Well done, you're really smart'. The 'smart' kids now focus on protecting what they have by making sure they don't expose themselves to anything which would risk them looking stupid.

Other researchers failed to replicate Dweck's results leading to some controversy in their acceptance in the academic world. A 2013 study did not find any statistically significant difference between the two groups. Another study published in 2018 by Professor Sherria Hoskins of Portsmouth University found that although there was some evidence of mindset having an effect, socioeconomic factors also played a part with those in disadvantaged groups tending to be more 'fixed' thus compounding their disadvantage. The concept is popular though and two recent books by Matthew Syed, *You Are Awesome* and *Dare to Be You* which encourage kids to develop a Growth Mindset have been best sellers.

The whole concept correlates with Charles Darwin's evolutionary premise that the species that survive aren't necessarily the strongest but the most adaptable. I think there would be little argument that a healthy dose of ability is a good starting point and that mindset alone is insufficient unless paired with good raw material. The argument that there is room to improve is attractive, though critics worry that it might become yet another yardstick children will be measured against. Cast your mind back to our chapter on firefighting where we met Sabrina Cohen-Hatton who described her experience of trying to manage at school without letting her teachers know that she was homeless at the time. Although she has a Growth Mindset in abundance, many others may have been crushed by circumstances such as hers. A Growth Mindset may be helpful, even necessary, but it certainly isn't sufficient to guarantee success.

A New Attitude to Error in Education

Teaching kids that error is inevitable and not a source of embarrassment or shame is a valuable lesson which has been shown to have a major effect on Safety Critical industries like aviation where accident rates are exceptionally low partly due to the Growth Mindset concept of continuous improvement. Whether this would have a measurable effect on educational outcomes is yet to be confirmed but some work has been done comparing an 'error tolerant classroom' to a more traditional teaching style.

A study of German maths students aged 12-15 years compared two styles, one where teaching focused on learning the correct technique and saw errors as an interruption to the work, and another which welcomed error as an opportunity to learn how we can go wrong and therefore better define the boundaries between correct and incorrect techniques. The study found that students were less afraid to make mistakes and found teachers more supportive when mistakes happened, but interestingly the addition of teacher training on how to help students analyse their mistakes and devise strategies to avoid them wasn't even noticed by the students – perhaps the psychological safety of error tolerance was sufficient and students devised strategies whether or not they were taught them. It isn't reported in this study, however, whether students actually improved their results in this environment.

Techniques for 'error prevention' rather than simply 'error correction' are being used successfully including in online training modules. These monitor students' work and intervene when a delay in responding suggests that they are stuck. It then suggests techniques to approach the problem rather than simply giving the correct next step, thereby helping them analyse their mistake and build confidence. Stronger students can often work out their own strategies without prompting, but weaker students may struggle without this intervention.

Hopefully education will be able to embrace and expand Thomas Edison's sentiment when explaining the value of his many new inventions which didn't work:

> Just because something doesn't do what you planned
> it to doesn't mean it's useless.

An interesting example of this is when the 3M company in the USA failed to develop a new Superglue. What Spencer Silver came up with in 1968 was slightly tacky but wasn't anywhere near as strong as the glue they hoped to develop. Six years later in 1974, a fellow employee, Arthur Fry, found a use for the product in what we now know as Post-It notes, although it took 3M until 1980 before they finally bought in to Fry's idea and commercialised it.

Many exam systems still focus on the ability of students to memorise and regurgitate reams of information at a set piece event such as GCSEs, International Baccalaureate or Leaving Certificate exams. This rewards many who can store lots of information but may not be particularly adept at doing anything useful with that information subsequently. Many of our most successful entrepreneurs failed at school but flourished when in an environment which rewards creative thought and innovation – that is, the real world! It's

195

probably more accurate to say our education system failed them, not the other way around.

Artificial Intelligence is rapidly overtaking our education system. The advent of the ChatGPT app in late 2022 has now created a conundrum for educators in that students can ask the app to write an essay and have a plausible result within seconds. Will exams have to revert to supervised testing again? Results of the app are admittedly still quite hit or miss – its output can sound convincing but be factually wrong – but since when did we need an app to produce that type of outcome?

Another interesting failure of the education system was exposed shortly after Ireland's Leaving Certificate results when the department admitted that the code used in producing the final marks had errors in two sections. Instead of the class profile being gauged by assessing their English, Maths, Irish and two best subjects from their Junior Cert state exams, Canadian firm Polymetrika International coded for the two weakest subjects instead. It also included one subject, Civic, Social and Political Education, which wasn't supposed to be considered at all. This error resulted in 10 per cent of students (6,500 of them!) being marked down by up to 10 per cent, substantially impacting their course options at university. By the time this error had been discovered, the college places which students had now unfairly missed had been filled, some no doubt by other students who had been incorrectly marked up! Perhaps this debacle may be an essay question in next year's IT or Sociology papers?

Encouraging Experimentation and Error?

The late Sir Ken Robinson's legendary TED talks have made him the most viewed speaker on TED with over 66 million views of his first talk alone. This talk in 2006 focused on his concern that our schools kill creativity. The unpredictability of trying to educate people for skills which don't exist yet leaves teachers and those who draw up the curriculum with a problem, but we solve it by focusing on what we did previously even though we know full well it's likely to be irrelevant by the time our children graduate. He says:

> If we are not prepared to be wrong, we will never come up with anything original.

Robinson says our businesses and education systems stigmatise mistakes. Children are prepared to take a chance but we educate them out of these creative capacities. He worried about the hierarchy of subjects with maths, sciences and languages at the top and art, music and dance near the bottom. He pointed out that we progressively educate our children from the waist up, then from the neck up and finally, only one side of their head, the left! He paints a memorable picture of professors using their bodies only as a form of transport for getting their heads to meetings! Academia is seen as the only measurement of intelligence leading to 'academic inflation'. Robinson focused on training the interaction of various parts of the brain rather than sub-dividing it. Our education system needs to change the perception of error and allow our children to flourish with whatever talents and skills they have, not just the narrow set we currently celebrate.

Robinson's 2012 TED talk argued that the focus on only STEM subjects, far from leaving 'No Child Left Behind', actually disadvantages them all. He feels that a certain amount of ADHD diagnoses were actually children bored with the curriculum because it doesn't reflect their talents.

This focus has led to a narrow, easily measured curriculum which punishes errors and teaches children to avoid them. This instils a mindset which treats error as unacceptable both for themselves in school and for society when they leave education, and sets up the intolerant and litigious culture which is contributing to problems which are crippling healthcare. If we process our young people through an exam system which rewards a narrow band of achievement but is intolerant of failures, it's not surprising that when these young people have entered society, they apply the same standards.

Ishan Goel, writing in *Entrepreneur* in 2018, voiced a similar view arguing that our modern education system is out of date. Students generally follow a set syllabus with predefined ideal outcomes. The focus on results in order to progress to the next stage of the treadmill forces teachers to ensure the required knowledge is transferred for reproduction at a set event, the exam. When these young people enter the world of work, what employers want is a creative worker who can take information, process it and hopefully do something creative with it that their competitors haven't thought of. They also usually require them to do it as part of a team which will involve a full suite of 'soft skills' such as communication, team-working and decision-making, none of which are generally taught in our education system (quite sensibly since our exam system doesn't reward them). Intelligence Quotient (IQ) makes up only about 20 per cent of the factors needed to succeed in life according to Daniel Goleman, the psychologist who pioneered the idea of Emotional Intelligence (EQ) in his 1995 book of the same name. EQ involves understanding your own emotions and therefore being better able to regulate them as well as displaying empathy and superior social skills which enhances relationships with others.

A poll published in 2019 by 'OnePoll' surveying 2,000 adults showed that 47 per cent of millennials (roughly 25 to 40 year-olds) have already had a complete career change since their first job, many changing after only four years. Most change position every 5.5 years and 32 per cent said they didn't see themselves in the same career for life. The availability of online or distance learning is giving people the ability to retrain while still in their current role and per-haps explains why over half of the 2,000 interviewed had changed career (as I did myself at the age of 30), with rea-sons cited being better salary, better training opportunities or better work-life balance.

Dell Technologies published a report in 2018 which esti-mated that 85 per cent of jobs which will be available in 2030 haven't even been invented yet.

> The pace of change will be so rapid that people will learn 'in the moment' using new technologies such as augmented reality and virtual reality. The ability to gain new knowledge will be more valuable than the knowledge itself.

Many jobs will be automated or we will be persuaded to do them ourselves – when was the last time you booked an airline ticket with a travel agent or checked in for that flight with an airline representative? Many will be augmented by Information Technology and Artificial Intelligence – healthcare is slowly adjusting to the reality that staff simply cannot acquire and store the amount of data now available and algorithms guiding them through the thought processes and decision points in the diagnosis and management of illness will contribute greatly to the Patient Safety discussed in an earlier chapter. Hospitals still use antiquated paging systems to 'bleep' their staff (I still have flashbacks …) and some still communicate using fax machines. Readers under 30 may need to Google 'fax machine' to understand what I'm talking about!

Meanwhile, staff use platforms such as WhatsApp to communicate amongst themselves and life-saving supports such as the *Oxford Handbook of Clinical Medicine,* which lived permanently in the pocket of my white coat during my intern year in St. James's Hospital in Dublin, have been replaced by an easily searchable app on our phones.

In summary, life is not as linear as it is sometimes portrayed in school.

Education in the world of continuous, life-long learning is not about transferring information, it's about teaching our students how to learn. This ability to learn, rather than our ability to reproduce information that may soon be out of date, is what will serve our society better. Unfortunately, while we cling to our out-dated examination model, teachers will have no option but to focus their time helping pupils over that hurdle while under-utilising the real skills of both students and teachers. Is that the biggest error of our education system in the twenty-first century?

This will hopefully give some reassurance to young people choosing which courses to study and what career path to follow (as my own children are at the moment) by highlighting that there's a fairly high chance they'll end up doing something completely different by the time they are 30 anyway so the decision is maybe not quite as life defining as they think. They are free to make mistakes safe in the knowledge that they won't be trapped by them for life in the way previous generations may have been. Their early jobs will only enhance the diversity of training and outlook employers claim to be seeking in their staff. To go back to Edison's logic, and also to paraphrase the legendary late Irish broadcaster, Larry Gogan, 'you haven't failed, you simply found some careers that didn't suit you'.

The Misuse of Information and a Threat to Privacy

To return to Facebook's world, Cambridge Analytica was a British company established in 2015 and an example of the new industry of 'information manipulation' which Facebook has fostered. It's no longer about learning reams of information, it's about accumulating information from multiple sources, processing and repackaging it and selling it to other businesses for their own, possibly nefarious, uses.

Chief Executive Alexander Nix, who in 2016 claimed to have 4,000 to 5,000 data points on every one of the 220 million adults in the USA, was caught by an undercover Channel 4 camera crew boasting that the company was working on over 200 elections across the world. Two of the highest profile were President Trump's election campaign and the UK's Brexit referendum. Nix stated that Cambridge Analytica 'ran all the digital campaign' for Trump. He said they used communication that would self-destruct (like Snapchat) leaving no incriminating evidence. After the report was broadcast, CA distanced themselves from the comments and suspended Nix.

Many political analysts dispute the significance of voter profiling and targeting of advertising accordingly, but given that the annual global advertising spend is currently around $625 billion, if people aren't influenced by marketing, someone is wasting an awful lot of money. By 2016, unprecedented amounts of data had been culled by companies such as Cambridge Analytica and social media assumed ever greater importance in influencing events. The platforms which sold them the information on their users and their users' friends without their knowledge were then used to disseminate advertisements, news items, opinion pieces and so on which were judged as likely to persuade them to vote in a given direction. It was only after the shock election of Donald Trump that America started to question what was happening regarding the sale of our privacy.

Many websites give access to special offers in return for answering some simple questions and giving up some of our privacy, thus coining the phrase, 'If you're not paying for the product, then you probably *are* the product'. The extreme version of this, which we will cover in Chapter 10, is Fake News whereby we can now get our news for free (no premium TV or newspaper subscriptions) but the information we receive is very likely to be unreliable or even false, designed to promote a certain political worldview. Even error itself is now a product!

Artificial Intelligence is now being used to enhance the harvesting of information with Google admitting to scanning e-mails for keywords which are then used to drive targeted advertising, and Apple and Amazon admitting that their iPhones and Alexa devices listen to our speech (even when we think applications such as Siri are not activated) and harvest keywords for the same reasons. Remember, we saw earlier that we are exposed to between 5,000 and 10,000 ads per day, many subconsciously. This may be useful in showing us only ads we are likely to be interested in but we now run the clear risk of being constantly misled and manipulated with biased information or even being fed misinformation encouraging erroneous decisions.

Much of the interest in the sale of our privacy is thanks to a whistleblower named Christopher Wylie who told *The New York Times* and *The Guardian/Observer* about Cambridge Analytica's practices. Just before the news broke, Facebook banned Wylie, Cambridge Analytica and some of its top executives from its platform, but the horse had already bolted.

Facebook's share price fell and Zuckerberg was summoned to testify to Congress. The penny was dropping that the lax approach we have allowed to develop round our privacy has real world consequences. Cambridge Analytica's input to the Leave campaign in the UK Brexit referendum is felt to have tipped the balance in a very close contest. Many questions regarding the funding of the campaign are still unclear with some of the major backers standing to gain significantly in the outcome they helped finance. This of course is how politics has worked for centuries, but now the influence these donors exert is much more substantial due to our access to instant, global communications with no filters on content for accuracy.

For the foreseeable future, 'The Four Horsemen' of Apple, Facebook, Google and Amazon will continue harvesting our data and we will likely continue to co-operate with them in return for convenience and some 'free' toys such as WhatsApp and Instagram. The very notion of privacy is long gone and we will have to learn to live with the consequences of that in whatever our post-Brexit and post-Trumpian worlds throw at us next! Applying our Error Management approach by questioning everything we read or see will give us some protection against being misled by deliberately misleading information. Our education system needs to ditch the twentieth century mindset and catch up in order to prepare our citizens for this new reality. The tools are already available and Safety Critical industries like aviation focus on appraisal of information with a high level of scepticism and awareness of biases. We need to work at this like our lives and well-being depended on it – because they do.

Chapter 10

Are We Ready to Accept Error Yet, or Is That Fake News?

Although we associate the term Fake News with recent events, particularly during the presidency of Donald Trump who has made the term his own, the idea actually goes back quite a bit further. In the UK, King Edward I passed a statute in the late thirteenth century which made it 'a grave offence to devise to tell any false news of prelates, dukes, earls, barons or nobles of the realm'. The rest of us plebs were apparently fair game! Another term for it is, of course, 'propaganda', a tool used by governments for centuries to present information in a way that benefits their aims, varying from mild distortions of the truth to downright lies. It was usually justified as being in the national interest, especially during wartime.

Media outlets have of course often been biased in favour of the views of their owner, one reason many powerful people have been keen to buy radio stations or newspapers. Many media outlets are known for their political leanings. In the UK, the *Telegraph* is well known to be sympathetic to the Conservative Party (and often publish articles written by senior members – hence its nickname, the Torygraph) whilst the *Guardian* is acknowledged as being broadly supportive of the Labour Party. And in the US, Fox News has enjoyed enormous success proudly promoting the views of Donald Trump and other rightwing politicians. This results in articles and editorial viewpoints which tend to favour one side or the other. Whilst maybe not qualifying as 'Fake News', this certainly leads to manipulation of opinions by focusing on one point of view only.

In this chapter we will delve more deeply into communication (and also, mis-communication). All our studies on adverse events, regardless of whether they are in aviation, healthcare or any other Safety Critical industry, suggest that 70 per cent are caused by errors in communication. It is essential, then, for us to learn a bit more about this fascinating topic which may be the most critical of the six Crew Resource Management (CRM) pillars.

At its most basic, communication involves a transmitter, a message and a receiver. Errors can occur at any (or all) of the three stages and often involve subconscious biases and have a substantial overlap with the other pillars of CRM. With this in mind, let's have a look at how the media has developed and how it now has such a major influence on our lives.

The invention of the printing press in 1439 led to an explosion of information, previously only available in rarified settings such as monasteries where handmade books such as the exquisite *Book of Kells* which resides in the library in Trinity College, Dublin, were created and used by monks. As publications spread, an ethos of responsible journalism didn't and by the seventeenth century, historians had started including footnotes citing their sources to try to combat this. By the eighteenth century, the problem was the subject of laws combatting it with The Netherlands banning one publisher, Gerard Lodewick van der Macht, four times. In the USA (or American colonies as they were at the time), Benjamin Franklin wrote false stories about murderous Native Americans working alongside the English King George III (brought to life memorably in the musical *Hamilton*) in order to sway public opinion in favour of independence.

Fake News reached new heights in the twentieth century during wartime. Unfounded rumours of 'German Corpse Factories' were circulated in the Allied press such as *The Times* and *The Daily Mail* but were shown afterwards to be fictitious. Nazi Propaganda minister Joseph Goebbels then used the story as evidence of British propaganda to try to provide cover for the Holocaust. Both sides had their Fake News teams (Reich Ministry of Public Enlightenment and Propaganda versus the British Political Warfare Executive) distributing misinformation to bolster support on their own side and foment disillusionment on their enemies. Towards the end of the century, it had even led to a new job title – Spin Doctor! This is a derogatory term for a public relations professional whose role is to exaggerate or emphasise one particular side of an issue – that of the person or group employing them! They 'spin' stories to make their side look good regardless of the reality. One of the best-known Spin Doctors in the UK was Alastair Campbell, Tony Blair's Press Secretary and Director of Communications and Strategy.

Whilst its history goes back almost a millennium or further, Fake News has really mushroomed in the twenty-first Century due to the preponderance of Social Media and our easy access to convenient mobile devices. It varies from satire (which some may interpret as real) to outright fiction, often with the intent of making people click on a story to find out more and having to wade through a plethora of ads in the process – the real point of the exercise for the creator. This type of article is known as click-bait.

American comedian Paul Horner was known for his fake stories which he intended as satire, but after promotion by Google's news search and by Facebook, ended up being shared widely by members of Donald Trump's campaign team. The *Chicago Tribune* referred to him as a 'hoax artist' and *The Huffington Post* called him a 'performance artist'. After the election of Trump in November 2016, he expressed regret that what he thought would satirise Trump and his supporters may have inadvertently helped get him elected! Horner has spoken at the European Parliament on the spread of Fake News and the need for fact checking. The tendency for people to find like-minded groups online and avoid dissenting voices leads to 'echo chambers' and discourages independent questioning. This can result in misinformation like Horner's being rapidly accepted as fact regardless of how outlandish it may be. The presentation of facts in 'bubbles', a convenient but incomplete and one-sided version of the 'facts', also contributed.

Facebook was one of the key gateways for fake stories and fake news websites. Fact checks of these stories were rarely seen by consumers despite an abundance of sites such as Snopes which provide this service. In 2017, inventor of the internet, Tim Berners-Lee, declared Fake News as one of the three big trends which needed dealt with if the internet were to truly serve humanity.

> A lie can travel halfway round the world while the truth is still putting on its shoes.

This is a quote attributed to Mark Twain, though that is probably in error and it is actually the modification of a quote by Dublin writer and churchman, Jonathan Swift (of *Gulliver's Travels* fame) in 1710. Social media has however accelerated this sentiment many-fold and the advent of Fake News sites and the use of 'bots' has even automated it. Fake News is a subset of a group known as disinformation, that is, having the appearance of credible news stories but being factually false and created or spread with the intent to deceive. Once it is passed on by consumers who mistakenly believe it to be true, it becomes misinformation. We now exist in a society with many Fake News outlets, sites which have the appearance of regular media but without the rigorous fact-checking and which mix a substantial number of fake stories with real ones to distract from their true motive.

Matthew Hindman of George Washington University and Vlad Barash of Social Media Intelligence firm Graphic carried out a large study assessing the impact Twitter had on spreading Fake News during the 2016 US Presidential election campaign. They looked at 600 media outlets and studied 10 million tweets from 700,000 accounts that linked to these sites. Their study looked both before and after the election. They found 6.6 million tweets connected to these Fake News outlets in the month leading up to the election but, interestingly, six months later they found 4 million in a month, showing that it isn't simply an election-based phenomenon. Of these, 65 per cent went to only 10 sites and 89 per cent went to the top 50. These figures didn't change after the election so these outlets aren't 'fly by night' operations, they're stable and thriving.

This news is distributed in two ways, through professional trolls – human-run accounts and cyborg accounts, or 'bots', which combine human-generated content with automated posting. Bots have trackable characteristics such as posting rates with no obvious downtime (such as sleep), thousands of tweets but few followers (if no one's listening, humans generally stop talking), high retweet activity with little content production and multiple tweets of the same link so 'bots' are generally detectable. New, more 'social bots' are constantly being developed in order to stay one step ahead. Professor Mike Kearney of the University of Missouri has developed the 'Tweetbotornot' package which he claims is 93 per cent accurate in detecting bots. We also need to look for co-ordinated activity across seemingly unconnected sites which can push a story or link. Spotting bots starts with analysing some Fake News channels and then tracking the accounts which access them to assess whether they meet characteristics like those discussed above.

How prevalent are bots? It is estimated that of the top 100 most followed accounts on Twitter, 33 per cent are 'bots'-automated accounts. A random sample of all accounts found 63 per cent to be 'bots' despite the fact that 15 per cent of accounts from before the election had been suspended, suggesting that over 70 per cent of accounts are actually automated. Fake News sites received around 13 per cent as many hits as the big mainstream media outlets and 37 per cent as many as regional newspapers. Clearly, their influence is significant and far-reaching. The heavy co-followership of these big accounts allows news to be propagated very quickly and widely.

Two years after the election in April 2018, around 90 per cent of these accounts were still active contradicting claims of a crackdown on them. However, aggressive action can be effective when applied. The Real Strategy, a site which promoted the 'pizzagate' untruths which linked Hillary Clinton with a Satanic child abuse ring operating out of a

Washington pizza parlour, had its account deleted and was blacklisted on other social media platforms. To understand the significance of this, consider that in November 2016 one million tweets were tagged #Pizzagate, and in early December, a 28-year-old from North Carolina opened fire on the premises. Despite no evidence being found by reputable outlets, a survey of 1,224 US voters that month found 9 per cent believed Clinton was linked to a child sex ring while 19 per cent weren't sure.

Deliberate error has clear, real world implications.

Although Fake News was an issue before 2016, the use of the term since by President Donald Trump has cemented its place in the public psyche and the term has become almost synonymous with Trump. For Trump, however, his use of Fake News appears to refer to any news that isn't sufficiently complimentary to him or is unsupportive of his aims and beliefs. Public concern has intensified with Trump's use of 'alternative facts' (a term used by spokesperson Kelly-Anne Conway in relation to the turnout for Trump's inauguration), his self-proclaimed 'war' on journalists and the prevalence of Fake News in what has become known as the 'post-truth era'. This confusion has led to a drop in trust in mainstream media outlets and, as we have seen above, a stable cohort of channels propagating misinformation to the extent that we now are no longer sure what is real and what is error.

In 1976, shortly after Watergate, trust in the media reached 72 per cent in the US. By 2016, this was down to 32 per cent. By attacking the 'lamestream media', Trump managed to sow confusion which makes it easier to deny events or opinions when necessary. Since democracy is dependent on the informed consent of the governed, undermining this information undermines democracy itself. Media literacy companies are now training students in initiatives like fact checking.

It's commonly accepted that politicians are known for telling the occasional untruth. Trump isn't like most politicians, but perhaps this aspect of his approach is a little more traditional. Tony Schwartz, who ghost-wrote Trump's best-known book, *The Art of the Deal*, described him as having a 'loose relationship with the truth' and coined the phrase 'truthful hyperbole' to describe Trump's exaggerations when trying to cut a deal. The website FactCheck.org declared Trump the 'King of the Whoppers' within six months of declaring his candidacy for the Presidential election and stated that:

> . . . in the twelve years of FactCheck.org's existence, we've never seen his match. He stands out not only for the sheer number of his factually false claims, but also for his brazen refusals to admit errors when proven wrong.

Several other fact-checking groups present a similar story with an average of 15 'alternative facts' being presented per day! Glenn Kessler, fact-checker for *The Washington Post*, said in 2017 that 'the pace and volume of the president's mis-statements means that we cannot possibly keep up'. Indeed, that paper's running total of Trump's 'untruths' since taking office exceeded 20,000 in July 2020, a day when they racked up another 62.

Since we are now dealing with how we are being manipulated by various agencies, it's probably a good time to have a look at the various classifications of error so we can get an idea of the ways we can be misled.

CLASSIFICATIONS OF ERROR

There are many different classifications of error depending on the context (scientific, human, computer programming and so on) but for our purposes, we are going to concentrate on the increasingly important topic of Human Error. This type of error, apart from being one of the most common, is one which is at least partially fixable, and is worthy of study because of the exponential increase in Artificial Intelligence (AI) in our twenty-first century world. In order to train computers and machines to perform human-type acts reliably, we need to work out where they can go wrong and then try to engineer these errors out of the system.

Reason's Four Part Model

One of the best known models was developed by a giant of the human performance and safety management field, Professor James Reason of the University of Manchester in the UK, probably best known for his Swiss Cheese Model of error as shown on the following page. He broke error down into four main elements which basically cover all the possible causes of an error. Each of these can then be studied in more detail using other models depending on which is most relevant for the error in question. Reason divided error classification into failure at the level of Intention, Action, Outcome and Context.

For the purposes of explanation, let's pretend that you have presented at your local Emergency Department with pain in your lower right abdominal area and a temperature, both of which have been present for almost twenty-fours. Enter your local surgical registrar. Where can this go wrong?

213

EXPECT THE UNEXPECTED. ASSESS YOUR RISKS. PREVENT INCIDENTS.

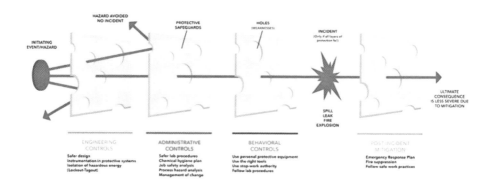

1. Intention

The first hurdle which both you and your diligent doc-tor must clear is the intention to treat the correct illness. Misdiagnosis at this early stage may lead to treatment that is carried out competently but doesn't resolve your symp-toms as it treated the wrong problem!

So first, our intrepid surgeon must diagnose your con-dition – the first opportunity to err! To tip the odds he will take a history – previous illnesses, medications, family his-tory and so on will help him to narrow the list of possible options. Having done this, he will then examine you, both generally (temperature, pulse rate, blood pressure, general appearance) and specifically (feeling your tummy for ten-derness, lumps and so on) in order to refine the diagnosis. Next up will be investigations (blood tests, x-rays, ultra-sound scan if necessary) before finally making a diagnosis, which will presumably be run by a consultant. Having decided you have acute appendicitis, the doctor decides to remove the inflamed appendage in the operating theatre which is performed flawlessly.

Unfortunately, you didn't actually have appendicitis – you were suffering from mesenteric adenitis, an inflammation of the lymph nodes in that area of the abdomen, often caused by a virus and which gets better by itself. It is a common condition in the same age group which commonly gets appendicitis so can easily cause confusion. In fairness to our medic, appendicitis is misdiagnosed in about 15 per cent of males and about 30 per cent of females. In males it can be confused with an inflamed gall bladder, kidney stones, a urinary infection or Crohn's disease, amongst others. In women it can be confused with all of the preceding but also ectopic pregnancy, ovarian cysts, pelvic inflammatory disease etc, the extra options accounting for the increased rate of error. Our young doctor's error was that of intention. Errors of intention can also be classified as a simple mistake – the plan was wrong.

2. Action

Let's assume that you actually do have appendicitis after all – you and your surgeon have cleared the first hurdle and you are in theatre for your operation. The next opportunity for a blunder is in the action of the surgery itself. It turns out that our friend's anatomical knowledge is a little below par and he actually removes your gall bladder in a flawless demonstration of a cholecystectomy. Again, his surgical technique is beyond reproach other than the fact that he erroneously removed the wrong organ. This is an error of action. It can also be classified as a 'slip' (he removed the wrong organ) or potentially a 'lapse' (he got distracted and forgot to remove anything at all).

3. Outcome

Let's backtrack slightly. Our surgeon is not removing your gall bladder but has correctly identified and removed your inflamed appendix, thereby resolving your underlying condition successfully. Where else could things go askew? This brings us the error of outcome.

Unfortunately, when closing the small opening in the bowel at the base of the now removed appendix, the suture material was from a dud batch and disintegrated on your way back to the ward. By next morning the contents of your bowel were leaking into your abdomen and you are now, through no fault of yours or the surgeon, suffering from acute peritonitis, the very condition the operation sought to avoid. This is an error of outcome. Everything was done correctly but things didn't work out as planned.

4. Context

The final opportunity for our surgeon to go astray brings us to the error of context. You are waiting patiently in theatre for your operation. Your surgeon, unfortunately, is next door performing a flawless appendicectomy on the wrong patient.

That patient has been the victim of a Never Event which is defined as:

> Serious Incidents that are wholly preventable because guidance or safety recommendations that provide strong systemic protective barriers are available at a national level and should have been implemented by all healthcare providers.

Our unfortunate surgeon arrived in the theatre designated for emergencies where 'his' patient was anaesthetised and ready on the table. The anaesthetist and theatre team know our medic well, assume he is aware of who this patient is and see no need to question him until he has removed the appendix and they realise things aren't progressing in the direction they were expecting.

As noted earlier, the most recent report on this topic by NHS Improvement recorded 423 Never Events over a nine month period to the end of January 2019. Wrong site surgery of which this would be the most extreme version accounted for 165 of these.

Preventative measures adapted from aviation, including the WHO Surgical Checklist, team briefings and time outs before starting the operation to ensure that everyone is on the same page, have been mandated for a decade now but studies and chatting to theatre staff show that implementation can be a little patchy.

Each of these four classifications is a starting point in our exploration of how errors occur and how we can strive to either avoid them completely, trap them before they go too far or at least mitigate the fallout from them as we've previously discussed. Let's now look at an alternative error classification.

Rasmussen's SRK Model

Jens Rasmussen, a Danish psychologist, developed the Skill-based, Rule-based, Knowledge-based (SRK) error classification in the mid-1970s. This separated the causes of error into three areas progressing from the level needing the least conscious input to the one requiring the most, a system which generally displays an increasing risk of error.

Again, for simplicity of explanation, let's nip back to the hospital to see how the patient is doing. You are recovering from your surgery but need intravenous antibiotic treatment to prevent any infection complicating your recovery. Let's have a look at the three levels to assess the risk areas of where this can go wrong.

1. Skill-based Error

Our surgeon's more junior colleague isn't available so it's up to him to insert an intravenous cannula (a little plastic tube) into one of your veins to allow the antibiotic solution to be administered. This is a skill learnt largely on the job as a junior doctor and junior staff are often the most proficient since they are most practised at it. They easily identify a suitable vein and deftly slip the cannula into it with minimal fuss, an almost automated procedure which is fortunate as it is often performed while sleep-deprived. Our friend, being too busy doing more complex work, rarely performs this task any more so has to slow down and think about it. He is slower and also at more risk of erring – getting it wrong by missing the vein and inserting the cannula into the sub-cutaneous tissue so that the antibiotic will not enter the bloodstream but instead collect painfully under the skin without achieving its aim. There is also the more serious error of mis-identifying the vein and inserting the cannula into an artery instead. This can lead to the higher pressure blood travelling up the cannula or else the antibiotic heading directly into the smaller vessels without being diluted in the venous bloodstream potentially causing toxicity and serious damage.

2. Rule-based Error

Let's assume our surgeon managed to successfully insert the cannula into the vein and is preparing your antibiotic solution. He has also noted that you have an under-lying kidney condition which means your body can't process this particular drug as efficiently so you need a reduced dose. He is diligently applying an accepted rule developed by renal and pharmaceutical specialists to let us tailor your treatment to your specific needs. Unfortunately, his arithmetic isn't quite as good as his surgical skills and he miscalculates the numbers and injects too high a dose which can lead to toxicity problems. He has committed a rule-based error. This type of error involves less automatism and more conscious thought (although perhaps not quite enough in our surgeon's case) and is therefore inherently more risky.

3. Knowledge-based Error

The highest level of this group involves the most risk of error as it involves the most thinking. In this case, our intrepid surgeon is blissfully unaware that your renal condition has any impact on the dose of the antibiotic so proceeds to give you the standard dose with no modification. His knowledge of this area is inadequate so he commits a knowledge-based error. We can try to reduce the risk of this error by highlighting the risk in an eye-catching manner in either the paper version of the reference manual for dosages, or in the computer-based prescribing system if the hospital has invested in one. We could also introduce a prescribing checklist to try to prompt thought about possible errors before proceeding. We'll address these ideas (and their pitfalls) in more detail later.

Planning/Execution Model

In this two-stage model we can separate the error according to whether it occurred in the planning stage, in which case it is a 'mistake', or during the execution of the plan, when it is either a 'slip' or a 'lapse'.

A mistake in planning is a fundamental error which basically means that you were never going to achieve a good outcome. Current error management training tries to identify this error by encouraging regular reviews of decisions to assess whether they are achieving the desired outcome. Hopefully, an erroneous plan can be spotted and reversed to allow a better one to be developed before the situation becomes irrecoverable. For example, a mistake would be to prescribe a penicillin-based antibiotic to a patient who is allergic to penicillin. If actioned, the result is never going to work out well.

A slip is an incorrectly actioned step in an otherwise perfectly good plan. It is by nature an active event, although often performed unconsciously. It can be an action which is common and well practised (hence it being amenable to automatic action) but incorrect or inappropriate in our particular scenario. A slip would be when we are aware that our patient is allergic to penicillin so prescribe a suitable alternative but then accidentally give them the penicillin-based one anyway. We have clutched defeat from the jaws of victory!

A lapse is a failure to perform an action. In the above patient, we are aware that they have the allergy, prescribe a suitable alternative, but then forget to actually give them any medication at all.

There are many more classifications or taxonomies of error, but for our purposes the above three should be sufficient. They give an idea of how error is not as simple as we might have initially thought and may be either an individual issue or an accumulation of several. We will look at how errors follow common patterns due to how we think and how we approach problems. For instance, we are convinced that we gather the available information, assess it rationally and then make an appropriate decision which we then action. Scientific research suggests that we do nothing of the sort! Firstly, we don't have time for that in our fast-moving world, and secondly, that's not how our brains are programmed. Now that we are armed with a little more information on error, let's go back to our political leaders to see how misleading information can be deployed.

We have seen how Donald Trump has turned Fake News into a spectator sport. In the UK, his friend and counterpart Boris Johnson has also told some howlers but has a lot of ground to make up if he's going to surpass 20,000! His most famous is probably the red Brexit bus emblazoned with 'We send the EU £350 million a week, let's fund our NHS instead. Vote Leave'. The media company Full Fact and others have shown that this is an overestimate by £100 million per week and, of course, it doesn't factor in money coming back from the EU or changes to the economy and trade deals after leaving. The UK Statistics Authority called the claim 'misleading'. If the claim actually turns out to be true, my former colleagues in the NHS are looking forward to what they can achieve with that £350 million per week!

The preponderance of Fake News can cause problems in mainstream media outlets which are obliged to provide balance and ensure both sides of a story are given equal airtime. Irish Foreign Minister Simon Coveney highlighted this issue in September 2020 on the Andrew Marr programme discussing Johnson's new Internal Markets Bill, which Northern Ireland Secretary of State Brandon Lewis sensationally announced would break international law (but only in a specific and limited way). Coveney said:

You seem to be suggesting that there are two sides
that are equal in this disagreement. There aren't.
There is one side that is breaking an agreement that
was signed by both.

To ensure 'balance', Marr was left to frame accusations as
serious questions including one on the EU blockading food
supplies to Northern Ireland to which Coveney replied:

Andrew, you've been following these negotiations
for more than three years now and you're a pretty
good detail person. And you know that is a completely bogus argument.

Next day in the House of Commons, Labour Shadow
Foreign Secretary Ed Miliband repeatedly challenged
Johnson to show where the bill addressed such issues with
no reply from an unusually silent Prime Minister.

The same day, Irish radio presenter Jennifer Zamparelli
tried to make a similarly one-sided issue into a reasoned
debate on 2FM by asking anti-mask protestors during the
Covid-19 pandemic on to her show to discuss the issue.
Social media outrage to the suggestion led to the piece being
cancelled. The general feeling was summed up by a tweet
by @grannies4equality:

This 'open discussion' will give airtime to people
advocating behaviour that puts all our lives at risk.
. . . Next week: how do you feel about brakes in cars?

Is there anyone trying to protect us from exposure to
this misinformation tsunami? Irish journalist Mark Little
decided to tackle this issue and in 2010 founded Storyful,
a Social Media Intelligence Agency offering news monitoring and reputation risk management to corporate clients.
Essentially, they verified news sources and social media

content. After finding and verifying this content, it distributed, licensed and commercialised it.

Storyful gained a reputation when processing content from the Syrian Civil War and the Arab Spring protests before being bought by Rupert Murdoch's News Corp in 2013 for $25 million. Examples of their work include analysis of the famous clip of CNN's Jim Acosta who appeared to strike a White House intern in November 2018. Storyful's software was able to detect that the 15 second long clip had been doctored by pausing three frames for a fraction of a second.

Another well-known example is of Nancy Pelosi, former speaker of the US House of Representatives, filmed in May 2020 where her answer to a question was edited to remove sections of her response and also slowed down in order to make her appear drunk and incoherent. Despite the video being debunked by both Snopes and FactCheck, who quoted Professor Hany Farid, who specialises in digital forensics, saying that parts were slowed down by 75 per cent giving the impression of slurring, the video was shared 2.5 million times on Facebook.

We can see that both the commercialisation of error and its detection are now well established so it is important that we be aware of such spin and manipulation. Given the easy availability of information in the digital age, perhaps people should be taught how to spot or at least be suspicious of manipulated content, and how to practise Error Management in order to not be easily misled. It's a shame we need to have suspicion as a default setting, but that, unfortunately, seems to be the price of having unfettered access to creating and consuming content in the twenty-first century.

As we reach the conclusion of our exploration of error in its many and varied incarnations, we approach the question which the book has been leading up to.

ARE WE READY TO ACCEPT ERROR YET?

The title of this book, *Oops! Why Things Go Wrong,* emphasises our initial reaction of embarrassment or even shame when we make a mistake. Equally, the original working subtitle, *The Inevitability of Error,* was intended to absolve that embarrassment with the assertion that error was going to happen anyway so there's no reason to be ashamed of it. The final subtitle, *Understanding and Controlling Error*, is perhaps a little more straight forward and hopefully less likely to miscommunicate my intention.

'It's not your fault' to quote Robin Williams' character in the movie *Good Will Hunting.*

As my six-year course in Medicine in Dublin progressed from the pre-clinical years on campus on College Green to the clinical training with patients in St. James's Hospital, avoidance of error literally became a matter of life and death. Our training focused on how to extract a diagnosis from a patient and then to decide on an appropriate treatment strategy to give them the best possible prognosis.

For example, if a patient presents with chest pains we take their history, do an examination and once we collate all this data, we might make our pronouncement that, 'This patient is having an Acute Myocardial Infarction!' Bit of Latin always sounds more impressive than saying, 'He's having a heart attack!'

At this point, we briefly acknowledge the possibility of an error by offering an alternative diagnosis in case we are wrong, although each step in our carefully followed process is intended to reduce this chance of error further and further.

Research shows that once we have invested our reputation in a diagnosis, we are loathe to change it to avoid losing face and looking incompetent. Studies also show that colleagues are loathe to correct you too and will not contradict your diagnosis unless it's very far off the mark.

A study in the *BMJ* published in 2000 asked a group of clinicians and also a group of pilots in the USA if your senior colleague (consultant/attending or captain) made a mistake, would you speak up and tell them? Of the pilots, 97 per cent said yes, they would. But only 55 per cent of the clinicians (made up of junior surgeons and scrub nurses) said they would! In other words, we pay lip service to the possibility of error but our fragile egos don't allow us to seriously consider it as an option. In the case of the junior surgeons, the constant six-month contracts probably don't entice staff to speak up either, although some units now encourage assertiveness using an escalating ladder to express concern. A simplified version of this goes along the lines of:

'I'm not sure that's a good idea.'

'Are you sure that's a good idea?'

'That's not a good idea!'

'Okay, stop now!'

Our healthcare chapter showed that a patient admitted to the hospital has a 10 per cent chance of suffering an adverse event caused by an error in our care, not because of the underlying illness. The emphasis throughout my training was on being right. I remember very little coverage of the possibility that I might make a mistake, nor do I remember being taught a strategy that would reduce the chance of an error or its impact if it's not spotted until late in the process. They were simply called 'complications', which lumped together genuinely unfortunate bits of bad luck along with our self-made failures. We weren't encouraged to admit that we may have messed up to the patient so as not to prejudice any possible legal proceedings in the future.

Having successfully navigated medical school, I was now released into the wild as an Intern on the cardio-thoracic surgery ward where I started learning the practical skills that would keep me afloat, largely with the help of the hugely experienced nursing team there. The system dictated that I had an SHO (Senior House Officer) above me who I could call for help or advice but the really senior team members (registrars and consultants) were often in our main cardiac unit in a different hospital across town. At night, two of us interns covered around 350 surgical patients from various specialities, clocking up a 36 hour shift every four or five days with little or no sleep and sporadic food. So, given what we have learnt so far, what was the chance of error? High to certain, I would guess. Yet there was no discussion of error and no mention of an Error Management strategy. Speaking to staff now when I give presentations in hospitals, little appears to have changed. Some hospitals are making in-roads to a Human Factors approach with some pockets of excellent work such as Professor Peter Brennan's Head and Neck Surgery Unit in the Queen Alexandra Hospital in Portsmouth, but no hospital as far as I'm aware is regularly training all staff in Human Factors and Error Management, despite it being one of the biggest issues in healthcare.

After jumping ship to aviation, the transformation of my understanding of the value of error began. The whole concept of error being accepted and, indeed, welcomed was totally alien to me and it took a while to get my head around the idea. My understanding at the start was that error is a sign of incompetence and was to be rooted out by studying and working harder. This was the mindset that was trained into me during my medical career and, after twelve years of training, I found it hard to let go. The turning point was the realisation during my command check training that it really wasn't expected that I would know everything and perform flawlessly whilst in command of a $100 million aeroplane. It was expected that I would be able to access and find the information I needed using the extensive resources made available, and that I could keep the plane and everyone on it safe whilst I was doing that.

My understanding of error has moved on immeasurably since my schooldays and it has freed up much of my already quite limited mental capacity. This extra capacity has, I hope, been put to better use managing the inevitable errors that I still make every day, even after twenty years in aviation, than it was spent furiously trying to be perfect and totally error-free. Life in a fast-moving, risky, complex industry doesn't afford that luxury; we need to learn to work safely within the parameters of the inevitable errors. Most Safety Critical industries have embraced this idea already but there are other areas such as agriculture, finance, education and the justice system where this approach could pay dividends both in cost savings and in transforming lives.

The only prerequisite is that those industries need to accept error as being inevitable and not something to be ashamed of. Assuming that they feel this will be worth the investment, what next? Let's have a look at the road map.

THE WAY FORWARD

In her 2015 book *Signals*, economist Pippa Malmgren refers back to Greek mythology when she describes economics as a balancing act similar to the never-ending battle between the two Greek goddesses, Hubris and Nemesis.

Hubris is the spirit of over-confidence that lights the fire of greed and compels us to take risks to achieve what the ego desires. It is, however, also what creates innovation and gets things done. Nemesis is the goddess of retribution, punishing those who indulge in too much hubris and brings us crashing back down to earth. In industry and indeed all human endeavours, error is our Nemesis which, as even Greek mythology shows us, is a given in every enterprise involving human input.

If we want to avoid our endeavours becoming Greek tragedies, we need to learn how to manage these errors successfully. So how do we implement an Error Management strategy? Those readers who have made it this far have probably guessed by now that it is broken into three sections!

Just Culture

The foundation of the whole Safety Management System concept is in acceptance and implementation of a Just Culture. This is a culture which tolerates genuine error and doesn't penalise anyone who makes an error as long as they report it and co-operate with the investigation to analyse *what* went wrong (not *who* went wrong) and try to find a way of reducing the chance of recurrence. It's not a 'get out of jail free card' though. It does not excuse gross negligence or wilful and malicious behaviour, both of which tend to be thankfully rare in most industries. In these cases, best case is demotion, suspension and re-training, and at worst disciplinary action, dismissal and possibly even criminal charges.

A Just Culture is not to be confused with a No Blame Culture. It is still expected that we take responsibility for our errors, but given that the staff member has probably carried out a similar task thousands of times before, we need to find out, 'What was different this time?' Why did this make sense to the person doing it at the time? Most industries are slow to dismiss otherwise competent staff in whom they have invested time and money. It is a much more profitable exercise to use their experience to better design and improve the systems. When incidents are studied, there are usually multiple causes and it's only when they all align (as in the case being investigated) that the error slips through the net. Cast your mind back to Reason's Swiss cheese model!

Systems Thinking

The second step in the process is to analyse the error and work out how it happened. Generally, we find a 'trip wire' that the staff member has fallen over. We now try to engineer that trip wire out of the system if possible and also try to insert 'safety nets' which will trap similar incidents in future before they progress to an accident. Changes can be approved quickly by a team representing various parts of the business and, in aviation at least, are promulgated with little delay – within weeks if not very urgent or within hours if necessary, given that information can now be transmitted to staff electronically and manuals updated rapidly.

Serious events like the 2009 AF447 crash involving an Air France Airbus A330 over the South Atlantic which cost the lives of 228 passengers and crew involved physical modifications to the aeroplane as well as training changes in how we handle a stall (both under way within weeks of the accident occurring) or, if less serious, simple tweaks to procedures or checklists. The least serious may only involve a reminder of existing procedures or perhaps addition to a database of concerns which can then be considered for inclusion in a future block of the continuous training we 'enjoy' if a pattern seems to be developing amongst crews.

As per our decision-making model, it is crucial that changes get reviewed looking for 'unintended consequences'.

In large, legacy-type industries like healthcare, change is difficult to effect. In many cases, changes such as increasing staff numbers or redesign of the physical environment in which staff work may be what is really needed. It may involve changing long established work practices. An example is the limitation on the number of hours staff are now permitted to work continuously in order to mitigate the errors caused by fatigue. This has effectively led to the break-up of 'the firm' of the old school training system which involved a hierarchical team working together to the new shift-based model where staff are continually rotating through teams and wards leading to poor 'continuity of care' and the inevitable errors which that causes. Trade-offs need to be carefully assessed and reassessed once established. When I was training, 80 hour weeks were common and ensured continuity of care, but at the cost of staff burn-out and of errors due to fatigue.

Healthcare talks about 'Evidence Based Practice' but despite no shortage of evidence on tiredness causing errors (although it is doubtful we need research to tell us that these shifts are unlikely to be safe) this problem still hasn't been meaningfully addressed. Hospital doctors often still work 24 hour shifts which other Safety Critical industries like aviation would baulk at – as would our passengers – so why should patients be forced to accept these risky work practices jeopardising their care?

Improved technology is also a tool we should be utilizing more to avoid error. Staying with healthcare, the Information Technology systems in the NHS, for example, are archaic and provide little support in avoiding error for staff. Notes are generally unavailable electronically and are not shared between institutions, leading to delays and miscommunication which contributes to the staggeringly high adverse event figures we discussed in the healthcare chapter. Some NHS hospitals still use fax machines while staff struggle to access clinical information (but communicate instantly in other areas of their lives using smart phones).

Electronic prescribing has algorithms which will highlight possible errors, yet the UK alone still has over 230 million medication errors per year. While we boast expensive new Da Vinci robots to enhance surgery, we tolerate twentieth century technology on the day to day issues like note keeping, investigations and referrals for opinions from specialist staff. Most likely a few Workload Management, Situational Awareness and Decision Making errors are contributing to this flawed system and resolving these would transform the working life of the staff, the efficiency of care of the patients and ultimately reduce errors saving a substantial proportion of the eye-watering financial drain on the system. After ten years of trying to share how aviation has addressed similar problems successfully, I have made minimal progress.

Aviation leverages technology differently to healthcare. Airplanes send a certain amount of basic information back to their company base by telemetry whilst in flight. Issues flag up on the technicians' computers in real time alerting them to problems. For instance, I was part of a crew which shut down the number two engine of an A330 over Eastern Canada en route to Los Angeles in 2008. After we had the flight stabilised and were safely en route to our diversion airport, Montreal-Pierre Trudeau International, I called our Flight Operations team back in Dublin using our on-board satellite telephone to let them know what was happening. They were able to respond straight away, 'yeah, we know!' The engine shutdown had flagged up on our engineering team's screens and Operations Control were then able to zoom in on our satellite trace to see we were diverting off our planned track in the direction of Montreal. We were then able to get our team in Dublin working on a strategy to resolve the problems we were about to encounter.

In the case of the 2009 AF447 crash discussed earlier, Air France and Airbus were able to assess what information they had and piece together a best guess of what happened. The 'Black Box' flight recorder and Cockpit Voice Recorder (CVR) weren't recovered until two years later when the wreckage was located, but it confirmed that their assessment was close to the mark. They had guessed that the pitot tubes, the metal tubes which stick out of the fuselage to measure speed, had iced up thereby giving erroneous readings. This led to the autopilot dropping out and the subsequent mishandling of the plane led to an irreversible stall and the loss of the airplane and all on board.

Within weeks, Airbus had sent a notice to all its A330 owners globally on how to modify these tubes and we were given revised training in the simulator straight away on how to manage a stall situation in the aeroplane. Further analysis revealed the bigger problem that training had focused so much on pilots as managers and the need to use automation to free up monitoring capacity that we had lost many of the basic handling skills acquired during early training, especially at high speeds and high altitudes where planes handle very differently. This led to a new training module called Upset Prevention and Recovery Training (UPRT). A compulsory part of our flight simulator conversion course and recurrent training now is a UPRT module where we fly the plane well outside its normal flight parametres. We learn an easily remembered technique which applies in all of these situations. Human Factors teaches us that if we need complex assessment and decision making, we will have missed the limited chance to recover safe flight so instead we 'Keep It Simple Stupid'. This is carried out at various altitudes to demonstrate the difference in handling techniques required. All this stems from investing in technology, studying accidents and applying the learning quickly and globally.

We all know that necessary systemic changes in healthcare involving more staff, better IT or infrastructure aren't likely to happen this side of Christmas, so what can we fall back on in the meantime? The third leg of our stool is the Crew Resource Management system we first looked at way back in Chapter 1 and will study in detail in the final chapter.

Crew Resource Management

In the absence of major staffing or structural change, we need to fall back on our CRM approach which effectively functions as our Personal Protective Equipment, our PPE. This is the strategy we studied earlier and forms the operating philosophy which we have embedded so successfully in aviation. The six pillars give us tools with which to intercept errors if we can't block them completely or a means to mitigate the consequences as a last resort.

Leadership styles can make or break a group. Encouraging followership and empowering staff to do a good job has been shown to be at least as motivating as monetary rewards, if not more so. People want to believe in what they are doing and feel that they are making an impact. Allowing staff to contribute to how work gets done builds trust and a feeling of ownership. They may see more efficient approaches involving new and evolving technology. Fresh eyes with experience in other industries may see opportunities that more established practitioners miss. Artificial Intelligence is likely to transform the area of Workload Management in the near future. Reassessment of our decisions to allow correction of unsuccessful calls and constant questioning and updating of our mental models helps us minimise errors.

To re-iterate how we summarised all this earlier:

'Where Can This Go Wrong?' and 'What's Plan B?'

HOW TO FOSTER AN INCREASED ACCEPTANCE OF ERROR IN SOCIETY

It is essential that we all buy in to the idea of error being inevitable and not a sign of incompetence or carelessness, especially in healthcare. Unfortunately, our system has been structured against a healthy approach to errors. To give feedback, patients often have to lodge a complaint. Our family had personal experience of this dysfunctional approach a number of years back when we were obliged to lodge a complaint when we simply wanted to address an error regarding a position on an out-patient waiting list.

When something goes wrong, hospital legal departments in the past had often advised staff not to admit an error and not to discuss the issue with the patient or their family, a wholly unsatisfactory position for both patient and staff alike. A new 'Duty of Candour' or 'Open Disclosure' approach is now being implemented in many countries, but given the examples in our healthcare chapter of how whistleblowers have been treated, staff may need quite a bit of convincing that they are genuinely safe to put their head above the parapet. A study published early in 2021 of about 600,000 NHS staff in the UK showed 25 per cent didn't feel safe speaking up. Also, although legally, an apology does not constitute an admission of liability in Civil (Tort) Law cases, it is much less clear in Criminal Law leaving staff open to disciplinary proceedings and potentially even criminal charges. It also would potentially negate the protection offered by their defence associations which operate similarly to insurance cover for clinicians. Indeed, the Medical Defence Union in its guidance to doctors states: 'Duty of Candour applies to organisations rather than individuals, but individuals will inevitably be involved in managing and resolving incidents.' This leaves conscientious staff in an unenviable position.

Staff therefore are understandably still reluctant to highlight their failures, partly due to this fear of litigation, even more so in the USA where the litigation route can be even costlier. Two main studies are often quoted addressing this issue, one by the University of Michigan and the other by Lexington Veterans Administration Medical Centre, both of which show a significant reduction in the number of claims and in legal and compensation costs. Figures generally show the chance of litigation is actually quite low. If, as figures show, 10 per cent of admissions suffer an adverse event, that totals about 1.5 million events per year in the UK alone. Of these, around 16,000 (1 per cent) submit a claim and roughly 5,000 (30 per cent) of these lead to legal proceedings. Only about 100 go to full trial and around 200 are resolved by mediation. Research shows that most patients actually don't want to sue but they find it is often the only way to get the information they deserve in order to find out what happened. One study reported in the *Journal of the American Medical Association*, albeit almost thirty years ago, showed that almost half of parents who filed malpractice suits for peri-natal injuries sued because they felt their doctor tried to mislead them. Given the stress and expense for both sides, the statistics we have suggest that a policy of Open Disclosure is likely to give increased satisfaction to both patients and staff, as well as reducing costs allowing funds to be better spent on patient care. In the UK, annual cash costs due to adverse events are currently around £2.3 billion so that leaves a lot of room for manoeuvre as well as ethically being the right thing to do. As Sir Liam Donaldson, former Chief Medical Officer in the UK, put it:

> To err is human, to cover up is unforgivable but to fail to learn is inexcusable.

The two most recent healthcare scandals in the Republic of Ireland originated from information being withheld from patients or their families.

The country's CervicalCheck cancer screening service performed an internal review in 2014 which discovered that fifteen women, including Vicky Phelan, had cervical smear tests which were incorrectly reported as being clear when they in fact showed early cancerous changes. Phelan, however, was not informed of this finding until 2017 so received no treatment leaving the young mother terminally ill. A case against the US laboratory which reported the test was settled without admission of liability for $2.5 million. In 2018, however, it became clear that Phelan was not alone. The Health Service Executive (HSE) reported that 206 women had developed cervical cancer following a misread test. More shockingly, 162 had not been informed of the error. CervicalCheck's clinical director, Dr Grainne Flannelly, stepped down two days later after it was revealed she had advised a gynaecologist not to inform women but simply to file the report. The Director-General of the HSE, Tony O'Brien, resigned two weeks later.

Phelan, despite her illness, continued to campaign for better treatment of the group including access to medication. Her work also led to closer scrutiny of other cancer screening programmes in the country including BreastCheck and BowelScreen. She died in November 2022.

The death of Savita Halappanavar in 2012 from sepsis in University Hospital Galway has also highlighted the cost of a lack of clarity in the legal system around healthcare in certain circumstances. The case arose when she was denied an abortion following an incomplete miscarriage due to a lack of clarity in the law which precluded abortion when a foetal heartbeat was still present unless there was an immediate threat to the mother's life, punishable by life imprisonment.

Savita and her husband had accepted the inevitable loss of their baby but she was refused treatment due to the unresolved legal situation arising from a high-profile case twenty years previously known as the 'X case'. This delay resulted in avoidable sepsis and Savita's death at the age of 31, which led to a public outcry and contributed to the referendum to repeal the 8th amendment of the constitution to allow abortion under limited circumstances, which passed in 2018.

These two cases, along with the recent outpouring of appreciation for the NHS for their selfless dedication during the Covid-19 pandemic, would suggest that the public would respond positively to being treated openly and fairly in this way, which is consistent with the aim of including the patient in their own care as opposed to the old-fashioned paternalistic model which has held sway for decades. With an aging population, we may have no option but to do this anyway in order to make more efficient use of the limited staff and finances available.

The 'Second Victim'

There has also been little consideration of the emotional impact of an adverse event on the staff member, the 'second victim'. A study published in *Current Oncology* surveyed surgeons and oncologists in a unit in Calgary, Canada who had been involved in incidents of unintended patient harm. Out of the 51 staff who responded, 55 per cent scored 24 or above on the 'Impact of Event Scale-Revised' assessment putting them in the category of post-traumatic stress. Many studies back up these findings yet support for these staff is thin on the ground.

The current system only adds to the stress experienced and referrals to accrediting bodies such as the GMC along with litigation can drag on for years, hanging over the staff member like a cloud. Figures are hard to come by, but it is generally accepted that this leads to burn-out, substance abuse and even self-harm or suicide. One study from the *Annals of Surgery* in 2010 surveyed almost 8,000 surgeons in the USA. where 8.9 per cent reported that they were concerned that they had made a major medical error in the previous three months and over 70 per cent felt personally responsible rather than blaming the system they worked in. This group showed a statistically significant correlation with a deterioration in mental health, burn-out and symptoms of depression. It is not clear which came first, however, the error or the burn-out.

The Financial Case

Using a Human Factors approach has been shown to intercept at least half of adverse events in several studies. Given the accepted figure of 10 per cent of admissions experiencing avoidable harm, this would lead to 750,000 fewer people suffering such harm in the UK alone, including around 250,000 avoiding serious harm. The number of deaths prevented in the UK alone could be anywhere between 5,500 and 25,000. The current compensation claim costs to the NHS due to avoidable harm is well over £2 billion annually (with total costs nearer £8 billion) so savings would amount to something in the region of £1 billion in claim costs and nearer £4 billion in total – about 5 per cent of the total hospital budget! All this while giving a much more efficient use of resources, increased patient satisfaction and more fulfilled staff, thus reducing staff turnover and sickness rates. We saw at the start of this chapter that communication issues accounted for 70 per cent of 'sentinel events' leading to errors, so addressing even that one area alone would have substantial benefits.

I hope I have provided a better understanding of error and its causes, and shown the enormous damage resulting from our failures in this area. I would like to finish our trip through error by focusing in more detail on what we can do about it.

Chapter 11

Tripwires and Safety Nets

Now that we have seen the enormous impact of error in a wide spectrum of industries, it's perhaps time to explore in more detail what we can do about it. Aviation is often held up as the Gold Standard for managing error and the application of Human Factors in organisations. The same principles are applicable to many industries so let's dig a little deeper into aviation's Safety Management System to see how much of it is relevant and transferable both to other industries and to our everyday lives.

Crew Resource Management is now in its sixth generation and has morphed from a relatively simple emphasis on training pilots to work better as teams into a full-blown Human Factors approach. CRM is now one of three supporting columns of aviation's overall Safety Management System, known as SMS. Take away any of the three and safety is at risk. So, what does our modern SMS in aviation look like? We must return to the Big Three.

JUST CULTURE

As discussed earlier, the main foundation for our safety system is the acceptance of a Just Culture. This isn't a woolly idea of 'how we do things around here' but is actually enshrined in our Operations Manuals as the over-arching ethos of the company and is accepted by airlines and regulators globally. It states that error is accepted as normal and inevitable in a high risk, Safety Critical industry so when it occurs we are expected to raise our hand and admit to it. If the staff member has made a genuine error, they will not be disciplined or dismissed if they are open and honest and participate fully in investigating how the event arose and what can be done to prevent its recurrence. It is not about apportioning blame and finding scapegoats, but rather finding why an actual or potential adverse event happened that compromised safety margins and how to make our system safer.

Importantly, while it involves forgiveness for genuine errors, it does not absolve gross negligence or deliberate sabotage. As mentioned earlier, it's not a 'Get Out of Jail Free' card.

SYSTEMS THINKING

In tandem with the Just Culture mindset, we apply Systems Thinking, that is, when something goes wrong, we approach the issue with the thought that the individual has carried out similar procedures many times before without incident so the underlying cause is more likely to have been a defect in the system.

Our Safety Office receives around twenty reports per day (and we are a relatively small airline). Reporting is made as quick and easy as possible with multiple options available. Reports can be submitted on our company supplied iPads with simple drop-down menus and text-boxes allowing free text to elaborate if necessary. We can also use our company internet portal or make a simple phone call. We can even call into the office which is on site. Lastly, a paper version can be submitted which gives the option of

Oops! Why Things Go Wrong

anonymity, although this is rarely felt necessary. All staff members are encouraged – indeed expected – to report any issue they feel could potentially impact on safety. The reports are often about small issues which staff feel could possibly have led to an incident. The office is headed by one of our most senior captains and aided by a diverse group including other pilots, ex-cabin crew members and non-flying staff in order to give as wide a view as possible. All reports are followed up with whatever sections of the company felt appropriate and often with the staff member involved, and either a change to systems or procedures is made (which is then promulgated quickly through our staff notification system) or else logged to spot patterns which can highlight underlying training issues or maybe slippage in the ways procedures are followed. This can then be addressed as necessary during recurrent training programmes.

The focus is very much on finding where the holes are in the system and how can we plug them. We use the reports as an opportunity to analyse our systems and procedures searching for tripwires which we had previously been unaware of and then try to engineer them out of the process, and ideally add one or more safety nets instead. The current management buzz-word for this is 'resilience'. We see this as the ability for a system to go wrong but still be safe by building in redundancy. This thinking informs everything from aircraft design to staff training and procedures. In short, we train staff to continually think:

'Where Can This Go Wrong?' and 'What's Plan B?'

CREW RESOURCE MANAGEMENT

Six Pillars of CRM

Crew Resource Management (CRM) has been split into six main pillars. A more recent update has reduced this to four but two of these are subdivided so totaling the original six essentially. The CRM pillars comprise:

1. Communication

2. Leadership

3. Stress and Workload Management

4. Decision Making

5. Situational Awareness

6. Threat and Error Management.

Research across many industries show that 70 per cent of adverse events are caused by communication issues so let's start there.

1. Communication

The word 'communication' is derived from the Latin, *communis,* meaning to make common. Communication is defined as 'the imparting or exchanging of information'. It 'makes common' the information or idea we wish to express – it creates a shared mental model. Communication involves three things: a transmitter, a message and a receiver. That should be fairly straight forward then. Evidence, however, shows that miscommunication is rife. As George Bernard Shaw famously noted, 'The single biggest problem in communication is the illusion it has taken place'.

So, where does it all go wrong?

Transmitters. Errors occur at all three stages and at multiple levels. Let's start with the transmitter. We need to be clear on what information we want to actually impart and not to distract from it with unnecessary details. Receivers have short attention spans – we need to cut straight to the relevant bit of the message before our target audience loses interest. As pilots, we receive very focused training on effective communication. Before we go into detail, let's have a quick look at how we as pilots are taught to communicate.

First, it helps to set the stage to make the receiver aware of what type of message is coming. For instance, in an emergency event in aviation, if we call our Senior Cabin Crew member into the cockpit and immediately tell them about what is happening when they were unaware anything was wrong, chances are they won't retain much of the information. This is due to the 'startle reflex' processed by the amygdala in the brain. To mitigate this, we set the scene by saying, 'We have had a major technical problem so I'm going to give you an emergency briefing. Let me know when you're ready.' This gives the receiver time to get into an emergency frame of mind and maybe even get a pen to write down the important points. We also use a standardised format which helps the transmitter structure the message and the receiver to be on the same wavelength to aid understanding. Ours is known as a NITS briefing.

- **Nature**: What is the problem, for example, a major hydraulic system failure.

- **Intention**: This is limited to whether we intend to perform an emergency landing or a normal one. This leads to one of two pre-determined procedures for the cabin crew.

- **Time**: How long until we are on the ground?

- **Special Instructions**: Will we be stopping on the runway? Do we expect any particular issues after we land?

Critically, we now ask the receiver to relay the message back to us to ensure that they have received all relevant information and understand its importance since we are relying on them to manage the cabin and passengers. This is known as 'closed loop communication' – the message is relayed back to us coming full circle so we are sure it has been transmitted, received and understood correctly. We use this same NITS format when communicating with Air Traffic Control, ground staff and so on which improves the effectiveness of our communication and reduces the chance of error.

The way the message is delivered affects understanding. Body language, gestures, facial expression, intonation etc all impact transmission. Professor Albert Mehrabian, an Iranian-born Emeritus Professor of Psychology at the University of California (UCLA), is best known for having coined the Mehrabian Rule on the relative importance of words, intonation and body language. As a result of several studies, Mehrabian and his colleagues produced the '7 per cent rule' stating that communication was determined in the following ratio – 7 per cent words used, 38 per cent audible cues such as tone of voice and 55 per cent visual cues such as facial expression. Unfortunately, the research studies themselves are an example of the propagation of error. Professor Mehrabian himself issued caveats to his research and it has been pointed out that the conclusions of the study have been stretched beyond the limits that the underlying science can support.

Message. The same logic applies to the message itself. It must be clear and concise and must cut straight to the chase. Messages can be ambiguous without the transmitter being aware of it, mainly because they are clear in their mind what they are saying and haven't spotted that the message could be interpreted differently. For instance, consider this conundrum.

A patient goes into hospital to have his right kidney removed. The surgeon inadvertently removes the left kidney. Which kidney is now left? The wrong one – which is the right one!

This shows the minefield that communication can turn into in, even with a seemingly simple message.

Visual messages can be misinterpreted due to the fact our brain skims information and often fills in the gaps with what it expects to see – it often doesn't do detail! Look at the passage below for instance.

> Aoccdrnig to a rscheearch at Cmabrigde Uinervtisy, it deosn't mttaer in what order the ltteers in a word are, the olny iprmoetnt thing is that the frist and lsat ltteer be in the rghit pclae. The rset can be a total mses and you can still raed it wouthit porbelm. This is bcuseae the human mind deos not raed ervey lteter by istlef, but the word as a wlohe.

I'm guessing that you read that without hesitation. Our brains take shortcuts which can be very useful but leave us error-prone as well, so we need to try to avoid the potential for misunderstanding. This can be achieved by having someone else assess the message and read back their understanding before it gets released as they may see it from a different viewpoint.

Misread messages can also have a positive outcome, though. Legend in the perfume world says assistants of Ernest Beaux misread his formula for perfume samples for Coco Chanel and added ten times the amount of aldehyde in error. When selecting from the huge array of samples, Chanel selected the one with the error, sample number 5, thus launching iconic scent, Chanel No. 5. There is possibly some truth in the story given that No. 5 was the first scent to use such a large quantity of aldehyde in its recipe.

Receivers. This consideration of different interpretations by different people brings us to the cognitive diversity approach that Matthew Syed discusses in his excellent book, *Rebel Ideas*. He cites examples such as the unusual collection of individuals assembled at Bletchley Park in Buckinghamshire to break the Enigma Code, an encryption system developed by the German Armed Forces during the Second World War using a machine with an electro-mechanical rotor mechanism which scrambled the letters. The team at Bletchley have been credited as having shortened the war by up to three years and potentially altered the final outcome. It was headed up by Alistair Denniston, who recruited Alan Turing, a Fellow at King's College, Cambridge and renowned as one of the greatest mathematicians of the twentieth century. Denniston was an early believer in Cognitive Diversity and widened his scope to include scholars of German, historians, philosophers and even J.R.R. Tolkein, then Professor of Anglo-Saxon in Oxford. Tolkein ultimately declined the offer and spent most of the war years writing *Lord of the Rings* instead!

Denniston cast his net even wider and in an unconventional direction. The *Daily Telegraph* newspaper published a crossword in each edition and there had been criticism that it had become too easy, in fact, that it could be completed in minutes. W.A.J. Garvin, the chairman of the gloriously named Eccentric Club, posted a £100 prize to be donated to charity if anyone could complete one of the paper's crosswords in less than twelve minutes. The editor of the *Telegraph* organised a competition for anyone who wanted to take up Garvin's challenge and the result was thirty people turning up to tackle the following day's crossword. Four of them completed it inside the time limit and a few weeks later several were recruited to be considered for the Bletchley Park group. This eclectic selection of individuals coalesced into a team who could analyse a message and each pick up a different connection depending on their background knowledge and interests, thus giving the best chance of making the connections that would link the code together. The group were immortalized in the Oscar winning 2014 movie *The Imitation Game* starring Benedict Cumberbatch.

As we can see, the three parts – transmitter, message, receiver – overlap and blend together but all parts must be taken into account for successful communication. For instance, some people are more receptive to visual cues than words. Some respond better to sound. It also goes without saying that the language must be one that the receiver can understand (and the transmitter is proficient in), an important consideration again in aviation where English has been designated as the universal language used by all crew. A restricted vocabulary is used and we make an effort to slow down and speak more clearly when working with staff whose first language isn't English – alas, these people can struggle with my strong Northern Ireland accent (as do some of my colleagues native to Dublin!). We spell items out using the phonetic alphabet and have standardised pronunciations, all designed to minimise error.

People can process information much more efficiently when presented as a graph rather than spreadsheets of numbers, although graphs can be manipulated to mislead by skewing axes, units etc. Keep Disraeli's warning about 'lies, damn lies and statistics' in mind when analysing data where analysis is often stretched to fit the desired outcome.

We are influenced by physical appearance. Tall, dark and handsome men are perceived as more desirable – not that I'm bitter or anything! It is known as the 'halo effect' – if people have certain attractive qualities then they probably have other qualities we value too. It goes the other way as well. The premise of the film *Legally Blond* is that Elle, the main protagonist, is young, blond and pretty so therefore must also be vacuous and not worth taking seriously. Her fondness for baby pink coloured items reinforces our prejudice. Elle's trajectory through the film ultimately shows how we underestimated her. The story resonates because deep down we know that this is often how we prejudge people. Again, awareness of the existence of this error is the first step in trying to address it.

The same is true of voice – a well-paced, deep, resonating voice carries more credibility than a rushed, breathless squeaky one. Perception is often more influential to our decisions than reality as our politicians unfortunately often prove to us after we have elected them!

Let's move on to the next pillar of our CRM framework.

2. Leadership

There are many definitions of leadership and many courses offering formal qualifications in the topic. My favourite definition is by Kevin Kruse, author of several books on the subject, which I feel succinctly ticks all the boxes.

> Leadership is a process of social influence, which maximises the efforts of others, towards the achievement of a goal.

To me, this covers all the essential parameters. It involves effecting change (hopefully improvement) by motivating other people. It makes no mention of seniority or rank – the most junior person in the room may be the one with a vision that other people respond to. They don't necessarily have a domineering, charismatic personality nor do they necessarily see themselves as a leader. They are also not necessarily a manager – that's a different role which they may or may not also hold.

Many leadership issues stem from only appealing to the logical forebrain – we understand the logic but it doesn't make us want to go the extra mile. It appeals to our IQ but not our EQ – our Emotional Intelligence. Daniel Goleman and others have written extensively on how our effectiveness is related as much, if not more, to our ability to get the co-operation of others in achieving goals. This Emotional Intelligence appeals to our primitive hind-brain and then connects to our higher level functions leading to a motivated, resilient group who believe in their leader.

The term Emotional Intelligence was first coined in a 1964 paper by Michael Beldoch but really came to prominence with Goleman's 1995 book *Emotional Intelligence: Why It Can Matter More Than IQ*. EQ has its critics and there is dispute over whether it constitutes 'intelligence'. From personal experience, though, I can think of many extremely 'intelligent' people with whom I have worked who did not inspire me to follow them. Conversely, I know others who can connect much more easily and in whom I would be much more comfortable putting my faith. These are the people who could influence me to do my best to help them achieve their goals, the definition of leadership which opened this section.

There are three main models of EQ, namely the Ability model, the Trait model and the Mixed model. Goleman's is probably the best known and is representative of the Mixed model. It considers five different areas:

- Self-awareness – understanding one's own emotions

- Self-regulation – controlling one's own emotions

- Social skill – managing relationships with others

- Empathy – understanding and considering the emotions of others

- Motivation – understanding what drives other people.

It's important though to remember that EQ is in addition to, not instead of, IQ and ability. We can all think of examples of leaders who can rally a crowd and channel that energy, but unless this is allied to a clear cause and the ability to deliver, it doesn't benefit either that group or the wider society. The mis-match between the two is the source of many errors so studying the balance between them is often quite illuminating.

Styles of Leadership. There are many types of leadership styles in academic and business literature but they are staging posts on a spectrum from total control to no control. Basically, they can be sub-divided as being based on Me, Us or You! Let's expand this to a model suggested by Bruna Martinuzzi, a columnist for *Business Trends and Insights,* working from maximum control to none.

Me:

- Autocratic – this can be summarised as 'Do as I say!' This leader believes they know more than the rest of the team (individually and collectively) and neither asks for nor accepts team input. This type of leader is becoming quite rare as people generally don't want to work under them.

- Authoritative – 'Follow me.' This leader is confident, has a clear view of where they are going and takes the time to explain it to their staff. They allow a little flexibility.

- Pace-setter – 'Do as I do!' This is appropriate as a short-term style in a motivated, self-directed group such as a start-up but in the long-term leads to stress and burn-out.

Us:

- Democratic – 'What do you think?' This is a participative style which shares information with the team and values their input. It promotes a cohesive, motivated team who have demonstrable input to decisions and therefore ownership of them.

You:

- Coaching – 'Consider this!' This style sees the team as a pool of talent to be nurtured and developed. They try to bring out the potential in all who work with them.

- Affiliative – 'People come first'. This is a style which sees the leader connect to the emotional needs of the team and tries to draw out their best while directing them towards the ultimate goal. It creates a harmonious group but requires capable, motivated staff.

- Laissez-faire – 'Whatever you're having yourself!' This is the extreme version of 'hands-off' leadership. It basically gives people the facilities and tools they need and then sits back and lets them get on with it. It can work in a creative environment and allows ideas to develop which weren't even under consideration, and can lead to products or services which hadn't even been dreamt of at the start. The risk is that the team can career off the tracks into no-control and achieve nothing.

The best leaders vary between the styles at different times depending on the development stage of the business or project and the environment they find themselves in. As an airline captain, I live mostly in the Democratic or Coaching area of the spectrum but the initial response to an urgent situation drives me quickly into the Autocratic mode to ensure the safety of the aircraft, crew and passengers, then quickly cycling through the Authoritative and Pace-setting stages back into the Democratic style to make best use of the resources available to resolve the situation. The Affiliative and Laissez-faire styles don't really fit well while in flight since we have a fairly well-defined goal which doesn't benefit much from the creativity these styles favour. We also have a finite amount of fuel to get us safely to our destination and back on the ground which limits the time available for test driving ideas. If we want to encourage creativity and try novel ways of solving problems, we tend to test it in the simulator first. Other than that, we stick to our Standard Operating Procedures (SOPs) of which more later.

3. *Stress and Workload Management*

Stress gets a bad rap. Like many things, stress exists on a spectrum but the general perception is only of the extreme where excessive or prolonged stress leads to physical or psychological damage. There is no one definition, but I think the most useful way of thinking of stress is as:

> Your body's way of responding to any demand or threat.

We need some level of stress to function just as a tyre needs to be inflated to a certain pressure or else it won't function – too little and it doesn't roll safely, too much and it bursts. Stress stimulates you to stay alert, say during a presentation. The Yerkes-Dodson graph, developed by two psychologists in 1908, is often used to illustrate this idea. As stress increases, so does our performance until we reach an optimum level. Beyond this, our performance starts to deteriorate as the 'fight or flight response' becomes excessive and dulls our judgment. The original graph showed that simple tasks didn't suffer from this overload effect but more complex ones did. This is often omitted in current interpretations of the graph as shown on the following page.

Stress can be categorized in various ways, reflecting our perception of it – what stresses me might not even register with you.

- **Hypostress**: This is a state of not being stimulated or stressed enough and leads to constant boredom. This person is restless, uninspired and certainly not performing anywhere near their optimum level.

- **Eustress**: A short burst of stress as in the 'fight or flight response'. It helps a person focus, increasing mental acuity and physical ability to react by increasing heart rate, blood flow to peripheral muscles and adrenaline release. After the threat has passed, the body reverts to a more normal level.

- **Hyperstress**: This is excessive stress when a person is forced to perform beyond what they perceive to be their limit. This 'stressed out' feeling is common in our

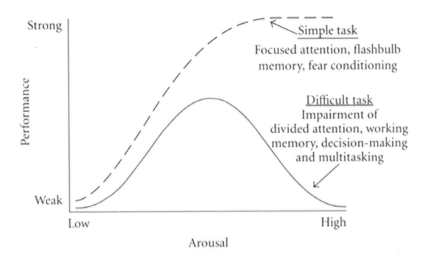

Original Yerkes-Dodson graph including hyperarousal

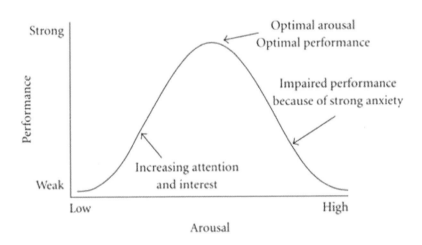

Commonly used variation known as the Hebbian version

twenty-first century world due to high workloads and tight deadlines. Because they are operating near (or a little beyond) capacity, the smallest extra stressor can tip the balance into an emotional outburst. It is managed ideally by reducing the workload or by better training to enable the person to cope with this level of activity.

- **Distress**: Distress is a negative stressor caused by changes in a person's lifestyle or circumstances, for example, a bereavement, job loss or illness, which lowers an individual's ability to deal with pressure.

- **Acute stress**: This is similar to eustress and prepares us for 'fight or flight' before subsiding after a short time when the threat passes.

- **Chronic stress**: This is stress which persists for a long time and is detrimental to physical and mental health, even contributing to depression. Acute can superimpose on chronic and tip the balance into overload.

Stressors can be divided into three types, namely:

- **Physical**: Environmental factors such as temperature, noise, oxygen levels and physical workload.

- **Physiological**: Tiredness or fatigue, diet, dehydration, fitness levels and so on.

- **Emotional**: Both in our relationships with our work colleagues (interpersonal issues, professional development issues) and with our spouse, children etc. and the events affecting their lives. Major life events such as births, deaths and marriages/divorces all have significant effects.

We can get so used to being stressed that we can end up considering it as a 'normal' state. Prolonged stress leads to cognitive, emotional, physical and social effects and being alert for these can give us early warning before our health crashes. Different things stress different people and to different extents. The self-awareness we discussed whilst considering emotional intelligence is of critical importance in being able to recognise stress in ourselves and others and to intervene to manage it. It goes without saying that too little or too much stress are both risk factors for error. We need to find the sweet-spot for optimum performance and to know how long we can realistically maintain this. Many factors influence our ability to manage stress including our attitude and general outlook, our sense of control over a situation, our expectations and preparation for the situation, our support network or colleagues as well as our appreciation for and ability to manage our emotions.

Aviation has designed a system which keeps pilots at an appropriate place on the Yerkes-Dodson curve. During take-off, for instance, we need to be well to the right side of the graph but still to the left of the peak so we are alert and ready to intervene quickly should anything go wrong, such as an engine failure at a critical moment, but still with some spare capacity to absorb this extra stressor without deterioration of performance. The most obvious way this is achieved is through training. We spend two days in the simulator twice per year carrying out takeoffs with engine failures, fires and so on so we are practised in handling them. This gives us the confidence that we can handle it should it happen for real. We also brief such scenarios at the start of each day so the actions are fresh in our minds, all of which mitigates the stress in the event of an emergency. We are also trained in Standard Operating Procedures (SOPs), which are routine behaviours we can default into almost automatically, freeing up cognitive capacity to deal with unusual aspects of the emergency (because the real world has a habit of not matching up exactly with what we had expected!).

Aviation's equivalent of 'airway, breathing, circulation' is 'aviate, navigate, communicate'.

Our initial goals are to make sure the plane is in a position to physically fly, so we focus on what pitch the nose is at, what power setting we have the engines at and so on. Next we make sure that we are heading somewhere safe and not towards a mountain and once we have all that under control, we talk to Air Traffic Control (ATC) to tell them what our problem is and what we would like them to do to help us! As Airbus pilots, we then have a standardised format of working through issues designed by Airbus and known as the Airbus Golden Rules. The 'aviate, navigate, communicate' is followed by three further assessments. Select the appropriate level of automation – use the autopilot or autothrust to free up cognitive capacity but not if they appear to be part of the underlying problem. Next assess the Flight Mode Annunciator section of our Flight Display to understand exactly what modes are available, and finally, if the aeroplane is not behaving as you would expect, intervene and fly it manually. This first phase ensures our safety regardless of what has actually failed.

We then prepare to move to the next phase of actually dealing with the problem clarifying both who will fly the aeroplane and speak to ATC. We confirm what the electronic notification system is telling us has failed and cross-check this against the parameters of the affected area to see if they make sense. The next relevant steps will be displayed on our upper Electronic Centralised Aircraft Monitoring

(ECAM) screen but these have sometimes been superseded by a modified procedure due to a technical change or glitch which has become apparent to an operator. This is transmitted to all affected airlines by a process known as an Operational Engineering Bulletin (OEB) which is effective until a permanent solution is found. We therefore check if there are any relevant OEBs in a physical manual known as our Quick Reference Handbook, a copy of which sits in the storage area beside each pilot, before launching into what would otherwise be an incorrect procedure. We then decide whether there is any urgency in dealing with the problem, or do we have more pressing issues to deal with first?

When ready, we then work through the electronic checklist displayed on the screen and end up at the Status page which will tell us what equipment we no longer have available. Before addressing this, we perform any outstanding normal checklists which wouldn't be addressed due to the failure we have encountered and try to reset any computers which have tripped out which may resolve part or all of the problem. Lastly, by returning to the Status page, we decide whether we can continue the flight, return to our departure airport or divert to an alternative airport to sort out the problem. A diversion increases the workload substantially and leads into another standard division of labour amongst the crew, but I think the gist of our approach at this stage is clear.

Although this sounds long-winded and convoluted, it actually flows quite quickly and because we have a standardised workload structure, it frees up capacity to manage our stress levels allowing us to make the best possible decisions. It keeps us in the optimum part of the Yerkes-Dodson curve to manage performance and minimise the risk of error. Having two of us also helps manage error by having a second pair of eyes and ears with perhaps a different viewpoint on what is happening. A good captain will encourage input from any relevant crew member, ATC, ground personnel (for example, the Fire Chief outside the aeroplane) and even the passengers who may see things outside our view which can be relayed to us by the cabin crew. All this is based on avoiding errors to achieve the best possible outcome, which is generally accepted as everyone getting home safely without us having wrecked the plane!

Once all this has been achieved, our inbuilt paranoia dictates that we go back to the start of the process and run through it again to check if what we have done is working and whether there is a better option that we missed first time. At all times, our focus is on 'have we got this wrong' and 'what else is likely to go wrong?' We assume error at all times.

These SOPs help spread the workload out so that we have maximum capacity available at critical times, that is, during take-off and landing when, statistically, the flight is at highest risk. A study by Boeing showed that 13 per cent of fatal accidents occurred during take-off and initial climb-out, and 48 per cent occurred during final approach and landing even though this only accounted for around 4 per cent of the flight time. To mitigate this, aviation applies a 'sterile cockpit' policy when below 10,000 feet from the ground. Pilots avoid any non-essential conversation in this phase and cabin crew are trained not to contact the flight deck unless the issue is urgent. We also try to get administrative work and briefings done in the relatively quiet cruise section of the flight.

The other main supports in workload management are checklists. These come in various formats and styles but our normal checklist covering all sections of the flight from switching everything on at the start of the day to switching it off at the end is contained on one side of a single, laminated A4 sheet which lives in the cockpit and doesn't get removed from it. Routine checklists such as the Approach check are in a 'challenge and response' format. This means that I have already set the plane up as necessary for the expected approach and the check simply involves the non-flying pilot reading the short challenges from the checklist and the flying pilot confirming aloud that each step has been completed and physically checking the switch, computer and so on. If we get interrupted during a check, for example by an ATC call, we generally start the check over again to avoid the error of missing a line.

In the event of an emergency or something failing on the aircraft, there are a small number of 'memory items', procedures, that we need to be able to carry out from memory due to insufficient time to use a checklist. For instance, if our brakes are failing on landing that is not the time to go rooting through a manual to find out what to do! Other non-standard checks are generally in a 'read and do' format – the non-flying pilot reads out each step, then the flying pilot actions it before moving to the next step. It's important, though, not to just follow these blindly without first thinking, 'is this appropriate for the situation I currently find myself in?'

Checklists are beginning to be used in healthcare. In 2009, the World Health Organisation (WHO) Surgical Safety Checklist became mandatory in the UK's National Health Service. Experience has been a little more mixed than in aviation, partly due to it being framed as further bureaucracy imposed by management (staff must sign the checklist and file it with the patient's notes, which is of benefit to no one other than the patient's legal representatives in a subsequent inquiry), in contrast to the aviation approach where the airline has no way of confirming whether the checklist was used or not. The difference is that, in aviation, we see the checklist as a safety tool to back us up in the management of error; it is there to protect us, not create unnecessary paperwork.

4. Decision-making

Decision-making is the process of selecting between two or more options.

This should be quite straight forward. We weigh up the information available and use our huge pre-frontal cortex to come to a rational, reasoned decision, no? That's what we would like to think happens but the reality, like many things in life, is a little messier. Emotions can trump rational thought and outweigh any amount of evidence. Our brain uses various shortcuts which may have served us well in our caveman iteration, but can let us down spectacularly in our modern world leaving us wide open to often costly errors.

Our mistaken view of our rationality can be traced as far back as Plato and the Ancient Greeks who saw us as rational creatures. This rationality is what defined us as humans and formed the foundations of our view of ourselves. Unfortunately, it is incorrect. It's not how our brain functions. The reptilian brain is connected to all areas of the brain by spindle neurons so that emotional responses are shared liberally and affect decisions whether we are aware of them or not.

Our brains can store huge amounts of memories which we can refer to when making decisions, but we can only handle around seven pieces of data at once. Strong emotional responses can reduce the number further. In the past, seven items was generally enough to make reasonable decisions but in our fast moving, data-driven world, seven is quite limiting. The brain tries to compensate for this by 'chunking', combining several items together, effectively making each block a single item. An example of this is how we quote phone numbers. We can't remember nine digits accurately but we can recall three blocks of three fairly easily.

When confronted with a problem, our reptilian brain often spits out a 'gut reaction' which emphasises its primitive connections rather than the higher level cortex. Our fore-brain then processes the information, accessing memories, previous failures and so on in order to come up with a response. It is easily misled, however, a trait we need to be aware of when we work in Safety Critical industries. It can be 'primed' by background information, a technique often adopted by charities, or 'framed', which involves planting ideas such as '£10 will feed a family for a day, £20 will pay for school books for a pupil' allowing us to picture how our donation would be used.

This simple pattern of a primitive response, tempered by the higher level brain assessment before making and implementing a decision, generally works pretty well. It is subject, however, to Human Factors. The acronym HALT is useful in assessing what can influence the brain's ability to process information. If we are Hungry, Angry, Late (or Lonely) or Tired, the higher brain function deteriorates and is less able to override our baser, emotional decisions making us more impulsive, cranky and, most importantly, error-prone. An awareness of this allows us to try to intercept these errors either by correcting the cause or by at least being vigilant.

An excess of information can also impair decision making. If we are presented with more than the seven items our brain can process, we can get so overloaded that we can no longer see the wood for the trees. Breaking a problem down to a small number of competing pieces of information can enhance the decision-making process.

Another major source of error however is confirmation bias where we seek out the bits of information which justify the answer we would like to be true whilst disregarding conflicting information. Our 'gut reaction' often gnaws away at us in this scenario prompting us to reconsider. This reminds us again of Matthew Syed's *Rebel Ideas*. By seeking out contradictory ideas, we get a broader view of an issue and are more likely to make good decisions as we saw in the Enigma Code team.

In aviation, one of the most discomfiting experiences is a Low Visibility Approach where we descend through cloud and land on a runway, potentially without actually seeing it until we are slowing down on the centre line (hopefully). We have a display on our Navigation Display screen with a representation of the runway on it, but what if it's wrong? That means we might actually be offset a few hundred feet to the side which will see us land on the airport terminal – not a good result! Rather than accept our information as definitely correct, we seek out contradictory evidence. For example, what does the co-pilot's screen show since it is fed by a different computer? But what if they're both wrong, possibly due to an erroneous database update by the mapping company? We can also cross reference it with the old-style radio beacons – what are our instruments telling us about their location and is this consistent with where we know them to be from either experience or our charts? Our Traffic Collision Avoidance System (TCAS) shows us where other traffic is – if it is lined up in a straight line ahead and behind us pointing at the runway, that's further reassurance. ATC also follow us on their radar screen – if they haven't commented on us being off track then we have a further source of confirmation. With these five independent sources all confirming the same result we can feel fairly reassured that we're heading towards a runway! This is at odds with our natural tendency to skim information, trading attention to detail for an overview of a situation which can lead to missing some very obvious things.

The famous 'door study' carried out in 1998 in Cornell University by psychologists Daniel Simons and Daniel Levin, had a new student, a 'stranger', stop a local student on campus to ask for directions. While they talk, two construction workers rudely push between them carrying a door – the 'stranger' trades places with one of the workmen who then continues the conversation with the student as if nothing had happened. Only 7 out of the 15 studied noticed that they were now speaking to a different person despite the interruption lasting only around a second! A follow-up study used two construction workers in hard hats (a 'foreign' group as opposed to students like them). Now only 4 out of 12 noticed the swap. They simply skimmed the information – the stranger was a 'construction worker' before and after so no change was noticed.

A different but no less dangerous bias is our brain's tendency to quit. If we don't see something we are looking for fairly quickly, our brain tunes out and can't see it when it does show up. This was shown by the 'Beer in the Refrigerator' study by Jeremy Wolfe, Professor of Ophthalmology at Harvard Medical School. A follow-up asked people to spot a tool (a hammer or a wrench) in photos which was cluttered with many distractors. When the tool was present 50 per cent of the time, their score rate was an impressive 93 per cent. When it was only present 1 per cent of the time, however, their score-rate plummeted to 70 per cent – they simply couldn't see it because their brain tuned out. From an evolutionary perspective, this makes sense. If our caveman ancestors watched intently for a rabbit to pass so they could eat but none do, their brains stop burning energy and tune out so that when a solitary rabbit does finally pass, it is essentially invisible.

Where this becomes an issue in our modern world is for workers such as a radiologist sitting in a darkened room looking through one hundred mammograms for an early stage breast tumour. If the incidence is too low (often around 0.3 per cent of scans have a tumour), it is quite possible to then miss the one that is there – studies have shown up to 30 per cent can be missed. To mitigate this error, many scans are now read separately by three independent assessors to protect against this error. A similar type study of airport security staff in the USA showed similarly concerning results. A 2006 study in Chicago's O'Hare Airport involving undercover TSA security officials testing security procedures by bringing bomb making material and explosives through scanners in their hand luggage found 60 per cent were missed. Similarly, 25 per cent of guns were missed in Newark in 2002 in another study. Human Factors are incorporated in by having 'positive' results electronically superimposed to keep staff attention levels high.

Crew Resource Management often uses decision-making frameworks to help with the process. The one which my airline used until recently was deceptively simple – the Six A's.

- **Aware**. Become aware that a problem or issue exists – often by a Master Caution light illuminating along with an auditory warning. A light and a bing in other words!

- **Assign**. Make sure one of the two pilots is actually going to look after flying the airplane to avoid both getting so focused on the issue that we inadvertently create a much bigger one.

- **Assess**. Read what the warning is telling us and study the relevant systems to work out what has actually happened and what other effects it may have.

- **Agree**. Ask for your colleague's opinion on what they see going on and what they think of your assessment of what needs to happen next.

- **Act**. Carry out whatever procedure the two of you have decided on.

- **Assess again**. Go back to the start and decide whether your input has solved the problem or whether you have misinterpreted it and need to start again.

Other airlines have similar frameworks such as DODAR (Diagnose, Options, Decide, Act, Review) or GRADE (Gather info, Review, Assess, Decide, Execute) amongst others. This structured approach gives consistency to the decision-making process because we realise its crucial role in flight safety, and widens out our Situational Awareness to reduce the risk of us missing important information and frees up capacity to explore several options rather than just the first one we think of. We also focus on the fact that there is rarely only one correct answer. The most important part of the system however is the Review part. We assume error and go looking for it even after we have made our decision. We are taught to look out for the traps which will disguise errors such as confirmation bias, reading the evidence in such a way as to see what we want to see. These are related to the three heuristics (from the Greek meaning 'to discover', using knowledge we have previously discovered whilst making decisions) that a Nobel Laureate, Daniel Kahneman, and Amos Tversky studied in the early 1980s in Jerusalem. These were availability, representativeness and anchoring.

Availability. This is making a judgment by referring to available examples from our experience. For instance, if a child arrives in the Emergency Department during flu season with a headache, temperature and shivers and the five previous patients have been children diagnosed with the flu, we are at risk of dismissing this one as the same without adequately assessing the alternatives such as bacterial meningitis. The first diagnosis is easily 'available' in our mind so is selected first.

Representativeness. This is basically stereotyping. When we ask people to pick out the rugby player in a lineup, they would rarely pick out Ireland's retired scrum half Peter Stringer who at 73 kilograms wouldn't fit everyone's stereotype of a rugby player. The average weight of an England player in the 2019 Six Nations, on the other hand, was 105 kilograms so this is what we presume the average player should look like.

Anchoring. This involves the first piece of information we get becoming the anchor around which subsequent decisions are made. For instance, when buying a second hand car we may do some research that tells us the average price for the car we are considering is £20,000. If we find one at £18,000 we quickly decide this is a good deal, whereas a little more searching might find an alternative at £17,000. We have anchored our definition of value on our initial price target.

There are now many more heuristics than the original three Kahneman and Tversky came up with, but all are examples of how our brains don't think quite as rationally as we'd like to believe. Armed with this awareness, we can avoid making common errors in our decision-making which in industries such as aviation and healthcare can have major consequences.

It's critically important that changing one's mind is not seen as weakness or a negative trait. On the contrary, having the courage to say 'I was wrong – let's reverse that and try a different approach' is the sign of someone with the confidence and self-belief to understand that error is an inevitable step along the way in most things we do. This ability to admit mistakes generally increases the loyalty of staff who accept that life doesn't always travel in one direction, and are much more understanding than they would be watching someone continue on a path which the dogs in the street can see isn't working. Feel free to insert your own example here . . .

5. Situational Awareness

Situational Awareness is knowing what is going on around you and therefore being able to predict what's likely to happen next. It involves building a Mental Model of what is happening and where we fit in to it. It is also important to enquire how a colleague sees the situation so that you can correct any errors and ensure you have a Shared Mental Model to work from.

This awareness can be thought of as like the layers of an onion. The deepest layer is you! How are you feeling? Physically, are you rested, fed, hydrated? Emotionally, are you calm, not overly stressed, content with your personal and professional relationships? All these issues will affect how you interpret what's happening and affect how likely you are to make a mistake – remember HALT (Hungry, Angry, Late or Tired)?

The next layer out is your immediate environment. Is it too hot, too cold, too noisy, too bright, not bright enough or generally not a comfortable place to live or work? The next layer is the people and equipment you immediately interact with, remembering of course that they have their own version of the first two layers as well. In a hospital, this will be the other staff members and ward, out-patient or theatre facilities. In aviation, it is the other pilot, cabin crew, passengers and the plane, including any failures which have occurred.

A further layer takes us into the corporate environment in which we are working. This encompasses labour relations, our interactions with management and whether we respect (and feel respected by) them. The final layer takes us into the general world we live in beyond our homes and workplace. Again, the Covid-19 pandemic of 2020 gives us an obvious example of how national and global events impact our situation and influence our decisions.

All of these layers, and the interaction with other people who all have their own layers which overlap partially with yours, make for a complex, dynamic environment when superimposed on to high risk industries like healthcare and aviation. Awareness that these layers exist is a good start at least.

So, how do we build up this Situational Awareness? We use our senses.

Sight accounts for the majority of the information we gather, totaling about 75 per cent of the input, with hearing contributing around 13 per cent. Touch adds around 6 per cent with smell and taste coming in last at 3 per cent each. These obviously vary with our role in life – a chef will use their taste and smell much more than say a healthcare worker.

The top three allow us to determine our orientation in space and maintain it. Our visual system contributes most and we will generally default to it in the event of a conflict of information (not always successfully as our visual illusions in the earlier chapter on neurophysiology showed). It accounts for 90 per cent of our physical position information. Visual illusions such as a wider than normal runway leading us to believe we are too low (because the 'picture' looks different), or auto-kinetic illusions where a dim light appears to move if stared at, are common but an awareness of the risk goes a long way to reducing the possibility of an error due to it.

It is assisted by the vestibular system in the ear which supplies information to the brain on orientation and movement such as turning. This can also give a bum steer, for example when we start a slow turn in a plane, the fluid in the ear is slightly behind the semi-circular canals which contain it and signals movement. If the turn is prolonged, however, the brain edits out this 'steady state' information (our brains get bored very quickly) so that when the turn eventually stops, the brain can interpret this as a turn in the other direction due to the inertia of the fluid continuing after the head has stopped turning. We use our visual input to override this feeling by referring to the horizon (or artificial horizon if we are flying on instruments such as when in clouds). Without this extra reference, we tend to steadily increase the bank of the turn whilst thinking we are maintaining the original bank angle which will eventually have a fairly significant effect on the plane's ability to stay airborne due to the physical laws of aerodynamics.

The somato-sensory system which takes nerve signals from our muscles and joints to the brain also contribute to our balance – a system known as proprioception. Sportsmen and women who have ankle injuries will often find difficulty in staying upright if they close their eyes as the nerves carrying the information have been disrupted and they need a visual input instead. This is why these athletes are given exercises to build this balance system back up to enhance long-term poise and reduce the risk of further injury. G-forces in pilots and racing drivers also work from this system.

These various sources of information feed into our memory to draw on previous knowledge before making a decision on our 'situation'. Our ultra-short sensory memory lasts for a few seconds before the information is either processed or lost. New information dislodges previous information due to the capacity issue. Long-term memory appears to be unlimited and permanent. It stores two types of data – semantic memory which is the general knowledge we accumulate, and episodic memory which stores specific experiences in our lives. The issue with it is not the storage but the retrieval of information. It appears that recall from long-term memory is actually more of a reconstruction than an exact replay. Our memories change without us being aware, and two people's memory of the same event can be very different. This can lead to errors with significant repercussions as we saw in our look at the criminal justice system.

'Flashbulb memory' is a specific type of episodic memory when a highly significant event gets recalled along with our own circumstances when we heard the news – the 'I remember exactly where I was when I heard JFK had been shot' effect. My own most memorable 'flashbulb memory' was the death of Princess Diana in 1997. I was the junior cardiac surgeon on call in the Royal Victoria Hospital in Belfast. After a rare few hours of undisturbed sleep, I bumped into a staff member in our Intensive Care Unit whose first words were, 'Did you hear, Niall? Diana's died!' My immediate reaction was to frantically look around the unit trying to remember which bed Diana had been in and saying, 'But why did nobody call me?' Then she added, 'Princess Diana – she died in a car crash in Paris last night.'

We absorb the information we need through attention. There is sensory input coming at us all the time, more than we can possibly process, so we filter out the majority whilst trying to capture the bits that are important to us. Our attention acts as this filter. It operates as a single channel processor – it can only handle one signal at a time. The multi-tasking function we think we are using is actually a rapid switching from one information stream to another with inevitable inefficiencies and errors inherent.

Information overload is a constant risk in areas such as an Intensive Care Unit or on a modern flight deck. This is a challenge for designers who need to consider Human

Factors while deciding how much information to present and in what format. There is no correct answer, but poor design is a significant handicap to users leading to an increased risk of errors and to poorer outcomes for patients or passengers.

Divided Attention. Staff may try to make the most of the equipment available in a number of ways. In aviation, we have already looked at Workload Management – we often delegate a specific role (such as flying the aircraft) so as to free up extra attentive capacity to assess an issue. One of the first things pilots are taught is to 'scan'. Our instruments are laid out focusing on a Primary Flight Display which contains an artificial horizon giving us a visual indication of the aircraft's position relative to the horizon, indicating whether we are banked to the side, pitched up or down and the rate at which it is changing. Further information such as speed is displayed usually to the left of this whilst altitude and rate of climb/descent are displayed to the right. A compass showing the bearing we are maintaining is below this display whilst engine indications such as power settings are displayed on an adjacent screen. The artificial horizon is our most important instrument so our scan works in a T-shaped format from it to the speed, back to the horizon then across to altitude information before going back to the horizon en-route down to the compass then back to the horizon. This is combined with glances across to the power settings since all these will interact with each other giving a flight path – the combination of pitch and power.

When flying manually such as on approach to landing we constantly tweak each setting which then has knock-on effects to other settings which need to be fine-tuned accordingly in a continuous dance until we're back on the ground.

Looking out the window gets brought in to the scan with our judgment on final touchdown based largely on what we see outside rather than using instruments. A gradual transition ensures this is done safely. Correct management of this divided attention is critical to safety.

ICU nurses scan monitors similarly, examining pulse rate, arterial pressure, venous pressure, oxygen saturation and so on, in conjunction with drug infusion pumps supplying medications which modify arterial tension, heart contractility etc. which all interact to affect the parameters making their job quite similar to flying an approach. Alarms alert them when parameters are drifting outside pre-determined limits (although the readings themselves can be erroneous making interpretation even more complex) prompting interventions such as changing infusion rates. In aviation, when parameters are not going to be recoverable in a timely manner, we perform a 'go around' by applying full power and discontinuing the approach by climbing away and coming back around for another go. In cardiac surgery, the equivalent when a patient deteriorated rapidly in ICU was to re-open their chest immediately using the pre-prepared thoracotomy tray or, if time permitted, return them to theatre for a more controlled re-opening.

Selective Attention. This is when we screen out inputs to focus on one which most interests us. Pilots listen to radio calls in the background but focus when they hear their call sign as this is an instruction specifically for them. We can focus on extraneous information and miss the one meant for us when selective attention strays into distraction.

Focused Attention. This is selective attention to the point of blocking out all other input. We become fixated on one input. This is rarely positive but can be especially dangerous when we fail to notice other parameters deteriorating due to our determination to address the one we are focused on. An unfortunate example of this is the case in 2005 of Elaine Bromiley, the young mother who was being prepared for routine, low risk surgery but suffered hypoxic brain damage and died after two consultant anaesthetists failed to successfully intubate her.

In the stress of the incident, the two developed 'tunnel vision' and were barely aware of what was happening outside their narrow focus. They lost awareness of how long Elaine had been without oxygen and unaware of the suggestions from the nurses of the option of emergency tracheotomy to remedy the situation. Elaine's husband, Martin, was an airline pilot and after the event assumed that the case would be investigated to find out what could be learned, but was shocked to hear that no follow-up was planned. Martin selflessly turned his wife's death into a turning point in UK healthcare by producing a well-known video, 'Just a Routine Operation', which is now part of the Patient Safety learning programme. Martin also set up the Clinical Human Factors Group in 2007 to promote learning and good practice and was awarded an OBE in 2016 in recognition of his work to embed a Human Factors approach in healthcare.

Perception. Perception is the next step in the process of Situational Awareness. The input now registers rather than simply 'going straight out the other ear'. Our perception can become our Mental Model if it fits what we expect to experience, but this leaves us open to error due to illusions. What we see is not necessarily what we are getting! We are prey to the various biases, such as confirmation bias (only registering the information that suits us) or availability bias (picking the first matching conclusion in our head) which if not counteracted by being open to other possible solutions will lead us into making errors.

Perception allows us to build our Mental Model of a situation as it is now and as it is likely to become and make the appropriate decisions – it helps us tell the future and manipulate that future into one that is positive. Good communication both in and out allows us to gather information, share it, compare our understanding of it with others and feed it into our decision-making process. Workload management using Standard Operating Procedures and checklists can aid this process. We can see now that far from being unrelated components, our CRM pillars are all actually closely linked and work in unison giving the best possible outcome. They aren't a substitute for good system design but they can be thought of as personal protective equipment (PPE) for when the system is inadequate or breaks down. They bring a Human Factors approach to the workplace in order to avoid, trap or mitigate error, depending on how early in its evolution the error is intercepted.

Sixth Generation CRM added one final pillar, namely:

6. Threat and Error Management

Threat and Error Management (TEM) was added following collaboration by the University of Texas Human Factors Research Project and Delta Airlines in 1996 on their Line Operations Safety Audit (LOSA) programme, which assessed flights in a non-jeopardy basis from the jump-seat in the cockpit. It involves constantly assessing a situation for where the potential errors are and how best to deal with them. As well as being a stand-alone concept, it can also be applied to each of the other CRM pillars to strengthen them and expose any weak points. Some organisations have tried to substitute TEM training for CRM training, but it's generally accepted as being insufficient on its own. It can, however, be used to summarise the whole concept of CRM and Human Factors into:

'Where Can This Go Wrong?' and 'What's Plan B?'

The aim then is to avoid the aircraft reaching the Unanticipated Adverse State (UAS) such as not being appropriately configured for landing, an unstable approach or, at worst, an accident.

Threats are events or conditions beyond your control which can compromise safety. These are considered in three groups, anticipated, unanticipated and latent.

Anticipated. In aviation, this would include issues such as weather conditions, congested airspace, language issues at the destination airport and so on. Healthcare examples could include a complicated and complex operation, previous surgery leading to scarring and difficult dissection, multiple co-morbidities, increased risk of bleeding and so on.

Unanticipated. This could include aircraft malfunction, an emergency situation involving another aircraft blocking the runway or a passenger becoming critically ill. In healthcare, this could be an anaphylactic reaction, sudden arrhythmia or failure of video equipment during a laparoscopic case. We try to think of as many of these as we can and brief them with the team to push them into the 'anticipated' threats section.

Latent. These are underlying threats that no one is aware of yet. These would include organisational weaknesses, poor rostering which doesn't account for long-term fatigue, sub-standard personal protective equipment (PPE) for healthcare workers, failure to plan for major adverse events and so on.

Errors are failures in responding to threats. As before, they can be classified as mistakes (response is inappropriate or simply wrong), a slip (correct response but failure in carrying it out correctly) or a lapse (failure to respond at all). Since TEM is all about Error Management, there is a three-stage intervention, namely Avoid, Trap, Mitigate.

Avoid. The principle is to look ahead to try to intercept the error before it happens at all. Briefings and Checklists from our Workload Management section help here.

Trap. The error has already occurred but we trap it before any adverse state can develop. A checklist can address this as in our Before Take-off Check allowing us to spot that the flaps haven't been set correctly before we reach the runway and therefore have time to correct the issue.

Mitigate. The error has happened and we don't have time to correct it but we can still avoid an adverse outcome. For instance, our final check shows that we have forgotten to lower the landing gear and we are now too close to landing to do it safely. We mitigate this by 'going around', applying full power and climbing away before coming back around for a second approach.

At all times we assume the possibility of error and have various CRM tools such as Standard Operating Procedures to try to anticipate them and, critically, a heightened expectation so we are constantly on the look-out for what we may have missed.

These CRM and Error Management principles have been honed through bitter experience in aviation but are equally applicable to all Safety Critical industries with a little tweaking to keep them relevant for each specific environment. They can't simply be 'transplanted' as aviation and, for instance, healthcare are two very different industries, but their underlying DNA is close enough that the approach can be 'genetically engineered' in. There are now quite a few healthcare leaders who are doing just this – taking the learnings from aviation and tailoring them for their own environment and applying a Human Factors approach to healthcare to reduce the number of adverse events. Hopefully, this will gather momentum and transform healthcare as it did aviation and other Safety Critical industries.

So, now what?

We have reached the conclusion of our trip through the sometimes amusing, occasionally devastating but, I think we can all agree now, omnipresent guest at our table – error!

We have considered its effect on our aviation sector, on sport, our emergency services, policing, science, education, the finance sector, on politics and in its possibly most dangerous incarnation so far – in social media where it has become a tool capable of destabilising the world order.

We have looked at how we can try to deal with it and have provided a toolkit which will hopefully equip you to address error and its management in whatever setting you find yourself. I would like to finish, however, back where my career started and where, in my opinion, Error Management is still most needed, in healthcare.

We have reports going back decades outlining how healthcare has lacked a Human Factors approach yet, despite some pockets of great work, there has been little systemic change and the problems continue unabated. There is, however, an opportunity to finally address this omission on a global level which could transform our approach to patient safety courtesy of the World Health Organisation.

THE WHO'S GLOBAL PATIENT SAFETY STRATEGY

In May 2021 the 74th World Health Assembly adopted the Global Action Plan on Patient Safety 2021-2030 (GAPPS). It sets out the admirably simple goal of:

> Achieve the maximum possible reduction in avoidable harm due to unsafe health care globally.

It aims to combine the two schools of Safety 1 (focusing on what went wrong and why) as well as Safety 2 (focusing on what went well and why). It acknowledges that healthcare hasn't promoted the concept of resilience which pervades other High Reliability Organisations (HROs) and has made this aim one of the seven strategic objectives of the project. They acknowledge the work of Professor Kathleen Sutcliffe who holds a number of appointments in Johns Hopkins University including at the Armstrong Institute for Patient Safety, and who in her books, *Managing the Unexpected* (2001) and her 2020 follow-up, *Still Not Safe*, outlines the five characteristics of High Reliability Organisations.

Acceptance of the need for Human Factors specialists in healthcare is gaining ground and the UK's NHS has called for a staff member to be designated as a Patient Safety Champion in every hospital in the country. This has been delayed by Covid-19 but is now under way. This in conjunction with the Freedom to Speak Up Guardians in many hospitals will hopefully start to change the acceptance of error. We also need to greatly increase the number of qualified

Human Factors professionals in our healthcare systems to augment what has been described as enthusiastic amateurs – a group which I would consider myself as belonging to. As I said at the start of the book, I'm not a Human Factors professional but I am a professional whose very survival depends on my successful application of Human Factors. The NHS with over 1.3 million staff has approximately 10 qualified Human Factors professionals as of 2023, highlighting the lack of emphasis the issue has suffered from for decades. This needs to change urgently.

The WHO plan calls for improved teaching on the awareness of risk and error both at undergraduate and postgraduate levels. It has already published a Patient Safety Curriculum Guide for Medical Schools as well as a Multi-Professional Edition which have been adopted in some member countries. It acknowledges the reluctance of many institutions to move outside their well-established clinical disciplines and also the lack of experienced trainers in this new area. There are, however, many of us in High Reliability Organisations, especially aviation, already sharing our Error Management approach in healthcare settings who will be more than happy to open channels for learning in both directions. We have already given clinicians access to our flight decks, simulators and training centres to demonstrate the relevance and transferability of our skills leading to pockets of excellent work which will only benefit from being adopted more widely across healthcare.

This ambitious global plan, along with the appetite for change I see regularly at the coalface of healthcare, bodes well for the transformation needed to progress towards the elusive goal of reducing avoidable harm and achieving a win-win-win situation for patients, staff and management alike. The WHO estimate the social cost of patient harm globally to be between \$1 to 2 trillion per year – that is up to \$2,000,000,000,000 written another way! The third decade of the twenty-first century looks like it's going to be the one when we finally get our heads around the elusive goal of managing error in healthcare.

I really hope I'm not mistaken on this one . . .

Notes on Sources

Chapter 1

'The Evolution of Crew Resource Management Training in Commercial Aviation'. *International Journal of Aviation Psychology*, 9(1), 19-32. Robert Helmreich, Ashleigh C. Merritt and John A. Wilhelm.

'Are we all less risky and more skilful than our fellow drivers?' *Acta Physiologica,* Vol. 47, Issue 2, February 1981, pages 143-148. Ola Svenson.

Chapter 2

'How Do We make Sense of What We See?' *Science Daily.* 20 November 2007. Johns Hopkins University.

The Three Pound Universe by Judith Hooper and Dick Teresi, 1986, Macmillan.

www.illusionsindex.org.

How to Fail by Elizabeth Day, 2019, Fourth Estate.

Black Box Thinking by Matthew Syed, 2016, John Murray.

The Business of Winning by Mark Gallagher, 2021, Kogan Page.

The Wisdom of Crowds by James Surowieki, 2005, Abacus.

Chapter 3

'Analysis of errors made by line umpires on ATP tournaments'. *International Journal of Performance Analysis in Sport*. 16(1): 264 275 April 2016. Jan Carboch, Katerina Vejvodová and Vladimir Süss.

Djokovic: Fine Umpires for Errors. *Tennis Now*. September 2018.

'Perceptual uncertainty and line-call challenges in professional tennis'. *Proc. Biol. Sci*. The Royal Society Publishing. 2008 Jul 22; 275(1643): 1645-1651. George Mather.

'So McEnroe had a point'. *The Daily Mail*. 27 October 2008. David Derbyshire.

'Antoine Demoitié's death should be a wake-up call for cycling's crowded races'. *The Guardian*. 1 April 2016. Suze Clemitson.

'Furious Lewis Hamilton demands "bulletproof" answers over Mercedes blunders. *The Telegraph*. 1 July 2018. Phil Duncan.

Chapter 4

'Risky business: The extraordinary life of firefighter Sabrina Cohen-Hatton'. *The Guardian*. 7 April 2019. Paula Cocozza.

The Heat of the Moment by Sabrina Cohen-Hatton, 2020, Black Swan.

ACT UP Demonstrations on Wall Street. NYC LGBT Historic Sites Project. 2017. https://www.nyclgbtsites.org/site/act-up-demonstration-at-the-new-york-stock-exchange/

How To Demand A Medical Breakthrough: Lessons From The AIDS Fight. *The Health Newsletter – NPR*. 9 February 2019. Nurith Aizenman.

'The reason why white cars are being stolen to order and shipped abroad.' *The Mirror*. 8 October 2017. Alex Scrapens.

'Forgetting of Passwords: Ecological Theory and Data.' Xianyi Gao et al. Paper from Proceedings of the 27th USENIX Security Symposium. August 15–17, 2018 • Baltimore, MD, USA.

'Police officer numbers in England and Wales' www.full-fact.org. 8 November 2019.

'Malware (malicious software)'. www.techtarget.com. April 2019. Margaret Rouse, Rob Wright and Debra Lee.

'Fifteen sex offenders in NI to have convictions rescinded due to accidental error in law.' *The Irish Times*. 23 September 2020. Freya McClements.

'The lessons to be learned for court practitioners from research conducted in New Zealand into jury dynamics.' *Journal – Law Society of Scotland*. 1 July 2001. John Carruthers.

'Extraneous factors in judicial decisions'. *PNAS*. 26 April 2011, Vol 108, No 17,6889-6992. Shai Danziger, Johnathan Levav and Liora Avnaim-Pesso.

The Secret Barrister: Stories of the Law and How It's Broken by The Secret Barrister, 2019, Picador.

'Juries are "too large for correct verdicts".' *The Telegraph*. 4 September 2001. Robert Uhlig.

'Many Prisoners on Death Row are Wrongfully Convicted.' *Scientific American*. 28 April 2014. Dina Fine Maron.

Being Wrong: Adventures in the Margin of Error by Kathryn Schulz, 2010, Portobello.

A Frolic of His Own by William Gaddis, 1995, Scribner.

Chapter 5

The National Institute for Occupational Safety and Health.

'Fatal injuries in agriculture, forestry and fishing in Great Britain 2018/19.' *Health and Safety Executive*. July 2019.

Farmwise – Your essential guide to health and safety in agriculture (Third edition). The Stationery Office. 2017.

'Farm Safety Week: Statistics.' *HSENI*. 18 July 2019.

'Farming: The UK's deadliest industry'. *BBC News*. 22 August 2019. Ed Lowther.

'Farms and Farmers'. *Statistical Yearbook of Ireland*. Central Statistics Office. 2018.

'How many people died in farm accidents in Ireland in 2019?' *That's Farming*. 14 January 2020. Catherina Cunnane.

'Risk taking and Accidents on Irish Farms.' *Health and Safety Authority, Ireland*. May 2017. Dorothy Watson, Oona Kenny, Bertrand Maître and Helen Russell.

'Tipperary students' pioneering farm safety video initiative goes nationwide'. *Tipperary Star*. 16 June 2020.

'Ireland 2002: Article IV Consultation – Staff Report and Public Information Notice on Executive Board Discussion.' International Monetary Fund. August 2002.

Follow the Money by David McWilliams, 2010, Gill Books. '"Economic doom merchants threaten our future", says Bertie'. *Irish Independent*. 2 July 2007. Michael Brennan.

The Black Swan by Nassim Nicholas Taleb, 2010, Penguin.

Chapter 6

'Causal Analysis of WHO's Surgical Safety Checklist Implementation Quality and Impact on Care Processes and Patient Outcomes: Secondary Analysis from a Large Stepped Wedge Cluster Randomised Controlled Trial in Norway.' *Ann. Surg.* 2019 Feb; 269(2): 283-290. Arvid Steiner Haugen et al.

'Effects on Clinical Outcomes of a 5-year Surgical Safety Checklist Implementation Experience: A Large-scale Population-Based Difference-in-Differences Study.' *Health Serv. Insights.* 2018 Jul 23;11:1178632918785127. Stefania Rodella et al.

'The Irish National Adverse Event Study-2 (INAES-2): Longitudinal trends in adverse event rates in the Irish health-care system', *BMJ Quality and Safety*, 2016, Dr Natasha Rafter et al.

To Err is Human: Building a Safer Health System, by Dr Lucian Leape, 1999, National Academy Press.

'Implementation of the WHO Surgical Safety Checklist Correlates with Reduced Surgical Mortality and Length of

Hospital Admission in a High-Income Country.' *World J Sure*. 2019 Jan; 43(1): 117-124. Elzerie de Jager et al.

'Medical error—the third leading cause of death in the US,' *British Medical Journal*, 2016, Marty Makary.

Safe Patients, Smart Hospitals: How One Doctor's Checklist Can Help Us Change Health Care from the Inside Out by Peter Pronovost and Eric Vohr, 2011, Plume.

The Checklist Manifesto: How to Get Things Right by Atul Gawnde, 2011, Profile.

'Surgical checklists: a systematic review of impacts and implementation.' *BMJ Quality and Safety*. Volume 23, issue 4, 2012. Jonathan R Treadwell, Scott Lucas and Amy Y Tsou.

'Systematic review and meta-analysis of the effect of the WHO Surgical Safety checklist on post-operative complications.' *Br J Sure*. 2014 Feb; 101(3): 150-8. J Bergs et al.

'I was left to fight alone for NHS whistle-blowing protection.' *The Guardian*. 2 Oct 2018. Benedict Cooper.

'Junior doctor withdraws legal challenge arguing that whistleblowing ruined his career.' *Workforce and Training – National Health Executive*. 16 Oct 2018.

'Provisional publication of Never Events reported as occurring between 1 April 2018 and 31 January 2019.' NHS Improvement. 27 February 2019.

'Medical negligence payments cost over €265m in first nine months of year.' *The Irish Times*. 11 November 2019. Martin Wall.

Freedom to Speak Up – A Review of Whistleblowing in the NHS. www.freedomtospeakup.org.uk. February 2015. Sir Robert Francis QC.

Chapter 7

Ancient History Encyclopedia website, co-founder Joshua Mark.

'Understanding margin of error.' YouGov. Politics and current affairs. 21 November 2011. Anthony Wells.

'What journalists can learn from their mistakes during the pandemic.' Reuters Institute for the Study of Journalism. Dorothy Byrne.

'Seven mistakes politicians make when following "the science".' *The Spectator*. 16 May 2020. Tom Lees.

'Exclusive: "perverse incentive" contributed to slump in rape charges.' *The Law Society Gazette*. 13 November 2019. Melanie Newman.

'Downing Street plans rape prosecution targets for police and CPS.' *The Guardian*. 9 August 2020. Caelainn Barr and Alexandra Topping.

'Dominic Raab bodyguard suspended after gun reportedly left on plane.' *The Guardian*. 19 September 20202. Nicola Slawson.

Chapter 8

Brilliant Blunders: From Darwin to Einstein – Colossal Mistakes by Great Scientists That Changed Our Understanding of Life and the Universe by Mario Livio, 2014, Simon & Schuster.

'The real story behind penicillin.' PBS News Hour. 27 September 2013. Dr Howard Markel.

'Fleming and the Discovery of Penicillin.' 14 March 2019. Karen Berger.

'Alfred Nobel created the Nobel Prize as a false obituary declared him "The Merchant of Death".' *The Vintage News*. 14 October 2016. Alex A.

Chapter 9

'Facebook Changes It's "Move Fast and Break Things" Motto.' *Mashable*. 30 April 2014. Samantha Murphy.

'How Cambridge Analytica Sparked the Great Privacy Awakening.' *Wired*. 17 March 2019. Issie Lapowsky.

'10 Snapchat Statistics You Need to Know in 2020.' *Oberlo*. 3 January 2020. Maryam Mohsin.

'Political Microtargeting: What Data Crunchers Did for Obama.' *Business Driven Technology* (6th edition). Chapter 6, Problem 2CCQ. Paige Baltzan.

'Error Correction' British Council/BBC 2008. https://www. teachingenglish.org.uk/professional-development/teach-ers/assessing-learning/articles/error-correction. Jo Budden.

'Learning from Errors: Effects of Teachers Training on Students' Attitudes Towards and Their Individual Use of Errors.' *PNA*, 8(1), 21-30. Rach, S., Ufer, S. & Heinze, A.

'Strategy Instruction and Error Prevention: The Research Behind ThinkFast for Basic Math Facts'. www.ilearn.com. Robert L. Collins, PhD.

'New test for "growth mindset", the theory that anyone who tries can succeed.' *The Guardian*. 10 May 2016. Susanna Rustin.

'The Relationship between implicit theories of intelligence, attainment and socio-demographic factors in a UK sample of primary school children.' *British Educational Research Journal*. 28 May 2019. Prof Sherria Hoskins et al.

Mindset: The New Psychology of Success by Carol Dweck, 2017, Robinson.

'Leaving Cert: 6,500 students awarded lower grade due to code errors.' *The Irish Times*. September 2020. Carl O'Brien, Marie O'Halloran and Pat Leahy.

Chapter 10

'"Tsunami of untruths": Trump has made 20,000 false or misleading claims – report.' *The Guardian*. 13 July 2020. Lauren Aratani.

'Disinformation, "Fake News" and Influence Campaigns on Twitter.' www.knightfoundation.org. October 2018. Matthew Hindman and Vlad Barash.

'President Trump claims the media peddles fake news. Has it made itself an easy target?' Comtalk. Lara Ehrlich.

'Viral Video Manipulates Pelosi's Words.' www.factcheck. org. 3 August 2020. Saranac Hale Spencer.

'The Physician's Achilles heel – surviving an adverse event.' *Curr. Oncol.* 2019 Dec; 26(6):e742-e747. I Stukalin, BC Lethebe, W Temple.

'An exploration of the implementation of open disclosure of adverse events in the UK: a scoping review and qualitative exploration.' National Institute for Health Research. 2014.

Report on the Pre-legislative Scrutiny on the 'Open Disclosure' provisions, to be included in the Civil Liability (Amendment) Bill. Houses of the Oireachtas Joint Committee on Health. February 2017.

'Opening up to patients could lead to fall in litigation costs.' *The Irish Times*. 12 November 2013. Paul Cullen.

'Open Disclosure – doctors need on-going training and peer support.' *BMJ*. 11 February 2019. Dubhfeasa Slattery.

'Duty of candour and keeping patients safe.' *Surgery*. 38:10, 2020. Vinita Shekar, Peter A. Brennan.

Evaluation of the national Open Disclosure Pilot. Health Service Executive/State Claims Agency. 2016. Dr Jane Pillinger.

Signals: How Everyday Signs Can Help Us Navigate the World's Turbulent Economy, by Pippa Malmgren, 2017, Weidenfeld & Nicholson.

Chapter 11

'Sensitivity to expression of emotional meaning in three modes of communication,' in J.R. Davitz et al., *The Communication of Emotional Meaning*, McGraw-Hill, pp. 31-42. Beldoch M. (1964).

'The 7 Most Common Leadership Styles (and How to Find Your Own).' *American Express*. 16 October 2019. Bruna Martinuzzi.

Rebel Ideas: The Power of Thinking Differently by Matthew Syed, 2021, John Murray.

Emotional Intelligence: Why it Can Matter More Than IQ, by Daniel Goleman, 1996, Random House.

Managing the Unexpected: Resilient Performance in an Age of Uncertainty by Karl Weicke and Kathleen Sutcliffe, 2017, John Wiley.

Still Not Safe: Patient Safety and the Middle-Managing of American Medicine, by Robert Wears and Kathleen Sutcliffe, 2020, OUP USA.

Index

Index